M 7.

Scif W9-CBI-264

THINKING ABOUT
NATIONAL SECURITY
Defense and Foreign Policy
in a Dangerous World

Harold Brown

THINKING ABOUT NATIONAL SECURITY
Defense and Foreign Policy in a Dangerous World

Westview Press / Boulder, Colorado

All rights reserved. No part of this publication may be reproduced or transmitted in any form or by any means, electronic or mechanical, including photocopy, recording, or any information storage and retrieval system, without permission in writing from the publisher.

Copyright © 1983 by Westview Press, Inc.

Published in 1983 in the United States of America by
Westview Press, Inc.
5500 Central Avenue
Boulder, Colorado 80301
Frederick A. Praeger, President and Publisher

Paperback edition published in 1984 by Westview Press, Inc.

Distributed to the book trade by
William Morrow & Co.
105 Madison Avenue
New York, New York 10016

Library of Congress Cataloging in Publication Data
Brown, Harold, 1927–
  Thinking about national security.
  Includes index.
  1. United States—National security. I. Title.
UA23.B7845   1983   355'.033073   82-23859
ISBN 0-86531-548-5
ISBN 0-86531-702-X (pbk.)

Printed and bound in the United States of America

10   9   8   7   6   5   4   3   2

To all my colleagues and associates,
past and present

Contents

Preface

The issues that, taken together, have traditionally defined national security policy rarely determine the outcomes of Presidential elections. They are, however, debated in the campaigns. Candidates sometimes take firm positions, but more often they convey impressions of their foreign and defense policy intentions. Whatever mandates Presidents receive from the voters are primarily economic and domestic. They must then define and implement their own national security policies and do so in a real world that is much more complex and constraining than most at first appreciate. Events beyond the control of even a superpower complicate the best-laid plans. Military strength, economic influence, and diplomatic skill prove to be limited in both extent and effect. Even if a mandate exists, it will soon erode, especially in a government whose structure diffuses power both within the executive branch and between the executive branch and the Congress. Bold innovations in national security policies are transformed into slow, incremental changes. Journalists, commentators, and political opponents, foreign and domestic, will then tend to emphasize the inconsistencies, the departures from campaign promises and from initial policy statements, of the new Administration. Historians will later note the essential consistency with earlier U.S. national security policy.

This well-established pattern is likely to repeat itself even if great departures are promised. Nevertheless, the issues of U.S. national security policy are important. In this book I have undertaken to outline the agenda of national security issues for publics who must think about and debate them, for government officials in both the executive branch and the legislative branch who must make decisions about them, and for students with a general interest in them. I place these issues in a brief historical perspective, try to tie together the political, economic, military, and other elements of U.S. national security policy, and suggest a way of arriving at policies that are both rational and practical.

National security issues have been the subject of continuous public discussion, but in quite different contexts. Officials in the executive branch and in the Congress set forth foreign and defense policies in speeches, as do those who aspire to office. Such speeches, however, generally deal with individual subjects rather than with the broad sweep of national security policy. The annual statements of the Secretary of State and the Secretary of Defense cover a broader range, but they are necessarily restricted by the responsibilities of the individual departments; they focus on the present rather than on policies for the next decade or two. The statements of journalists and commentators who deal with national security issues are usually circumscribed by a narrow range of subject, a relatively short perspective, and restricted length. Scholars deal with these subjects exhaustively, weighing history and the opinions of other scholars, but they write unhampered—and uninformed—by the responsibility and the urgency of real experience.

This book is written in analytic and policy terms, but from the perspective of one who has had national security responsibilities. As a result, it draws more on my own thinking and experience than on scholarly literature, and it includes prescriptive conclusions that would be less appropriate to scholarship or journalism. The views I express in the following chapters do not differ greatly from those I held in office; but a broader range of topics, a freer format, more shades of gray, and greater candor are available to one who is out of office.

The book as a whole proceeds with more logic and in a clearer sequence than the real world can offer. Beginning with a definition of U.S. national security and a description of the goals of national security policy, it moves through analysis of the functional and geographical elements of national security to an examination of the organizational and managerial factors in the formulation and execution of national security policy. In following this sequence, I emphasize the need to design a political, economic, and military strategy toward the Soviet Union, our major adversary on the international scene. I discuss the steps to improve the condition of the U.S. economy and to reduce U.S. dependence on foreign energy supplies that will be essential to a successful U.S. national security policy. I focus on the stark facts of the nuclear age and define the complex requirements of nuclear deterrence.

Next I address the question of the appropriate division of responsibilities in the NATO alliance, in which the relative economic
weight of the U.S. and European partners has changed markedly
since 1960, and in which major differences have arisen over appropriate
economic and military policies toward the Soviet Union. I present
the sensitive political issues the United States faces in the Far East,
with its ally Japan—now an economic competitor but a military
dependent—and with the People's Republic of China (PRC), an
important military and political counter to the Soviet Union, although
PRC political objectives often differ sharply from those of the United
States. I outline the complex political and military issues involved
in designing a strategy for preserving peace and protecting U.S.
interests in Southwest Asia. I treat in general terms the rest of the
Third World, in which the nature of the military threat is less acute
than elsewhere. Then I turn to U.S. naval forces and their role all
over the world and suggest priorities in U.S. planning for multifront
conflicts. In the final policy chapter I set forth the objectives of and
assess the modest prospects for arms control.

Decisions on national security policy, and still more their implementation, require large organizations involving millions of people.
Accordingly, I proceed next to several issues of management and
organization. Can the U.S. Government as a whole be organized to
provide and execute better policies, given resource constraints? Can
the Department of Defense be managed more efficiently? How should
the United States take advantage of its advances in technology? Can
the United States ensure that its forces include enough military
personnel, and personnel with the right training, to carry out the
military missions that its overall political and military strategy calls
for?

I am not principally concerned here with military hardware or
with weapons systems, which enter into the presentation only insofar
as they influence military strategy and overall national security policy.
This book is not intended to be a guide to this year's—or any
year's—five-year defense program. Nor is it a diplomatic compendium.
Although I do discuss the political relations of the United States with
other countries, some regions—for example, the Indian subcontinent
and the Western Hemisphere—have been given less attention than
the importance of their relations with the United States would seem
to merit. The reason is simple: I am setting forth in some detail the
political and military elements of national security where they are
most pressing, while dealing with the other elements in more general
and global terms.

This book is neither a study of personalities nor a sketch of specific events. In the arguments set forth, however, I do address the need to achieve the political strength and skill that are indispensable if we are to create the domestic political base from which a wise national security policy can be formulated and implemented. The methods and domestic policies required to establish such a political base are beyond the scope of this book, but without that base little or none of what is recommended here is possible.

Each of these foregone subjects deserves many volumes, but the present work is not one of those volumes. Its purpose, rather, is to help establish a framework for thinking about national security. Public and political leaders need such a framework more than they need a prescription for what to think. In the final chapter I draw some summary conclusions and make some recommendations on U.S. policy, based on the analysis that has gone before. Both conclusions and recommendations are, inevitably, tentative. Whatever their validity, I hope that the agenda set forth and the analysis of the issues presented will provide readers with an approach that can be followed to reach independent judgments about present and future national security issues. If this book contributes to a better understanding of ways to analyze and draw conclusions about these issues, it will have served its purpose.

As you proceed through the book, you will notice that certain themes are stated and repeated. Briefly, they are as follows:

• U.S. national security must now be defined to take into account nuclear weapons—a potential threat to the very existence of the nation—and the greatly increased economic interdependence that has sharply altered U.S. relations with the rest of the world since World War II. That security must be sought in a world of instant communications, technological innovations, and declining internal political cohesion.

• The Soviet Union, now a global superpower, poses *the* major military threat to U.S. interests and values, and a substantial political threat through the possibility of military action or intimidation around the world.

• The United States must safeguard its national security interests with greater skill than it has heretofore, because the growing relative military and economic strength of other powers has made infeasible its reestablishment of the military and economic preeminence it enjoyed in the 1950s. Alliances and alignments are now even more necessary as elements of national security policy than they were before.

• Political, economic, and military strategies, along with other elements of national strength and with efforts toward arms control, must be integrated and coordinated in a national security policy. Military forces are an essential element of that strength. Without sufficient military capability, no amount of political or economic strength will be adequate. The world is dangerous, and the Soviet military threat is real. Even in peacetime, the military balance and perceptions of the likely outcome of a military conflict have political consequences in international affairs. But the usefulness of military strength is limited; it is not freely substitutable for other elements of strength. Indeed, therein lies one of the principal limitations of Soviet power.

• The national security of the United States will in the end depend on whether the industrialized democracies are able to sustain their military, political, and economic strength, postponing present consumption as necessary, even during difficult economic times. Failure to carry through such a program is a sure recipe for deep decline in the United States and in the industrialized democracies as a group. The United States must lead its alliances and coalitions, through example and consultation rather than through compulsion, to join in attaining common goals and making common sacrifices.

The history of national security policy in the United States since World War II displays remarkable continuity, despite significant shifts in attitude toward the Soviet Union and significant changes in declaratory policy—containment, liberation, the long twilight struggle, détente, cooperation and competition, and negotiation from strength. U.S. policy has been successful overall, and its major elements should be retained even while it is modified in response to new situations and trends.

I believe that the United States has the internal resources and the strength of will necessary to preserve its security and well-being. To do so will require a certain amount of good luck. It will also require an informed and determined public and a skillful and dedicated leadership.

Harold Brown

Acknowledgments

Any attempt at a comprehensive examination of a complex and extensive subject owes much of its substance to the ideas, impressions, and experiences that its author received from or shared with many associates and colleagues. In my own case, these comprise the substance of more than thirty years of participation in national security affairs. I must thus content myself with recognizing specifically here only a few of those people and institutions to whom I am indebted for particular assistance. For the rest, the dedication of the work to all of my colleagues and associates, past and present, will have to suffice.

My wife, Colene, and my daughters, Deborah and Ellen, encouraged me to write the book and patiently accepted my resulting personality changes. I am grateful for the sympathy and support they have given me through many years of public life.

The School of Advanced International Studies of The Johns Hopkins University has provided me during the past two years with intellectual stimulation, pleasant collegial surroundings, an office, secretarial help, and student assistance. For all of these I wish particularly to thank Dean George Packard. Elaine Clark and Maryllis Bartlett patiently typed the initial drafts of the manuscript, and David Fuhrmann and Proctor Reid provided invaluable research assistance and helpful discussion.

Nancy Brady, who was my secretary and administrative assistant for eight of my twelve years in the Defense Department, gave generously of her personal time to prepare the final manuscript with her usual skill and efficiency. The Office of Security Review in the

Department of Defense, at my request, read the manuscript to see that it contained no classified information.

Various former colleagues read specific chapters, about which they made comments and suggestions and delivered constructive criticisms. These include Professor Richard Cooper, Dr. Fred Bergsten, Walter Slocombe, Ambassador Robert Komer, Ambassador Morton Abramowitz, Dr. William Perry, and Robin Pirie.

John Kester read the entire manuscript with an eye both to organization and to substance and made many specific comments. Dr. Lynn Davis reviewed every chapter, did extensive editing, suggested revisions and clarifications, and held me to a higher standard of analysis and intellectual rigor than I believed myself capable of. Without them I know I would not have completed the task.

I am grateful also to Frederick A. Praeger of Westview Press, my publisher, for his continuing encouragement; to Tim Kenslea, who edited the manuscript; and to Alice Levine, Kathy Jones, Deborah Lynes, and Susan McRory at Westview Press for their editorial help.

These are the individuals who are responsible for whatever polish, coherence, and consistency the book may have. Yet the first draft was mine, the final writing was mine, the ideas and conclusions are mine, and—needless to say—all the mistakes are my own.

H.B.

1

Defining National Security

U.S. presidents, opinion-making elites, and the public as a whole seek as high a level of national security as possible for the United States in the last two decades of the twentieth century. But by what yardstick do we measure that security? And to what lengths should we go to attain it? How, indeed, do we even define national security?

The preamble to the U.S. Constitution declares that one of the purposes of the new Federal Government is to "provide for the common defense." (It is notable that this goal appears immediately before another—to "promote the general welfare.") Indeed, a national government has no more fundamental responsibility than to safeguard the nation's security. When the framers of the Constitution wrote that document, they surely had in mind the need to defend the new nation from conquest or political domination by the actually or potentially hostile European powers that retained major footholds in North America. They may not have had so explicitly in mind the element of national security that lies in economic independence. The new nation imported many things from outside, but it had proved during the Revolutionary War that it could, if necessary, get along without them by finding substitute sources or devising substitute products.

Through the War of 1812, the new nation continued to feel threatened by the possible expansionist aims of the European powers, but after that war the United States had clearly become the dominant power on the North American continent, itself expanding at the expense of its neighbors. U.S. policies outside the region that was to comprise the forty-eight contiguous states continued to promote the aim of excluding European influence from the Western Hemisphere—by, for example, the purchase of Alaska from Russia and the overthrow of Maximilian in Mexico, both in 1867. U.S. activities also included the pursuit of private or presumed public economic benefits in the Caribbean and Central America and a carrying out of the concept that the United States had a moral duty to aid the oppressed or unenlightened both nearby and far away. Nothing exemplifies this last aim so well as President McKinley's stated determination in the Spanish-American War to "Christianize" the Philippines—an area that had been Christian since well before the first Anglo-Saxon settlers arrived in North America.

Neither in World War I nor in World War II was the physical existence or nature of the United States immediately threatened. But the U.S. perception, probably correct in the first case and certainly so in the second, was that a German victory would inevitably have led to a threat to the nature and even the existence of the United States—a threat that would have had to be faced on much less favorable terms should its allies have first succumbed.

NATIONAL SECURITY TODAY

How violent much of U.S. history has been! Yet it all now seems idyllic and simple when compared to the world we face in the final two decades of the twentieth century. The real world imposes severe limitations on any aspirations toward an ideal condition of national security today.

Since the late 1950s, the United States, along with the other countries of the world, has faced the possibility of nuclear destruction brought about by decisions that could be made by the leaders of another country—the Soviet Union. Such a decision would be irrational because it would bring immediate destruction to the Soviets as well. But that is only a modest comfort; there have been too many irrational decisions in history. This threat of total destruction represents a change from anything in the previous history of the world and is one measure of the limits of military power in assuring the kind of national security that the United States had enjoyed since 1815— and indeed even had during those periods of the Revolutionary War when it seemed that the new nation might not be born at all. If one takes as a measure of national security the ability of the people of the United States to determine their own future without being influenced by what happens outside their own borders, the threat of nuclear destruction means that U.S. national security has deteriorated markedly and probably irreversibly since the early 1950s.

Another measure of national security is economic strength and independence. In 1946 the United States had more than half of the world's Gross National Product (GNP). Now its GNP of more than $3 trillion is only about 30 percent of the world total. Economic interdependence, which has long characterized many other countries of the world, now also characterizes the United States. In 1960 neither exports nor imports constituted more than a few percent of the GNP of the United States, though U.S. agriculture and the U.S. automobile industry were significantly involved in overseas markets. But, as has the rest of the world, the United States has since World War II become much more dependent on imports and exports for its economic well-being. Most other major economic powers are even more dependent on world trade for markets or raw materials. The Soviet Union and the People's Republic of China (PRC) are both less dependent than the United States on external economic relations, but this circumstance is almost certainly both an effect and a cause of their being much poorer than the United States.

The United States is especially dependent on oil imports. Since the beginning of the 1970s, the United States has been subject to major political influence from the foreign oil-producing nations, from whom it recently imported more than half, and still imports about a third, of its oil. The recessions and the inflation that have disrupted the U.S. economy since the early 1970s and now threaten to continue through the 1980s and into the 1990s are in large measure a reflection of this dependence. U.S. oil imports alone still cost about $70 billion a year.

The United States is now also a net importer of manufactured goods by about $40 billion a year. To pay for these and other imports, the United States must export great quantities of its agricultural surplus and the products of its advanced high-technology industries. Total imports and total exports (including intangibles) each now amount to about 10 percent of the U.S. GNP. The balance of trade and capital flows, and the enormous quantity of dollars held abroad, can and do very substantially affect U.S. inflation rates, interest rates, and foreign exchange rates. One in six U.S. industrial jobs and two in five U.S. agricultural acres produce for export. Unemployment in the automobile and steel industries rises when the volume of imports of those products rises and their prices fall.

The effects of such competition, good and ill, depend not only on foreign relations but also—at least as much—on such matters as labor practices, the state of technology in the United States, industrial productivity, and tax policies. But the situation is a far cry from the one that existed during most of the nineteenth century and the first half of the twentieth century, when what happened in other countries, or what happened to U.S. relations with them, had little effect on the U.S. economy.

The United States's control of its borders has eroded. U.S. actions alone cannot control the flow of illegal immigrants across the U.S.-Mexican border. And the flow of Cuban refugees from Mariel Harbor to Florida in 1980 showed that it is difficult, given humanitarian impulses and political influences within the United States, for the U.S. Government to be the sole arbiter of who enters the country. Outside events, as in earlier times, determine the numbers who wish to come. In the past, many have mistakenly seen immigration as out of control and considered it a threat to the security and even the identity of the United States. Similar feelings exist today, but the physical difficulties of preventing illegal immigration from Mexico and the Caribbean are much greater today than they have ever been.

By each of these criteria—continued physical existence, economic well-being, control of borders—an ideal measure of national security might still be the ability to operate as if the outside world did not exist. But any attempt to behave that way in today's interdependent world is a futile exercise in nostalgia. Isolationism—the attempt to defend a "Fortress America"—however tempting, is not the road to security for the United States during the 1980s. The size of the United States, its geographical remoteness from much of the rest of the world, and its relative abundance of natural resources might make isolationism more feasible for the United States than for the other major industrialized countries, but these attributes do not make it feasible enough.

National security, then, is the ability to preserve the nation's physical integrity and territory; to maintain its economic relations with the rest of the world on reasonable terms; to protect its nature, institutions, and governance from disruption from outside; and to control its borders.

THREATS TO NATIONAL SECURITY

What are the actual or potential threats to U.S. national security? There are such threats, both short-term and long-term. Some of these threats are internal: a slackening of economic growth and static or declining productivity; a dissipation of natural resources; a loss of domestic cohesion as a result of generational and ethnic conflicts and fragmentation into special interests; a decline of ties to family, religion, and place (both home and nation) without the appearance of other loyalties to take their place; an erosion of the educational system; a decline in the work ethic; a feeling on the part of the poor, the old, and minority groups that they are being abandoned; and a loss of confidence in national political leadership, especially since the Vietnam War and Watergate. It is by no means clear that these internal issues, which pose real threats to U.S. domestic security, are on the road to being solved; at different times during the 1970s and 1980s progress was made and ground was lost.

A wide range of major external economic threats to U.S. national security exist as well. These include the cost and instability of energy supplies; terrorism, which (among its many other ill effects) can disrupt the functioning of economic channels; instability in nearby regions, with consequent mass physical movements of people; worldwide starvation; local wars involving major U.S. trading partners; and disruptions of orderly international economic and financial arrangements through political or economic failures within the advanced industrial countries. These concerns are also far from resolution. They can be expected to continue—and new ones to arise—not only through the 1980s and 1990s but also into the next century.

Finally, and most gravely, there are the international threats of a military or political nature. Nuclear attack would of course be the most catastrophically devastating by far. That nuclear weapons have been used only twice in the almost four decades of the nuclear age— at the termination of World War II—is somewhat reassuring, especially in light of the dozens of predictions during that time that nuclear weapons surely would be used in the next five to ten years. To that extent, the "balance of terror" has proved considerably better than nothing. But such reassurance can only be modest. The nuclear stockpiles of the two superpowers have grown in numbers since 1960 as large bombs have been replaced by smaller and more numerous missile warheads. Total megatonnage has accordingly fallen, but the time of flight is, for much of the strategic arsenal of both sides, minutes rather than hours. A conventional clash between the United States and the Soviet Union could well escalate to a strategic nuclear war. There is always the possibility of a miscalculation. Nuclear proliferation, though not nearly so rapid thus far as many had feared, continues apace.

More likely than nuclear war, though less immediately catastrophic, is military intimidation of, or conventional (nonnuclear) attack on, U.S. allies and friends. If such tactics were successful, the world military and political balance would tilt dangerously against the United States; and the long-run survival of the United States in a generally recognizable geographical and political form would be threatened. A further rise of disruption and anarchy throughout the

Third World is also a possibility. Such a development, while not immediately destructive to the industrialized countries, would render their situation shaky in the long run, as the starving and warring poorer countries were driven to desperate actions against the rest of the nations of the world.

In the array of threats and problems that face the developing countries and the industrialized democracies, particularly the United States, the part played by the Soviet Union must not be underestimated. It is an expansionist power of massive military strength, with a tight control over its population that gives its leaders considerable freedom from internal political constraints in determining what foreign and military policies to pursue. It is relatively ineffective and weak by most other criteria, but in light of its military and industrial power and its firmness of purpose the Soviet Union must be seen as the major national adversary to the United States throughout the rest of this century. The succession process through which the Soviet leadership is passing in the early 1980s increases the uncertainty of future Soviet behavior and with it the potential for trouble, not only for the United States but for the rest of the world as well.

But even if the Soviet Union were by some external miracle, or by an improbable complete turn inward on itself, to subside into unimportance as an international factor, that would by no means cause the disappearance of all the international complexities, problems, dangers, or even potential disasters with which the United States must cope and for which it must plan through the rest of this century. Remaining would be the economic competition from the industrialized countries of Western Europe and Japan and, increasingly, from those nations in the process of industrializing—South Korea, Singapore, Brazil, and Mexico, for example. This competition already creates considerable economic difficulty for the United States and can be expected to create more during the remainder of the century. A significant share of the stagnation in economic growth that has left the United States no better off economically than it was fifteen years ago can be traced to this rising competition.

The energy shortage and the behavior of the Organization of Petroleum Exporting Countries (OPEC), particularly of its members in Southwest Asia, including the Middle East, have already had major negative effects on the economic well-being of the United States. That situation retains the potential for much worse disruption and indeed for possible disaster through various future combinations of mishandling and mischance. The oil shortage, the actions of OPEC, the price rises, and the resultant economic misfortunes have not been caused by Soviet actions, though Soviet meddling has been signifi-

cantly unhelpful. But even without actual or possible Soviet involve-
ments, other factors make the situation dangerous: the Arab-Israeli
conflicts, the issue of a Palestinian homeland, the Iranian revolution,
the Iran-Iraq war, the recognition by the oil producers that the
ravenous appetites of the industrialized nations for oil have made
those nations ripe targets for extortion, and internal instabilities in
various oil-producing nations of the area.

Internal instability within, and regional conflicts between, the oil-
producing countries, or between some of those countries and Israel,
will remain the most likely (though not the only) possible causes of
a future oil cutoff or major price increase. Either a cutoff or a price
increase would cause the United States great direct damage and
produce even more harm through the secondary effects of the much
greater disruption to the other industrialized democracies. The Soviets
remain at least a complicating factor in this equation, showing every
sign of continuing to encourage instability in the Middle East and
the rest of Southwest Asia and retaining the option of a direct military
penetration into the region, or of major political intimidation based
on that possibility, despite the risk of escalation into a war with the
United States. For the United States and its allies, the temptation to
intervene in the region in order to ensure continued access to its oil
must be weighed against the risks of a direct clash with the Soviet
Union or of throwing the countries of the region into its arms. In
any event, the high risk of failure of intervention in situations in
which it is easier to sabotage complex pumping facilities, pipelines,
or oil fields than it is to ensure their continued operation makes such
Western action questionable. Thus the political and economic risks,
complexities, and dangers that spring from the dependence of the
industrialized democracies on energy supplies from an unstable region
will have to be reckoned with and lived with for the rest of this
century.

The poverty and instability of other developing countries in Latin
America, Asia, and Africa will also continue through the rest of the
twentieth century and into the twenty-first. Their economic interactions
with the developed world will continue, and the combination in the
industrialized world of proper ethical attitudes and often overstated
guilt feelings about the poverty and colonial history of the developing
regions will also exist, with or without the complicating factor of
Soviet attempts to use the Third World economically, politically, and
strategically against the West. Terrorism will also stay on the scene
regardless of Soviet actions. Environmental problems, social tensions,
conflicts between various segments of populations, economic dislo-

cations, and other domestic difficulties of the industrialized democracies are by no means the result of some master Soviet plot.

If there were no advantages to put on the scales against these problems and threats, the prospects would be daunting indeed and the maintenance of national security nearly hopeless. But the United States has enormous assets. In internal and economic terms, these include its democratic political system, its vast resources, the skills of its people, and the productivity of its economic system.

The United States also faces its external political and military threats together with allies and friends around the world. The United States has alliances or mutual security treaties with the countries of Western Europe and with Japan, South Korea, and the Philippines in the Far East. It has normalized relations with the People's Republic of China (PRC) and has begun to build alignments with countries in Southwest Asia. Each of these friendships poses potential difficulties, because the national interests of these partners will not always be congruent with those of the United States and may be perceived as differing by the respective citizenries even when they *are* congruent.

In Western Europe there is widespread concern about U.S. nuclear weapons, though Soviet weapons nearby or aimed from afar are accepted by many of the same people as a fact of life. Major differences exist between the United States and many of its European allies about how to deal with the Soviet Union in the light of such events as the invasion of Afghanistan in 1979 and the imposition of martial law in Poland in 1981. The United States has major differences with Japan on the appropriate level of Japanese defense efforts and on trade policies. The relationship with the PRC is still being formed, and a major clash over policies toward Taiwan could abort the development of closer ties. In Southwest Asia, complex questions involving Israel, Palestinian rights, U.S. and allied economic interests, and regional concerns about westernization and Western influence interact to invest each relationship with difficulty and potential conflict.

But the United States has friends, however difficult they may sometimes be. The Soviets remain isolated, engaged in a continuing economic and political struggle with the non-Soviet elements of their empire and confronted with economic failure, political stagnation, and demographic problems at home.

A national security policy for the 1980s and 1990s must come to grips with the Soviet Union and the relations the United States has with the Soviet Union. It must take into account the realities of the U.S. economy and confront world economic issues that make the United States dependent on other nations—especially the issue of energy supply. It must provide adequate strategic nuclear forces and sound nuclear doctrine; an overall political and military strategy for Europe, East Asia, and Southwest Asia; and conventional and nuclear forces of sufficient size, capability, and flexibility to carry out those strategies.

In devising and executing such a national security policy, the United States must use its resources and emphasize its comparative advantages to produce an effective military establishment, closely integrated with its economic and diplomatic activities. The government must also retain the support of the American people and foster the belief that this national security policy is directed at assuring, insofar as possible, that the United States will be free to evolve internally in the direction of its own ideals.

2

The Soviet Union

Probably the most vital task in designing a national security policy for the United States in the 1980s and 1990s—but also the most difficult—is to define a comprehensive political, economic, and military policy toward the Soviet Union. Such a policy will require an understanding of the motivations of the Soviet ruling class and its leaders, their military and political goals, the problems that face the Soviet Union, and how these may evolve under a new generation of Soviet leaders.

THE AIMS OF SOVIET LEADERS

The Soviet Union is the only country in the world with the power to destroy the United States as a physical and political entity, although it could do this only at the cost of being destroyed itself. But aside from having the physical capability, the Soviet Union is the only nation that might be motivated to destroy the United States, if the Soviet leaders believed they could do so without unacceptable damage to themselves. In doing so, they could achieve world rule.

Some argue that Soviet leaders seek world domination. Others argue just as forcefully that they are motivated by defensive aims, that their objective is only to preserve their present power in the Soviet Union and elsewhere. Proponents of each argument tend to see the Soviet leaders as paranoid, a perception that somewhat diminishes the distinction between the two views. To the degree that Soviet leaders consider their power over their own country and the integrity of their own country threatened by the existence of other great power centers in other countries, near or far, even a "defensive" motivation will cause them to want to dominate others—their neighbors and, insofar as the reach of Soviet power makes it possible, people in distant areas of the world as well. It also leads them to attempt to undermine the stability and strength of regimes anywhere in the world that are not subject to or dominated by Soviet power.

The Soviet leaders see themselves as the apostolic successors to the founders of a world religion more than a hundred years old—though they probably would not use those terms. Their belief in their inevitable victory as the instruments of history and of dialectical materialism may have weakened in recent decades, but if they no longer believe in the certainty of world revolution and the triumph of Marxism-Leninism within some finite period, they still dream of it and consider it their duty to work toward it. All of Soviet history and international relations since 1917 is consistent with this aim. Still, there have always been limits to their dedication. Preserving their power in the USSR is more important to the Soviet leaders than increasing it elsewhere. There have also been periods in Soviet as in non-Soviet history when different foreign and international policies have become tools or pawns in domestic political struggles. This may be increasingly so now, as internal differences emerge about investment priorities, military needs, and apparent Soviet passivity in the Middle East. In any event, it will surely be the case again in the future.

Central to the goals and values of the Soviet leaders, and of the groups from which they draw power, is their position as a ruling class in the Soviet Union. The improvement in the standard of living of the Soviet population since the early 1950s, along with the end of Stalinist terror, has given that ruling class considerably more stability and a degree of legitimacy within the Soviet Union itself. The life of the ordinary Soviet citizen and the state of political rights, freedom, and human values in the Soviet Union remain abysmal, but life in the Soviet ruling class itself is more pleasant and less dangerous than it was in Stalin's day, as is the stability in the leadership positions that has prevailed for most of this group since the middle of the 1950s. Now for the most part in their seventies, this group has been and is extremely cautious and conservative, both in foreign policy and in domestic matters.

As Soviet military power has increased and become global in reach since the early 1960s the leaders have become more willing to use it, but not in anything so rash as the Cuban missile venture of 1962. Instead, they have relied on arms transfers to Third World countries, proxies such as the Cubans and Vietnamese, and the threat or actual use of their own troops. They have used Soviet troops only in areas immediately peripheral to the Soviet Union: Afghanistan, Poland, Czechoslovakia, Hungary, and East Germany and in skirmishes with the PRC. Their intention is clearly to hold what they have, strengthen it militarily and economically, and control or intimidate everything on its periphery. Future economic development within the Soviet Union will depend heavily on the development of Soviet Central Asia, Siberia, and the Soviet Far East, so they have strengthened Soviet military forces there facing the PRC, which they see as a hostile and potentially dangerous military and ideological antagonist. The military policy of the Soviet leaders has increasingly become that they must be able to defeat any adversary or combination of adversaries on all of their borders simultaneously. This is a prescription for an enormous military force, and an enormous military force is what they have built.

The retention of Eastern Europe is the next highest priority for the Soviet leaders. It is, aside from the Soviet Union itself, the one area for whose preservation under their dominion they would take high risks of war with the United States. Soviet problems in Eastern Europe are compounded by the practically complete lack of legitimacy of Soviet hegemony among the peoples of Eastern Europe. If Soviet troops were to be withdrawn and the people assured that they could not come back, almost none of the regimes in the area—certainly not the Polish, Czechoslovakian, or Hungarian—would last more than a few days.

The Soviets claim parity with the United States as an influence in the developing world. They seek to buttress that claim by giving political support to revolutionary movements, making arms sales to client states and friendly regimes, and maintaining significant capabilities to project force considerable distances and to interfere with intercontinental lines of communication.

The neutralization of China and the expansion of Soviet influence in the Third World are undoubtedly seen by the Soviet leaders as essential prerequisites to the decline of the democratic-capitalist nations, a decline the Soviet leaders consider it their duty to hurry along. Their ideological beliefs lead them to consider this decay and demise inevitable. They probably see the ills of Western society as encouraging their beliefs, however much they must puzzle at the failure of the Soviet system to close the economic, agricultural, and technological gaps—or any other gap except the military one. But the Soviet leaders know that their system has its strengths: the ability to assemble such great military power and to make their own population accept the deprivations that this requires, the ability to pursue long-range goals, the ability to carry out massive industrial-ization of a sort that appeals to many in the developing world, and the ability to hold out to the potential leaders of the developing world the prospect of the sort of stable power and privilege within their own countries that the Soviet ruling class has maintained for decades. These strengths are significant assets.

The Soviet leaders undoubtedly see the United States as the major villain behind all their principal problems, though it is at least as unreasonable for them to blame the difficulties created by their own internal contradictions on the United States as it is for the United States to blame its economic and social difficulties on them. But it is inevitable that the Soviet leaders, seeing the United States in this light, should attempt to diminish and undermine U.S. influence wherever it exists in the world and to separate allies and friends from the United States. They can be expected to continue to do this no matter how the Soviet leadership itself may evolve.

PROBLEMS FOR THE SOVIET UNION

The major internal problems the Soviet Union faces in the 1980s will be worse than those of the 1970s. Soviet agriculture has a sixty-year record of disaster. Annual Soviet GNP growth averaged 5 percent from 1966 to 1970, 4 percent from 1971 to 1977, and less than 2 percent since. Industrial growth rates have fallen steadily since the late 1960s. The productivity of outputs from natural resources, the labor force, and capital investments will continue to decline for the Soviets. They will be forced to turn to more remote and climatically inhospitable areas for their natural resources. Their work force will shrink except in areas of non-Slavic ethnicity, which are far from the present centers of population and industry. Their managerial efficiency and investment choices will probably worsen still further as the increasing complexity of an advanced economy becomes even less suitable to centralized bureaucratic direction. Moreover, the brightest members of the professional and technological class will continue to turn as far away from ideology as they can, leaving careerists to rise to the top of the party and the government.

Economic failure and political dissent in Eastern Europe, and nationalist feeling there and in Afghanistan, are likely to become more acute problems for the Soviet empire. The trend that will make Slavs a much smaller majority and make ethnic Russians a minority within the Soviet Union by the year 2000 must be very disturbing to the Russia-centered Soviet leadership. The economic and demo-graphic problems are likely to cause the already slowing Soviet growth to flatten and may even produce a downturn in the standard of living, especially if the military budget continues to grow at a rate of 4 percent a year in real terms while the already lower overall growth rate of the Soviet GNP shrinks further. But the Soviet system is unlikely to break down during this century, barring the combination of a substantial worsening in the conditions of life and further major foreign policy setbacks. And the Soviet leaders, recognizing that their military buildup has brought them significant international advantages and that it remains (along with their single-mindedness and determination) their most effective tool in international affairs, are likely to continue that military buildup.

A NEW GENERATION OF SOVIET LEADERS

An unparalleled change in Soviet leadership is inevitable during the 1980s as a result of the persistence in leadership roles for the past thirty years of the generation now in their seventies. This wholesale change, which will extend through several levels of the party and the government, regionally and nationally, makes prediction of the behavior of the new Soviet leadership extremely difficult. The coming generation of leaders did not know the Stalinist terror personally. They did not experience the massive destruction and sacrifice of World War II from positions of responsibility. They do not remember the anxieties that the leaders of the 1940s, 1950s, and early 1960s felt in a world that seemed to them to be dominated by an intimidating U.S. power, a power that surrounded them, overflew their skies, and dominated the world's economic, political, and military affairs. The new Soviet leaders who assume power during the 1980s may decide to help solve the great domestic problems they already face by moving to ease their external relations. Or they may turn to foreign adventures in an attempt to win decisive advantage in the contest with the West, to obtain added resources to solve their internal problems, or to stabilize and expand their own dominance as a ruling class. It would be foolish of the industrialized democracies to assume that either course is inevitable. But whatever marginal effect (and it will be marginal) their policies and behavior can have in encouraging Soviet leaders to adopt the first of these alternative policies should be sought. The question is what policies and behavior are most likely to have that effect.

The period of leadership transition is likely to increase the influence of the military and security forces within the Soviet elite. Potential successors are likely to court those power centers because that power is physical, focused, and explicit, whereas the power of the bureaucratic, technological, and managerial elite is diffuse and remote. The public court paid to the military by Brezhnev in his last days and by Andropov (the ranking alumnus of the security organs) in his first days as General Secretary illustrates this conclusion, as does the upward movement of Aliyev (another alumnus of the security apparatus) and the public prominence of the military and police during the transition.

The new leaders will have risen to power through severe and probably protracted struggle of which we are already seeing the early signs. Keeping and expanding power will be their goal. They are likely to have much less experience in dealing with foreign countries on political and military matters than do the present gerontocrats, who have kept these matters substantially to themselves. They are likely, however, to be better educated and more sophisticated about internal and international economic matters. But sophistication is not the same thing as liberalism or good will. There is no way of knowing whether they will be easier or more difficult to deal with. The prospect of Soviet concessions is already being held out to Western Europe, China, and Japan by the first post-Brezhnev Soviet government. It also shows skill at exploiting U.S. government miscues and existing strains between the United States and those other power centers.

The only conclusion that can be drawn with some confidence is that the change to a new generation of Soviet rulers will create major new risks and opportunities for the United States in dealing with them. Other than that, the United States must deal with probabilities and possibilities, not certainties, so any other conclusions ought to be expressed with considerable caution and in very general terms.

THE UNITED STATES AND THE SOVIET UNION

The Soviets are likely to pursue an expansionist foreign policy for the rest of this century. Their massive internal and substantial external problems have only intensified the concentration of the leaders on their goals. The first of these goals is maintaining their power at home. They have a good thing going for themselves, and the end of the Stalinist terror and the improvement in economic output over the past few decades have made it better. Their other main goal is to maintain their power along the periphery of the Soviet Union and to extend that power, if possible, to more remote areas as well. Thus the United States and the Soviet Union will continue to be adversaries at least in political terms for the rest of this century.

Nevertheless, the United States and the Soviet Union have some common interests. The first is in avoiding the unimaginably and indeed terminally catastrophic destruction of a nuclear war. The United States ought to aim, and generally has aimed, at a peaceful world system in which the peoples of all countries can determine their own destinies with a minimum of outside coercion and disruption. The Soviet leaders seek, at worst, to gain a dominant position in the world. Both of these aims would be rendered impossible by a nuclear war, so both countries have the strongest possible motivation to prevent a nuclear war.

To say that the Soviets would greatly prefer to gain their ends eventually without a nuclear war and that the United States has as its most important goal the avoidance of a nuclear war is not to say that nuclear war will never happen. But it provides an important basis for pursuing joint policies. Examples are arms limitation, the hot line for communication in a crisis, and nonproliferation policies to increase stability in the rest of the world. In such efforts, each side will try to maximize its own relative advantage even as it attempts to develop some mutually advantageous cooperative policies. The prospects of success will continue to be limited by the adversary relationship and the existence of specific conflicting goals.

U.S. policy toward the Soviet Union must keep the Soviets from gaining dominion in the areas that are critical to U.S. security—specifically, Western Europe, Southwest Asia, including the Middle East, and the Far East. The United States with its friends and allies must be strong enough militarily to prevent a successful Soviet military attack or major political intimidation in those areas and to maintain a dominant military position in the Western Hemisphere. To that end, the United States must build up its political and economic as well as military strength. It must encourage alignments as well as strengthen alliances. At the same time, the industrialized democracies must not forget the factor of Soviet paranoia. An attempt on their part to destabilize Soviet leadership or its dominance of Eastern Europe by economic warfare or subversion would carry grave risks; it should not even be considered except as a response to a clear and direct Soviet threat to an area critical to U.S. security. An attempt to create an explicit military superiority over the Soviet Union of the sort that existed during the 1950s, and the appearance of a military threat to the Soviet Union implicit in such a military posture, would be dangerous and unlikely to succeed.

Given the difference in the ways the United States and the Soviet Union perceive the world, it is not clear that these goals—maintaining enough strength to prevent political intimidation in areas important to the United States while avoiding a threatening appearance to the

Soviet Union—are both possible. Seeking to walk that narrow line (if it exists) will challenge U.S. leadership skills to the maximum.

Are there carrots that the United States can dangle before the Soviet leaders to promote a change in the direction of less expansionist and disruptive Soviet policies? There may be. But some earlier carrots have not got the mule pulling in the right direction. The Soviet leaders sought military parity after the Cuban missile crisis. They now have it. The easing of their expansionist and paranoid tendencies that some thought would follow from such parity has not yet appeared. The Soviets want a part at least equal to that of the United States in influencing events all over the world. They have yet to achieve the economic strength or display the political responsibility necessary to lay claim to such a role. The "web of relationships" encouraged by the United States and its allies early in the 1970s, giving the Soviets the promise of economic benefit in return for more responsible political behavior, especially in the Third World, did not come into being—or at least did not produce the hoped-for behavior. But the Soviets have a legitimate argument that the United States reneged on such economic promises as most-favored-nation treatment. It is likely that what they expected from the United States was not what the United States understood by the bargain, nor was what the United States expected from them quite what they understood. Nevertheless, it would be worth trying such an approach again at the right time. But the two parties must be more explicit about the expected behavior of each. Moreover, a schedule of commitment should be included—on the U.S. side, a commitment not to change the economic rules within less than two, three, or even five years, at which time a review would be made; and on the Soviet side, commitments of corresponding duration and specificity.

Such an approach is inevitably a temporizing one. The goal of the United States should be to contain Soviet expansionist tendencies and at the same time to outlast them, hoping for but not assuming an eventual evolution in the Soviet political system or its acceptance of an international order that seeks stability and relative freedom for each country to find its own destiny. The existence of internal contradictions in Soviet policy suggests that over time Soviet motivations and behavior may change for the better. Such a change is rather unlikely in this century, but U.S. attitudes, words, and actions may be able to encourage such a shift in coming decades.

3

Economic Policies and National Security

Economic developments within nations and economic interactions between nations critically affect political and military balances and strategies. Economic interests and needs affect foreign and defense policy decisions. Military capability must rest on an infrastructure of economic strength (although in recent history there have been major regional military powers that were able to exert substantial temporary influence without a large economic base—Japan in the 1930s and early 1940s, Vietnam in recent years). The connection runs the other way, too. Military strength can be used as part of a political strategy to extract economic advantage. That worked for the Third Reich in Eastern Europe during the late 1930s. The debate continues, whether the cost of building major military strength critically detracts from economic performance, whether the economies of industrialized democracies can sustain a military buildup to meet the challenge of Soviet military power, and what economic policies should be pursued in the competition of the industrialized democracies with the Soviet Union.

THE EFFECTS OF MILITARY SPENDING

What are the effects of military spending on the economy of the United States? It is often asserted that military expenditures are a uniquely intense drain on the national economy, unlike either private or other public expenditures. The reason given is that military expenditures do not produce any goods that add to the consumer economy, but instead are "wasted." At the other extreme, it is argued that military expenditures, especially on the development of high-technology equipment, propel those technologies, and the rest of the economy, into a more advanced technological state and that they promote capital expenditures in the areas that make the economy technologically more sophisticated and more efficient. Neither of these arguments contains more than a kernel of truth; both, in fact, are substantially misleading and incorrect.

It is true that government expenditures on military hardware and on military salaries do not directly increase the productive capacity of the economy, as do capital expenditures made by industry. But the same is true of practically all other Federal Government expenditures—and of private consumption, for that matter. A more sensible approach would be to compare the effects of military expenditures on the overall state of the economy with the effects of the other largest category of government expenditures, income transfers. The comparison is particularly apt because income transfers are designed to "insure domestic tranquility" and "promote the general welfare"—the two goals that, in the preamble to the Constitution, flank "provide for the common defense."

Neither type of expenditure produces consumer goods or services directly. But both fund services—ostensibly, the preservation of peace and the establishment of social justice, respectively. They may or may not succeed; there are those who claim that each category of expenditure is counterproductive of its goal. But few would maintain that the intended goals are themselves wasteful or useless. The income transferred to recipients of Social Security, food stamps, or welfare, or paid on behalf of recipients of Medicaid, is used to procure a variety of goods and services. The funds from the military budget that go to workers and companies in defense industries, to active-duty military and civil service personnel, and to retired military personnel are also subsequently spent on a variety of goods and services. Each is distributed through the economy, thereby making a contribution to the GNP that multiplies as it stimulates further transactions. Both categories of expenditure contribute to overall demand without directly increasing the supply of consumer goods.

The effect on inflation of small increases in income transfers or in military expenditures is roughly the same. The portion of military expenditures that goes into procurement of weapons or other military hardware, however, is subject to bottlenecks and to shortages of materials and skilled workers if it is increased too rapidly from year to year. The seriousness of this problem will depend on the degree to which those skills and industrial facilities are already saturated with military and civilian production. An economy operating at full steam will be pushed toward inflation by increased government procurement expenditures, civil or military, more than one that is sluggish. Government nonprocurement expenditures, civil or military, have a similar but smaller effect. If the rate of increase in military procurement is too high (under present economic circumstances and at present procurement levels, more than about 15 percent a year in constant dollars), the cost per unit of military hardware will begin to inflate more rapidly than the general economy. The point at which this occurs will depend on the level of civilian demand for the corresponding skills and plant. In extreme circumstances the result could be increased expenditures with no increase in the volume of procurement. At a still more rapid rate of increase in military expenditures this inflationary effect can spill over into the general economy.

All of these effects occurred during the Vietnam War when substantial military expenditures were added to Great Society social programs in an economy already operating near capacity, without tax increases to pay for them. Later, the growth of demand for aerospace and electronic parts in the civilian sector caused an escalation of costs in those areas and in major military systems from 1977 to 1980, at a rate several percentage points higher per year than the rise in other prices. The economic slump from 1980 to 1982 allowed a more rapid growth in military procurement without as much of an inflationary effect.

It is also often asserted that military expenditures create fewer jobs than do other outlays. Of course, transfer expenditures of the government, unlike military expenditures, create no jobs directly. Public works expenditures, directly or through revenue sharing with the local or state government for that purpose, may create or at least reallocate more jobs per million dollars spent than do defense expenditures. Perhaps the most useful comparison is with the entire economy. In 1982, defense employment (civilian employees of the Federal Government, active duty military personnel, and private sector employees in defense industries) amounted to about 6 million, or about 6 percent of the employed labor force. Defense outlays were about 6 percent of the GNP. Thus, defense is just about as labor-intensive as the rest of the economy. Defense *procurement* is more labor-intensive than the oil industry, less labor-intensive than the fast-food industry, and probably about as labor-intensive as the average representative of the manufacturing sector.

The effect of government expenditures for military technology on the United States's more general technological and economic development is equally ambiguous. There can be little doubt that the civilian aircraft and electronics industries in the United States received a substantial boost during the 1950s and 1960s from military expenditures on those technologies. The computer industry and the jet aircraft industry in the United States both owe their start and their early predominance over foreign competitors to this injection of capital, technology, and skilled labor. Government expenditures on capital-intensive facilities for military production, unlike most government expenditures, increase the nation's productive capacity.

In recent years, however, the effect of government expenditures in those industries has become considerably less clear-cut. The civilian markets for integrated circuits, microcomputers and related electronics are much larger than the military ones. Military requirements predominate in a few specialized areas—very high capacity high-speed computers, for example. These technologies have applications elsewhere, but those are not the largest part of the market, nor do civilian applications inevitably arise for each new military technology. Similarly, though advances in military aircraft design continue to have some helpful applications for civilian aircraft manufacturers, the movement of military requirements into the supersonic range has made the spillover from military technology smaller than it was in the 1950s and 1960s. Where skilled personnel or facilities are a limiting factor, it has been suggested, military needs may divert them from the civilian high-technology industries, but at present this does not outweigh the beneficial spillover from military programs. Both factors are modest.

The effects of military expenditures on the economy and on inflation, then, are not very different from the effects of nonmilitary government expenditures. One possible negative exception is the case of a too-rapid expansion of military procurement activities, say, beyond 15 percent a year in real dollars. There will then be bottlenecks in, and competition for, special skills, materials, and technologies. But, except at times of rapid spending increases, any such negative results would probably be offset by the modest positive effects of government investment in high-technology developments that spill over into civilian applications and by the effect of government capital investments in plant that is useful for both military and civilian production. Rapid increases in real defense procurement will squeeze the civilian economy if it is near full employment and full use of civilian capacity—which was certainly not the case during the period 1980 to 1982.

Whatever the effects of defense programs on the economy, they are likely to be far less at the present level of defense expenditures—

less than 6 percent of the GNP—than at the 10 or 11 percent level that prevailed through the late 1950s. The fact that the economy is considerably more troubled now than it was then does not mean that the decrease in relative expenditure on military programs has hampered the economy. Labor productivity, management skill, investment and savings rates, the legislative and regulatory environment in which investment decisions are made, the flexibility and work ethic of the labor force, the cost and availability of oil and other natural resources, and other such factors are much more important in determining the growth rate and the health of the economy than is the level of military expenditures—at least as long as it stays between 5 and 10 percent of GNP.

MILITARY SPENDING IN
THE INDUSTRIALIZED DEMOCRACIES

The question remains whether the economies of the industrialized democracies can in practical political terms sustain a buildup of their military efforts and expenditures in response to the expansion of Soviet military capabilities, which has continued for twenty years at a real annual rate of about 4 percent. During this same period in the United States, defense expenditures in constant dollars fell slightly before the Vietnam War, rose substantially during it, fell even more substantially thereafter, and then began to rise again, slowly, in the late 1970s. As a percentage of GNP, they fell from about 10 percent to 5 percent and are now rising past 6 percent. The European allies of the United States increased their defense expenditures substantially in real terms from 1965 to 1975, while keeping the percentage of their GNPs devoted to defense about constant. There are variations among the Western European countries: The United Kingdom's percentage of GNP spent on defense actually rose, because its GNP fell; West Germany's spending as a percentage of GNP increased slightly; France's remained the highest in Western Europe throughout the period. Japan, starting from nearly nothing, increased its defense expenditures to about 1 percent of GNP. Because Japan's GNP increased more than fourfold from 1960 to 1980, this has produced a Japanese defense budget of about $12 billion, fifth among noncommunist industrialized nations. The United States spends about $200 billion; West Germany, France, and Great Britain all spend in the neighborhood of $25 billion to $30 billion.

In purely economic terms, these countries have the ability to increase their military budgets and capabilities substantially. Given that the total GNPs of the industrialized democracies add up to about

$7 trillion a year, an increase in defense expenditures of 1 percent of GNP would make available about $70 billion more, nearly half of it in the U.S. budget. The present percentages of GNP devoted to income transfers are about 14 percent in the United States, near 25 percent in Western Europe, and a little less than 10 percent in Japan. This suggests that funding could be made available to make a major difference in the military balance between the Soviet Union and the industrialized democracies.

Whether the latter have the will to do so and can overcome the serious political difficulties that would be entailed in such an expansion is quite a different question. In the nations of Western Europe, social welfare programs much larger than those in the United States have been embedded into the economic and political system. In Japan, where per capita social welfare expenditures are lower than they are in the United States, there are substantial political inhibitions to increasing defense expenditures, connected with both constitutional strictures and long-held party positions. In both Western Europe and Japan, defense programs are also limited by the public perception that there is no major military threat. Moreover, transfers of even 1 percent from domestic to military expenditures are particularly difficult politically when high unemployment, low economic growth rates, and substantial inflation are the general rule in these countries, even though underutilized industrial plant and unemployed youth make increases in the military less inflationary and disruptive than they would otherwise be. These factors strongly suggest that a major increase in military expenditures over the next five years is unlikely except in the United States—and even there it is only moderately likely, unless the Soviet Union were to undertake further expansionist or manipulative moves like its actions in Afghanistan and in Poland.

ECONOMIC POLICIES AND THE COMPETITION
WITH THE SOVIET UNION

The productivity of the industrialized democracies and the correspondingly high standards of living that prevail provide an extremely effective instrument for promoting their national security. First, they enable these countries to bear the economic costs of military preparedness. Second, to the extent that the citizens of these nations recognize the relative advantages of their economic situation over that of the citizens of the communist countries, their will to self-defense should be strengthened. Finally, the example of economic well-being set for countries in the Third World is also an important factor in forming their attitudes toward the democratic and the Soviet alternatives. Even those Third World leaders who are tempted to follow the Soviet model for the power that it confers on the ruling class in such societies seek the material benefits that so clearly favor the market economies.

All this is not to ignore the very real economic, political, and social deficiencies in the industrialized democratic societies. Unemployment has returned to levels unknown since the Great Depression. Inadequate or inefficient attention is still given to the needs of those who, whether through their own doing or through external circumstances, have fared poorly in economic competition. There is excessive preoccupation with material values. Long-range planning, both in governments and in many industrial enterprises, is so weak that avoidable dislocations still cause much pain. Industrialized democratic societies are sadly vulnerable to the effects of international economic cycles and unforeseen catastrophes. All of these factors weaken the appeal of the democratic-capitalist or mixed-economy political and economic systems. The results of the poor economic performance of the industrialized democracies in the 1970s imply that their poor prospects for the 1980s will produce continuing and even increasing stresses among them, political difficulties within them, and constraints on their abilities to maintain adequate military forces and to operate effectively in international affairs.

Another complicating factor is the unparalleled increase in prosperity together with the absence of war in Europe from about 1948 to 1973, which accustomed a whole generation to the idea that peace and steady improvement in standards of living constituted the natural order of things. This attitude makes the industrialized democracies fragile in the face of adversity, and a lack of resolve could well erode the willingness of their people to make sacrifices to preserve the democratic system and the market economy.

But taken all in all, there is really no contest between the economic attractions of the market economies and those of the Soviet system, whether to Third World nations or to the citizens of the industrialized democracies themselves, just as the attractions of freedom in the end outweigh its risks in the perception of those who have any opportunity to choose and also of most of those who lack that opportunity. The industrialized democracies can take advantage of this situation to strengthen their own security not by any specific action against or in response to the Soviet bloc but by using the economic, technological, and managerial skills they have to aid developing countries and by informing people in all countries of the world of this situation. The facts of life in the democracies, compared to what exists anywhere else, constitute the most effective propaganda of all.

Is it possible or valuable to use economic policies as a more direct and coercive instrument in this competition with the Soviet Union? In the early 1970s the industrialized democracies sought, but failed, through economic policies to influence importantly Soviet military and political behavior. For one thing, the Soviets have historically attempted to remain economically self-sufficient, in part to avoid becoming subject to just such pressures. (They have become dependent for grain on the United States, Canada, Australia, and Argentina. They will import 30 million tons or more annually for the rest of the 1980s. But these are primarily feed grains; even if all grain exporters were to place an embargo on sales to the Soviet Union, its population would continue to have an adequate diet, though Soviet meat production would suffer severely.) More important, the Soviet leaders see marginal or even significant slowing down in the rate of improvement of the material condition of the average Soviet citizen as less important than the expansion of Soviet power. Even if an economic boycott or embargo hurts Soviet citizens more than it hurts the citizens of the democratic countries that impose it (as would usually be the case), the Soviet government can constrain its citizens to endure this more easily than the democratic governments can constrain or cajole their citizens to accept the lesser pain. Then too, another reason the Soviet Union has refused to pursue economic cooperation with the industrialized democracies is that their governments, and particularly that of the United States, have tended to change the terms of economic relations with the Soviet Union relatively frequently based on year-to-year or even month-to-month fluctuations in U.S.-Soviet relations.

Should the industrialized democracies design their economic policies to try to inhibit Soviet economic growth? The argument for such policies is that the Soviets would face difficult choices in allocating resources between their military and civilian sectors if their economic growth were further slowed by the denial of markets in and credits from the market economies of North America, Western Europe, and Japan. The goal would be to slow the rate of Soviet military growth or else to damage the Soviet economy in other ways to make expansionism more difficult for the Soviets to pursue. The opposing argument is that such an economic policy would be seen by the Soviet people as an act of economic warfare, which would strengthen the solidarity of the Soviet masses with the ruling class by legitimizing the latter's claim that capitalist enmity rather than the deficiencies of their own system is the cause of Soviet economic troubles. It would also strengthen the hands of those leaders who advocate a more confrontational posture toward the United States. Finally, such an economic policy could not be expected to succeed unless all the industrial democracies participated. The United States would probably not be able to persuade its allies and friends to join in such a policy, and U.S. producers would suffer a loss of sales to no useful effect should the United States alone follow such a policy.

A separate issue is the degree to which it is feasible or even desirable to limit transfer of dual-use technology (civilian technology with potential military applications) to the Soviets, or to others in Eastern Europe or elsewhere who could be expected to transfer it to the Soviets. Again, as the United States is by no means the sole supplier of the industrial products and technologies the Soviets need, the pros and cons of a technology boycott can often be seen as principally a matter of what limitations the United States can persuade its allies to agree to and what inhibitions are imposed on the Soviet economy if the United States acts alone.

GUIDELINES FOR AN ECONOMIC POLICY
TOWARD THE SOVIET UNION

The Soviets have not been deterred by fear of Western economic sanctions from adventures in the Third World, either direct or through Cuban proxies, or from their actions in Afghanistan and Poland. Relying in part on their own ability to cope with such sanctions, and in part on their confidence that the capitalist rope salesmen will continue to compete for the privilege of supplying—on credit!—the rope by which they themselves will be hanged, the Soviets have been willing to have their citizens eat less meat and more bread rather than restrain their plans and actions in the cause of expanding their power.

If the Soviet leaders face a decision they regard as central to the maintenance of their power—such as a loss of control by the Polish Communist Party leadership—the threat or even the reality of economic sanctions will not fundamentally change the choice they will make. But it is nonetheless important for the industrialized democracies to impose such economic sanctions as they can muster when Soviet actions become unacceptable. Soviet leaders will then be aware that such actions do carry a penalty, even if they are prepared to bear it in a cause they regard as important enough. In such cases that perception could still affect the detailed nature of their actions; in less central matters it might alter their decisions in an important, even decisive way.

The economic forces that create dependencies can be seen to operate in both directions and sometimes to operate more strongly on Western sellers than on Soviet buyers. Western banks and governments lent more than $25 billion to Poland under circumstances and on terms that assumed a far too optimistic picture of future Polish economic advances. To some extent these loans were intended to promote closer ties between Poland and the West, and to some extent they were seen as creating jobs and markets for Western producers. For both reasons, Western governments encouraged them. The banks have since become concerned about the adverse effects of a default on their balance sheets and their outraged stockholders and on the international financial and economic structure. These legitimate concerns may have prompted a softer political, and economic, response to the Soviet-inspired repression in Poland by some nations than would otherwise have been forthcoming. U.S. farmers recognize that the higher demand for their products in world markets created by the Soviet need for feed grains to increase the amount of meat in the diet of Soviet citizens increases their world prices, so they opposed embargoes on the sale of grain to the Soviets in retaliation for Soviet actions in Afghanistan and in Poland.

Thus the ability of Western governments to impose economic penalties on the Soviets has been undercut by the economic interests of specific pressure groups within their own societies. This is not a reason to rule out any attempts to use economic leverage but it does suggest that these attempts may well be more damaging to relationships among industrialized democracies than to the Soviets unless they are carefully designed—and sometimes even then.

Given such limitations, what constitutes a reasonable policy for the United States and one to which it should try to persuade its allies to adhere? Without expecting much effectiveness from economic measures as a lever for Soviet behavior or as a punishment for Soviet actions, the United States should observe the following principles.

Individual corporate and financial entities in the industrialized democracies often find their transactions with the Soviets and with Eastern Europe profitable—or at least they may be temporarily able to reflect them as such in their financial statements. But competition exists among firms in the United States, Japan, and Western Europe and indeed among the overall economies of all those nations. As a result, the Soviet Union, operating as a single economic entity, can manipulate this competition—both in conventional purchases, sales, and loans and in the relations it establishes for capital formation and energy supply to serve its own political and economic ends. For that reason trade, credit, and energy relations with the Soviet Union and Eastern Europe should be governed in detail by policies set by the U.S., Western European, and Japanese governments rather than determined by individual firms. Soviet leverage on these governments through such firms would thus be greatly limited.

An extreme approach would be to require that all trade and loans be effected directly through the governments. The mercantilist implications of such an approach at a time when free trade even among market economies is difficult enough to preserve argue against its use, as does the fact that East-West trade would still not be monolithic on the Western side. A more modest approach would probably accomplish much of the necessary insulation: Only loans guaranteed by the governments of the industrialized democracies could be made— and the governments would decide which loans should be made, either case by case or according to a policy that could be reviewed periodically. This approach assumes that sales to the Soviet bloc of items not controlled as military or dual-use, for cash only, give the Soviets relatively little leverage either before or after the sale.

The banks, though insured against total loss for such future guaranteed loans, would still have to decide whether a particular loan to the Soviet bloc met the criteria of opportunity cost when compared with possible loans elsewhere. The democratic governments could charge the banks a suitable percentage as a premium for such insurance. Forbidding unguaranteed loans would reduce pressure on the banks, or from the banks on governments, to make concessions to prevent a Soviet-bloc default. The democratic governments would still face the pressures provided by their own potential losses in the event of a default. They would at the same time retain a carrot and a stick for use on the Soviets and Eastern Europeans—among whom distinctions should be made in such decisions on the basis of economic status, degree of adherence to Soviet foreign policy, and extent of domestic repression.

As for loans now outstanding to Eastern European countries, especially (in the delicate parlance of bankers) "nonperforming" ones, governments could purchase these loans at some fraction of their face value and thereby assume responsibility for the decision either to reschedule or to trigger a formal default. Such a step would reduce the inhibitions on causing formal default, because individual banks and the international financial system would be at less risk. But a government repurchase would require governments to assume these debts at a time when their budget deficits are on the rise. That makes the idea less likely to be implemented.

Poland currently owes $25 billion to Western banks and governments. It is completely incapable of repaying it. When arrearages on such a debt occur, banks usually demand interest payments but work out a rescheduling (stretchout) of principal payments at a higher interest rate and under conditions set by the International Monetary Fund (IMF) for the internal economic program of the debtor. Poland's economic situation is so poor that this procedure may not be feasible without a Soviet hard-currency subsidy. If this is so, the lenders will have the choice of tolerating unrescheduled arrearages in principal and even in interest or of imposing a formal default. Default would make all principal due at once and terminate payments. In either case, all new credits would almost certainly end, not only to Poland, but probably to other Eastern European governments as well, and perhaps even to the Soviet Union. Other Eastern European governments are not in the dire economic and political straits of Poland, but they are also likely to face credit crises in the near future. The credit situation of the Eastern European nations is such that lenders are unlikely to increase total credit outstanding to any of them now that the Soviet Union is no longer seen as their financial guarantor. (The Soviet Union itself is still seen as a good credit risk.)

The best approach, in my judgment, is to reschedule principal payments only on the basis of clear commitments about economic programs along the lines of the rules the IMF imposes. Arrearages should be allowed to remain in a temporary status, so as to exert continuing pressure on the Eastern Europeans. Loans should be formally placed into default only if interest payments are not met or as a penalty for unacceptable political behavior. Further loans and more generous repayment terms, financed by the governments of the industrialized democracies, should be held out as incentives for more acceptable political behavior—further loans to Poland, for example, in return for a genuine easing of repression there. The United States has some leverage in gaining support among its allies for this overall approach: It can threaten to force a formal default of the outstanding loans. Under present conditions, the international banking system would be damaged but not wrecked, even by defaults on all Soviet bloc loans. There is a much more severe risk of general default on loans to Third World countries.

During this time of deteriorated U.S.-Soviet relations, such commodities as agricultural products should still be sold to the Soviets and the rest of the Soviet bloc, but without preferential terms on either price or credit. The United States and its allies should not give the Soviet bloc the same concessionary terms they provide to friendly developing countries—a category into which the Soviets do not even try to put themselves except on this single issue. Embargoes on such sales should be reserved for use as a response to further unacceptable Soviet behavior such as a military invasion of Poland.

More favorable credit terms (even most-favored-nation status) should be considered if relations improve over a sustained period.

Export of technology that has direct military application should be denied to the Soviet Union and its allies. In the areas of indirectly usable technology and dual-use technology—microelectronic circuits, new materials, computers, lasers, and fiber optics—the issues become more difficult. Because leakage is inevitable, the goal should be to keep the Soviets four or five years behind in such technologies. The United States should put pressure on its allies to agree, recognizing that its leverage is limited, for loosening alliance ties would hurt the United States as well. But the United States has technology that its allies want, and this technology could be held back if the allies fail to agree to enforceable restraints on its retransfer to the Soviet bloc.

The industrialized democracies should give preference to selling products instead of manufacturing capability. The industrialized democracies should maintain as much control as possible over the long-term usefulness of equipment they sell the Soviets (auto plants, for example, or oil-drilling equipment) by controlling the availability of spare parts. The Soviets prefer turn-key arrangements—that is, plants built by an outside contractor but operated entirely by the purchaser—but they have not always been able to operate effectively turn-key operations constructed for them by foreign contractors. Democratic governments should encourage situations in which Soviet factory operation depends on the continued presence of foreign contractor employees. That dependence may provide useful leverage.

Cutoffs in trade or credit are inherently leaky and likely to be divisive among suppliers, so they should be either imposed for a limited time that is fixed at its inception or planned from the beginning to be eased at an undetermined later time, even if the act for which it was imposed has not been reversed. The rationale is one of a limited penalty for a limited though unacceptable act.

The balance of economic interest among the democratic nations differs for various commodities, technologies, and industrial products. This makes it difficult to reach a policy that is fair to the economies of the various allied countries (and those of other nonaligned but friendly nations, such as Argentina). But it is important to have a policy that gives evidence of continuity, even between successive U.S. administrations of different parties. One way to approach both problems is to attempt to reach agreement with Western European and Japanese suppliers of technologies and industrial equipment, and with Australian, Argentinian, and Canadian grain producers, to review Soviet behavior every two or three years and not to make major changes in policy except after such reviews. In return, the United

States should seek from its allies agreement that such sales would be subject to some sort of U.S. veto. An arrangement of this kind would be difficult to reach but it would offer the suppliers—and the Soviets—the advantage of relatively long-term, predictable decisions, which make planning easier for everyone. U.S. leverage is again limited. But U.S. technological and commodity production does outweigh that of other suppliers. The value of stable markets, and the implicit U.S. threat of undercutting such markets, should carry some influence.

Finally, what about the use of economic sanctions against countries outside the Soviet bloc? Trying to get Third World countries to support U.S. political views against those of the Soviets by cutting off normal trade relations is not only unlikely to work but smacks too much of Soviet-style coercion. Even for U.S. economic aid, the proper criterion should be whether or not the recipient is an active tool of Soviet interests, rather than whether it always supports U.S. political positions.

In summary, U.S. economic leverage is of limited use in persuading the Soviets to abandon or even moderate their policy of expanding their power wherever they can, whenever they can. The effect that the United States can have is too small, and Soviet motivations too strong, to expect this to be a decisive or even a major influence in cases the Soviets regard as central. But details in those cases, and entire decisions in less central ones, may be so influenced. Loans, technology transfers, and expanded trade would clearly ease the Soviets' worsening economic problems; they can be offered as potential rewards for cooperative behavior. As in the past, a military response to unacceptable Soviet behavior will often be unrealistic or inadvisable. But in some cases more than mere moral outrage will be necessary. In such circumstances, economic actions are an appropriate expression and can be something—if not much—of a carrot and stick.

In every case it will be desirable to get as much allied and friendly cooperation as possible, but there have been and will be occasions when the United States must proceed alone. Even in those circumstances, every attempt should be made to consult with other governments and to act in a way that divides the United States from its friends as little as possible. Discouraging increased European purchases of Soviet gas, for example, and impeding the funding of a new Soviet pipeline for that purpose, may well be strategically sensible; but after Western European countries had decided to proceed, unilateral U.S. attempts to prevent them from doing so became more damaging to the United States than to the Soviet Union.

The principal changes that must be made in U.S. economic policy toward the Soviet bloc are greater consistency and more stability. These can be ensured by regular reviews every few years or whenever major changes in East-West relations loom rather than whenever a new individual transaction is proposed; by more effort to devise common or at least parallel policies among the industrialized democracies; and by the imposition of penalties for fixed periods rather than until a change in the offending policy—or worse, a weakening of political will in the industrialized democracies—occurs.

The size and fundamental health of the U.S. economy, even deep in recession, is one of the greatest strengths of U.S. foreign and security policy. The use of its economic strength must be thought through and coordinated with its allies and friends. Without rational and effective foreign economic policies, the military strength and diplomacy of the United States will carry a severe extra burden.

4

The Energy Issue

One economic issue that will without question affect U.S. national security for the foreseeable future is energy—where to get it, how to get it, how to pay for it, and how to ensure a sufficient supply at a bearable price.

Energy is unique among economic issues and among natural resources. Energy consumption dwarfs most other economic activities. The total value of energy consumed in the United States alone is about $400 billion a year. And this energy is a vital input into all other industrial and manufacturing processes. Energy cannot be easily replaced by other resources, though conservation can reduce consumption rates significantly. Substituting other forms of energy for the natural hydrocarbons in fossil fuels has proved a difficult task.

Fossil fuels, in turn, are unique among energy sources. They are convenient, they are relatively compact, they are easily processed, and they are ideally suited to power transportation. (Several fossil fuels are also important in international markets because they can be made into chemical feedstocks.) Hydrocarbon consumption is particularly dependent on international trade, and thus on international relations, because the supplies of and demand for these fuels are not evenly distributed around the world. In 1980 the United States imported about 40 percent of its oil at a cost of about $76 billion. About 63 percent of the 42 million barrels of oil produced each day outside the communist countries is traded internationally, with an annual value of about $325 billion. Through the 1980s, at least a quarter of the noncommunist world's oil—half of its total oil imports—will come from the Persian Gulf region. Many of the nations in that region are developing countries in a politically unstable and militarily threatened part of the world. The sea routes by which that oil (and a much smaller amount of liquefied natural gas) is traded could be closed by military action. The double oil shocks of 1973–1974 and 1979–1980 left nominal oil prices sixteen times higher in 1980 than in 1970 (six times higher in real terms). The severe domestic economic consequences and international crises these events created are a measure of the importance of energy in general and of hydrocarbons in particular.

To ensure the continued availability of such vital resources, the United States, the other industrialized democracies, and developing countries must make major technological, economic, and political changes. But such changes will be difficult and time-consuming. The oil-importing nations began the 1980s in a weakened economic condition, so future supply difficulties will have even more serious effects. Only if the industrialized democracies—and especially the United States—build upon, expand, and accelerate the plans drafted and enacted during the late 1970s to ease this problem can a similar state of dependence and risk be avoided through the 1990s. The longer the dependence and political instability continues, the greater the likelihood of an economic catastrophe or of a war breaking out in a struggle over these resources.

THE DEGREE OF DEPENDENCE

The industrialized countries depend absolutely on energy for their prosperity, and their energy consumption has grown enormously, along with their GNPs, since World War II. During that same time, there has been a major shift from coal to oil and natural gas as the fuels of choice. From 1950 to 1970 oil prices were very low, perhaps even artificially low, but other reasons for the shift include the convenience of these fuels, their ease of transportation, and the smaller amount of polluting residues created by their use. In transportation, petroleum derivatives (or, in the future, synthetic fuels) have enormous advantages by virtue of their high energy per unit of volume and their usefulness in the internal combustion engine.

Energy resources in general and oil in particular have thus become an enormously powerful lever for those who control them or can control their flow. This is true despite the substantial variation in dependence on imported oil among individual nations. Of the industrial nations, Canada and the Soviet Union will probably be substantially self-sufficient through most or all of the 1980s. Among the smaller countries, Norway will be an exporter. The United Kingdom is practically self-sufficient in oil and other sources of energy, but its continued economic decline shows that such self-sufficiency does not solve all the problems of industrialized countries.

The rest of Western Europe and Japan are very much more dependent on imported oil than is the United States. Western Europe imports about 80 percent of its oil, and Japan nearly 100 percent. Various European countries have taken steps to reduce this dependence. In 1980, the government of French President Giscard d'Estaing introduced a drastic plan to reduce the percentage of oil in France's total primary energy consumption from 56 percent to 30 percent by 1990, to increase the contribution of nuclear energy to approximately 30 percent, and to expand the domestic market for coal greatly. (The Mitterrand government has modified these plans only marginally.) The discovery of substantial natural gas deposits under the North Sea has given the Netherlands a reprieve from dependence on imports, but that supply is likely to decline substantially during the next decade. The Federal Republic of Germany, Italy, and most of the smaller European nations have seen their nuclear programs substantially slowed by the antinuclear movement, so they will continue to be dependent on imports of oil and, to a lesser degree, coal and natural gas. Japan has had a considerable nuclear program, but it will continue to be almost totally dependent on foreign sources for its hydrocarbons.

The developing countries are in many ways even more dependent on energy, and especially on imported hydrocarbons. They are currently in a stage of industrial development and urbanization that requires greater volumes of energy per unit of industrial output than do the activities of the more advanced industrialized nations. (The centralized economies of the Soviet bloc fall between these levels.) Hence their rate of increase in energy consumption exceeds their rate of GNP growth. Moreover, they lack domestic alternative energy sources and do not have the financial reserves that would allow them to adapt smoothly to major fluctuations in energy prices or supplies. While oil prices remained relatively low, the relative industrial inefficiency of Third World industrializing countries and their lack of financial reserves did not inhibit the rapid expansion of their GNPs. Rapid growth in these countries, especially in exports, and an overall healthy growing international economy provided many developing nations with sufficient foreign exchange to keep the oil flowing to them.

But the sudden increases in oil prices during the 1970s exacerbated the incipient world recession and raised the demand for credit to finance oil imports throughout the industrialized world. This dealt a severe blow to the energy-importing developing countries. They were hit even harder by the oil shocks than were the developed nations. They had to borrow heavily to sustain growth rates near what they had experienced in the 1960s and early 1970s. The legacy of this borrowing to finance imports at a time when export earnings could not keep pace with the rising cost of foreign oil is a level of external debt that threatens their solvency. It also threatens the solvency of the major U.S. banks that made those loans, just as some Western European banks have similar problems with loans to Eastern Europe. Though the International Monetary Fund (IMF) and other actors in the world financial community have considerably increased their credit facilities for developing countries and recycled billions of petrodollars to these developing nations, the prospects for large-scale adjustment and economic recovery in the Third World are considerably less favorable than they are in the industrialized nations.

MILITARY AND POLITICAL FACTORS

There is no doubt that control over the oil supply can be used as a political lever by one country or another. The Soviet Union has used this lever on more than one occasion, sometimes with success, sometimes not. During the late 1950s in Finland, a government was formed that excluded the Communist Party. The Soviets strongly disapproved and cut off Finnish access to oil from the Soviet Union, Finland's principal source of supply. This was not the strongest sanction the Soviets might have chosen to apply, but it did prove sufficient: The Finns changed the composition of the new government. The Soviets applied a similar sanction to the People's Republic of China (PRC) after the split between those two countries in the mid-1960s. That time it failed to work, partly because the Chinese were not as dependent on Soviet oil as the Finns and partly because the implied threat of Soviet military action carried less weight with the Chinese than with the Finns.

The most memorable attempt to apply such leverage to the industrialized democracies was the Arab oil boycott imposed on the United States and the Netherlands in retaliation for their support of Israel in the Arab-Israeli War of October 1973. Because the dependence of the industrialized democracies on imported oil had increased since 1967, the oil boycott was a credible weapon, but it failed in its immediate political goal: Neither the United States nor the Netherlands altered its pro-Israel stance. But the boycott—and even more the threefold price increase that followed the 1973 war—did have its effects. If a commodity is vital to its consumers, no easy substitute is available, and enough of the supply to make the difference between surplus and scarcity is controlled by a few producers, prices can be manipulated upward quite significantly. The American public became much more aware of the power that the oil-exporting countries wielded. In Western Europe and Japan the lesson was much sharper and more effective, as is consistent with their greater dependence on oil imports. From that time on, Western European and Japanese attitudes shifted in a direction more favorable to the Arabs and less favorable to Israel.

The stagflation during the rest of the 1970s and a second oil shock after the Iranian revolution of 1979 showed that leverage exerted through control of oil supply and pricing policies need not be limited to the threat to cut off supply and cripple the industrialized economies. Supply reductions and price increases can have a protracted, debilitating effect on the economies of industrialized countries and on the economies of developing countries that do not produce oil. The latter have undergone more economic suffering as a result of those price increases than they can be shown to have undergone as a result of market barriers imposed on their products by the developed nations or of the failure by those nations to transfer new and valuable technology. Both in the industrialized democracies and in the developing nations whose geographical position may expose them to pressure from the Soviet Union or Soviet surrogates, the economic difficulties caused by the increase in oil prices have been a major factor in limiting their programs to build up their own military capabilities.[1]

This is not to say that the rise in oil prices has been unfair. Oil is the only substantial natural resource of many of the oil producers. Unless they get a price for it much higher in real terms than they commanded until the middle of the 1970s, their chances of creating

---

[1] A cutoff of imported oil would not jeopardize the ability of the U.S. military to operate. The military establishment now accounts for only 2 or 3 percent of U.S. oil consumption. Even in wartime, when that percentage might double or triple, diversion of oil from civilian consumers could ensure adequate supplies for the military overall, though reasons of flexibility make developing and using synthetic fuels in the military a good idea. In peacetime, the military gets about 20 percent of its petroleum, oil, and lubricants from foreign sources, but if those were to be cut off—either in peacetime or in wartime—supplies could be shipped from the United States. There would be some risk, though, and some shipping capacity would be diverted from other military tasks. Most of the European members of NATO would have much more difficulty obtaining enough oil to supply their military forces in a protracted war, unless it could be shipped from the United States. Their economies would be affected even more severely than their military forces.

an economy that is not totally dependent on it—and thus of surviving economically into the postpetroleum era that is likely to arrive in the early decades of the twenty-first century—are poor. It is hard to criticize a producer for selling a product at a price equal to its long-term replacement value, especially if the market will pay that price. Indeed, it is clear that the Saudis could have done a better job of maximizing current revenues, or perhaps even the total present value in constant dollars of their underground store of oil, by observing a more restrictive production policy and charging the higher unit price that would have been possible. But Saudi economic prosperity depends on a certain level of economic activity in the industrialized world, and should the industrialized nations fall into a deep depression, even the Saudis would suffer from a lack of customers. They also depend to a substantial degree on the United States for political and military support, and a policy that maximized their economic gain by crippling the economies of the industrialized democracies would lose them that necessary support.

There are substantial variations in the interests of the various oil-exporting countries. The heavily populated ones—Nigeria, Egypt, Iran, and Indonesia—need to sell all the oil they can. The lightly populated ones—Saudi Arabia, the United Arab Emirates, Kuwait, Libya—have greater freedom, but in general they are weaker and have more concern about regional military threats. Saudi Arabia, Kuwait, and the United Arab Emirates together have by far the bulk of the discretionary export capability (although Iraq will have a significant amount if and when it can resume the shipments disrupted by the Iran-Iraq War begun in 1980). For U.S. policy, the practical result of this diversity in their needs and oil-exporting ability is that the various countries must be dealt with in different ways.

The Soviet Union, which had considerable export capability through the 1970s, is likely to lose it in the mid-1980s; its own production will peak while its internal requirements will continue to grow. This is likely to have a greater economic effect on oil-importing Eastern Europe than on the Soviet Union itself, because the Soviets have been raising the price they charge the Eastern Europeans to a level closer to the world market price, and they can reduce the amounts they sell. The Soviets do not need to achieve a dominant position in Southwest Asia for their own internal energy needs. If they were to undertake such an adventure, their most likely objective would instead be to control energy sources vital to the industrialized democracies.

Such a possibility makes the Persian Gulf region and the areas surrounding it an arena of potential conflict, including military conflict between the United States and the Soviet Union. But there are other possible causes of disruption. Regional wars resulting from indigenous conflicts can have that effect: The Iran-Iraq War reduced exports by about 3 million barrels a day. Internal chaos or sabotage can do the same: Iranian exports had previously fallen by nearly 4 million barrels a day between 1978 and 1980 as a result of the revolution that overthrew the Shah.

The various oil-importing nations of the industrialized world differ not only in their degree of dependence on imported oil but also in their attitudes toward both the developing countries that export it and their various local adversaries. These factors combine with other economic and political frictions among the industrialized democracies to create and intensify a policy split between the United States and its allies. Increases in oil prices and increasing vulnerability to supply cutoffs or to further price increases have also exacerbated tensions between the developing world and the industrialized democracies. Developing countries have tended to blame their problems on the democracies rather than on the Soviet bloc, to which they feel vulnerable militarily, or on the petroleum exporters, to whom they feel vulnerable economically.

ENERGY DEPENDENCE IN THE UNITED STATES

Under these circumstances, what long-term plans and programs are needed if the United States and the other industrialized democracies are to manage the technological, economic, and political factors that govern the availability of a resource so vital to them?

In the United States, a continuation of the present degree of dependence on imported oil promises to create major national security risks, both directly in foreign and military matters and indirectly in its actual and potential effects on the economy. Even at the 1982 level of reliance on oil imports—30 percent, substantially reduced from what it was four years before—the U.S. economy and foreign policy are dependent on others to an uncomfortable degree. As is usually the case with vital commodities, a world shortage of 10 to 20 percent would cause a price increase of 50 to 100 percent. The U.S. economy would be damaged massively by a major international disruption that affected the price or availability of that much of its oil consumption. Controls and allocations previously seen only in wartime would be required to handle a cutoff of that magnitude. A doubling of the present price of imported oil, while in principle less disruptive, would still have a major negative effect on the U.S. economy. The United States would have to reduce its oil imports to approximately 10 percent of consumption to avoid major dislocations in the event of either a cutoff or a major price increase. At that level of imports, for example, the strategic petroleum reserve (nearly 300 million barrels at the end of 1982) and the elasticity of consumption could well be able to make up for a cutoff of many months.

What options are open to the United States, both to reduce the long-term concern that this vulnerability creates and to make short-term cutoffs more manageable? The most straightforward insurance against short-term cutoffs is the stockpiling of oil in the strategic petroleum reserve (SPR). Six months of imports at the 1982 level corresponds to about 750 million barrels of oil. A stockpile of this size could provide insurance against even the most extreme uses of the oil weapon against the United States in the short run. Moreover, consumption during an oil cutoff could probably be reduced to exceed domestic production by only a few million barrels a day, so such a stockpile might well be able to make up for a complete cutoff of imports for a year or more. (And a complete cutoff would be unlikely, considering that some fraction of those imports come from the Western Hemisphere.) Such a stockpile should therefore discourage potential disrupters from thinking that they can produce a quick effect and could well cause them to wonder whether they themselves might feel major negative economic effects before the United States does. The SPR program is not cheap—it would require an investment of up to $30 billion in oil inventory and a few billion more in storage facilities. But over five years, a careful program of purchases should make an effective reserve feasible and affordable. The program begun by the Carter administration and continued by the Reagan administration makes sense.

The producers—especially Saudi Arabia, which holds the most optional production capacity—can be expected to object to the SPR. Their way of putting the issue is, "Why should we sell you oil from under our territory to put under yours?" But the United States is putting oil from other sources into the SPR. One source is the Elk Hills fields in California; Mexico is another. Transferring this crude oil to the SPR stores it where it is better located for distribution within the United States and can be pumped at a much faster rate. Even during a time of long-term shortages, there will be temporary periods of excess of oil supply over demand, as happened in 1982. Oil-exporting nations then have less control and may even see advantages to SPR purchases in keeping prices up. As long as the SPR does not represent a direct transfer from Saudi Arabia, its buildup should be manageable.

Continued government and private efforts in energy conservation could substantially reduce U.S. dependence on foreign oil, at least over the short and medium terms. As much as 25 percent of all primary energy used in the U.S. economy could be saved under the present structure of the economy without lowering the standard of living. These figures are not directly translatable into potential oil savings, but they do indicate the important role energy conservation can play in reducing U.S. energy dependence. But conservation's role in cutting oil imports is essentially a complementary one; in the long run, conservation cannot replace the United States's need to diversify and expand its energy resource base.

Easing the long-term dependence of the United States—and its allies in the industrialized world, an even more vital and much more difficult task—will require additional actions. Deregulation of oil in the United States has encouraged further development of U.S. indigenous natural hydrocarbon sources. Deregulation of natural gas should have a similar effect. In the case of natural gas, the price increase resulting from deregulation will encourage more exploration for and production of gas from shallow depths. The accompanying loss of the current premium on deep gas, already deregulated, could, however, slow down the relative development of that gas. Coal would be one likely substitute in many central power stations for any gas not produced because of a change in gas prices. Concerns that imported oil would also be used as a substitute for this gas, thus increasing oil imports, could be addressed by levying an oil import tax that would counterbalance the greater capital cost of converting boilers to coal rather than oil. That tax and a wellhead or windfall profit tax on deregulated gas would also be effective ways to reduce federal deficits and to pay for defense program increases.

The United States has coal reserves that can satisfy its requirements for central power generation for several hundred years if necessary, and its cost per British thermal unit (Btu) in the United States is half that of residual oil. But there are environmental risks in the greatly increased amounts of carbon dioxide that would be produced if the United States burned much more coal, oil, or gas. Renewable resources can to a certain extent substitute for natural hydrocarbons and ease some of the environmental concerns that accompany increasing consumption of energy. So can nuclear fission energy, though it poses difficult environmental problems of its own. Those problems are soluble, but various accidents suggest poor quality control and lack of operational care in the nuclear power program. Such impressions combined with popular and legislative antinuclear actions, have delayed the construction of nuclear power plants and pushed up their costs. Thus nuclear energy production in the United States will grow very slowly during the remainder of this century. Such renewable resources as solar heating and cooling, biomass conversion, wind power, and (somewhat further down the track) solar electric power will be able to meet only a small percentage of U.S. energy needs for the rest of this century. Nuclear fusion energy is still further away. This means that the bulk of the energy growth for U.S. central power stations during the next two decades will come from coal; perhaps some will come from natural gas.

Hydrocarbons are required for use in transportation, which now accounts for about half of our oil consumption and about a quarter of our total energy consumption. They are also required for chemical synthesis of plastics, feedstocks, fertilizers, and other chemicals. To this end, a synthetic fuel program is vital. It is thus unfortunate that the Reagan administration so substantially cut back the synthetic fuel program approved by Congress during 1980.[2] The ability to produce by the mid-1990s a few million barrels a day of oil equivalent from the oil shale and coal so plentiful in the United States would greatly reduce the political consequences of the uneven distribution of oil around the world.

It has been suggested that the natural functioning of economic markets will ensure that oil substitutes are available once they are needed and economically feasible. That judgment is faulty (as it is, for different reasons, with respect to the development of nuclear power and the construction of the Alaska gas pipeline). It is difficult for the markets to respond in advance to international events that are not specifically predictable or at least specifically foreseeable. It is practically impossible for private investors to invest money now to ensure against events that might take place at any time in the next twenty years, or not at all. If the markets were perfect, and resources could be moved quickly without friction to the production and use of some alternative energy source after the price of oil exceeded its natural level, reliance on the market might suffice. But experience verifies that the market for oil and other energy sources is anything but perfect and economic adjustment to oil price fluctuations is far from frictionless. More important, private firms and economic markets cannot be expected to take into account national

---

[2]Only a relatively small fraction of the funds authorized in the synfuels program approved in 1980 would actually have appeared as Federal expenditures. The bulk of the program would have been synfuel purchases at a guaranteed price. Such guarantees do have some effect on government expenditures and more on the credit market. Over the next fifteen years, a reasonable expectation of government expenditures from the program adopted in 1980 is about $15 billion.

effects and objectives in planning their actions. Government planning and actions, however, must do so.

A few examples make the point. The national security and foreign policy difficulties and dangers created by excessive dependence on imported oil could lead to a major war involving the United States. The national macroeconomic costs of each of the past disruptions in energy supplies in 1973–1974 and 1979–1980 amounted to a reduction in level of GNP several percentage points below what it would otherwise have been. The economy has not yet recovered from those reductions. Actions that would prevent a repetition are worth hundreds of billions of dollars—if they can be confidently identified. In addition, if national and international actions to inhibit future price increases succeed, the terms of trade would improve for the oil importers over what would otherwise be the case. Even in the absence of a disruption this would have beneficial economic and political effects in the United States and in the other industrialized democracies. It is difficult to see how pure market forces can meet these objectives, although governments can make use of market forces in developing and carrying out programs to reduce dependence on imported energy resources.

The national government, living in a world of real constraints and potentially explosive short-term and long-term problems, must plan for future energy needs and implement policies that will at least minimize the threat to its own security of an energy shortage, real or artificial. The national security consequences of the energy situation are clearly a Federal responsibility, encompassed in the constitutional purpose of providing for the common defense. Federal encouragement of nuclear power, and of the Alaska pipeline, has been and is justifiable on similar grounds.

It could be argued that the much greater dependence of most of the industrialized democracies on imported hydrocarbons would vitiate any U.S. program for self-sufficiency. That dependence, however, actually reinforces the arguments for such programs across the board. Some U.S. allies have been proceeding in the direction of greater self-sufficiency on their own. The French effort in nuclear power is an example. But few of them are likely to be able to substitute synthetic fuels to the degree the United States can, because they lack comparable oil shale and coal resources. They are still less likely to be able to make the major investments needed to create the base for such a technology and such an industry on their own.

But U.S. coal would be—and it now is—an effective, feasible, and economical substitute in Western Europe and Japan for residual oil or for imported natural gas from the Soviet Union, Algeria, or Indonesia. Even with the extra transportation cost, the delivered cost per Btu of U.S. coal is 25 percent less than that of imported oil or gas. In the long run, a synthetic hydrocarbon capability based on U.S. oil shale and coal could also play a part in meeting the needs of U.S. allies. Such a program would provide them with alternative sources for at least some of their hydrocarbon requirements and much of their fuel for electricity. To the degree that such synthetic fuels can promote closer ties to the United States rather than to others, that would improve cohesion within the alliances and restore U.S. leadership.

In light of all these factors, it makes sense for the United States to undertake a major government-assisted program to diversify energy sources. Many of these sources would not compete on equal terms with the international price of oil now, but they may well do so in ten or fifteen years, when the United States will want to be free of the difficulties that its energy situation makes almost inevitable for its national security policy during the 1980s. The United States must now undertake the necessary technological developments and quickly establish at least a few rapidly expandable prototype and demonstration facilities to be integrated into its electrical energy and hydrocarbon supply systems. Otherwise the United States will not have a chance to iron out the inevitable bugs in such developments, gain accurate data on plant costs, or establish a base that can be expanded quickly in a future emergency. A synthetic fuels program can be advanced with loans of product purchases guaranteed by the government; the cost to the government would come five or ten years later and could amount to about one-fourth of the amount of funding appropriated. Nuclear energy can be assisted by tighter government standards of design and operation and by government insurance.

Thus, the United States should encourage synthetic fuels, nuclear energy, and renewable energy sources—aiming perhaps at an additional 5 percent of the total U.S. energy supply from each of them and an additional 10 percent directly from coal by the year 2000.

None of these individual approaches will solve the problem; as can be seen by these percentages, even all of them together will be only a partial replacement for present sources. But working on all of them and turning the more promising ones into actual and substantial contributors to the U.S. energy supply will, when combined with renewed conservation efforts, reduce U.S. dependence, limit the ability of foreign oil producers to set prices arbitrarily, provide examples for other users, and improve U.S. ties with its industrialized allies and the energy-importing developing countries.

Stockpiling six months' supply of oil imports is an obvious and sensible precaution. Its cost suggests that it should be carried out over a period of five years, depending on the availability and price of oil. Completing the present SPR program will therefore ease the potential short-term economic problems that will arise if U.S. energy production remains substantially and permanently below consumption.

Major unilateral U.S. programs must be accompanied by various international arrangements. Some of the more reliable oil suppliers are likely to have concerns about U.S. actions that reduce U.S. dependence. The United States must accordingly phase its actions over time, but it must nevertheless take those actions.

With its energy-importing allies, the United States should plan to go beyond the present International Energy Authority arrangements for pooling energy resources and sharing shortages in a crisis. One approach would be for the United States to commit itself in advance to pool its resources with its allies and friends in a crisis, once it has guaranteed some preestablished minimal level of internal consumption. Such an agreement would have to be accompanied by some prearrangements, which should include prior commitment to joint political (and in certain circumstances military) action. A major advance in U.S. energy resources across a broad spectrum of technology and capabilities would aid the United States in negotiating such a comprehensive arrangement, which would in turn increase U.S. international influence with its allies and friends, as well as with neutrals and adversaries, and provide a tool sorely needed in U.S. national security policy.

5

Strategic Forces, Deterrence, and Strategic Nuclear War

The factor that makes national security for the United States in the second half of the twentieth century most different from what it had been before is the possibility of strategic nuclear war. Nation-states have been destroyed before, and catastrophes both natural and man-made have wiped out up to half the population of large geographical areas. The Mongol invasion of the Khorezmian Empire, in what is now Iran and Iraq, killed most of the urban population and, by destroying the irrigation system, reduced the farm population as well. The Black Death in Europe a century later killed as much as a third of the population.

But those events took place over many months or years. Political and social structures could continue in recognizable form. The destruction of more than 100 million people each in the United States, the Soviet Union, and in the rest of the Europe could take place during the first half-hour of a nuclear war. These deaths would be caused by the blast and the heat of the fireball, and the ensuing fires and collapse of buildings. Many tens of millions of additional casualties would be caused thereafter by nuclear fallout, and the breakdown of production and distribution would cause further deaths and thoroughly disrupt the lives of any survivors. In societies much more urbanized than any in previous centuries, such a war would be a catastrophe not only indescribable, but unimaginable. Those societies would almost certainly cease to function, and the target nations cease to exist as physical entities. It would be unlike anything that has taken place on this planet since human life began. To some observers, such a war seems likely during the next few decades. To others, including myself, it appears improbable. But even if it is highly improbable, the effects of such a war necessarily make its prevention the highest priority of any U.S. national security policy. Defeats in earlier wars could have returned the United States to British hegemony, divided it in two, or put it in grave danger of isolation in a world dominated by a bestially totalitarian world power. But in all those cases, time, the possibility of a revival in military strength, and the existence of a political structure of sorts would have provided a chance for an upward turn in fortune. A thermonuclear war that destroys half the U.S. population in a half-hour and condemns the rest to an existence "solitary, poor, nasty, brutish, and short"— for most, very short—is a prospect of immeasurably greater severity than any of those earlier threats.

THE NEW REALITY

Beginning in the mid-1950s, when a Soviet nuclear attack would have been able to cause tens of millions of deaths in the United States, and increasingly in the 1960s and 1970s, during which the potential effects of a thermonuclear strategic war grew to 100 million immediate U.S. deaths, the United States has been unable to eliminate the threat of its own destruction in a thermonuclear war. Instead it has had to rely on deterrence to prevent a potential adversary from starting such a war. Such deterrence arises from the knowledge on the part of the leaders of the Soviet Union, the only nation able to inflict this damage on the United States, that such a war would also inevitably lead to the destruction of their own society, their own people, and their own leadership.

This situation has been, to put it mildly, difficult for the people of the United States, and for their political leaders, who had been accustomed, whatever else was at stake, to a national identity and a national existence free of immediate threats. In the United States this revolutionary change in the level and the nature of possible damage has led to several reactions, some of them excessive.

One is the idea that because nuclear war would be so horrible, it is inconceivable; nuclear weapons will never be used, so nothing much needs to be done to build up particular capabilities or maintain relative balances in strategic forces. In response, it should be noted that political leaders in the past—aggressive, but not necessarily irrational—have often made wishful, mistaken, and foolish estimates of consequences that have led to catastrophic wars. Nuclear deterrence must therefore be conclusive. It must present such a certainty of destructive retaliation that no chain of reasoning would allow a decision maker contemplating the initiation of a strategic war to conclude that such an attack would be anything other than the worst possible choice.

There have, however, been genuinely irrational leaders of great nations. Deterrence is a rational process. It depends on a conscious decision not to start a nuclear war, based on recognition of the consequence—destruction by retaliation. Irrational leaders cannot be deterred. But they may not be able to force their subordinates, loyal but usually rational or at least calculating in nature, to go along.

Furthermore, behavior in periods of tension can be (and in my judgment is) influenced by the nature of the strategic capabilities and the relative balance of strategic forces, even if the use of those strategic forces is very unlikely. Real consequences have followed the shift since the late 1960s away from a perceived U.S. strategic superiority. This U.S. advantage would have been of only marginal value in a thermonuclear war and was of limited political value, but its loss has had a significant effect on relations between the United States and its allies and on the attitudes of people in other countries toward the United States. That shift in perception was only one cause of these changed attitudes about the United States—the outcome of the Vietnam War and the loss of U.S. economic weight relative to the rest of the world were others.

The shift has probably had less effect on relations between the United States and the Soviet Union, because *Soviet* perceptions of the strategic balance probably do not involve Soviet superiority. They have judged that the balance in strategic forces is considerably more favorable to them than it was in the 1960s. But they probably include in their measure of the balance of strategic forces several factors that are ignored by the more pessimistic U.S. analysts, polemicists, and political leaders. One such factor is the strategic nuclear capabilities of other anti-Soviet nuclear powers. Another is their sense of the technological superiority of the United States and especially of the prospects for rapid U.S. deployment of new technologies in the strategic field. Soviet military leaders may also tend to measure their capabilities for defense and for limiting damage against a much higher standard than most U.S. analysts consider realistic. Nevertheless, the capabilities of U.S. strategic nuclear forces and the relative balance with the Soviet Union are still important, even if the destructiveness of these weapons sharply limits, and perhaps eliminates for practical purposes, their usefulness in an actual conflict.

Deciding to retaliate in kind after an attack on U.S. cities that killed 100 million Americans would raise grave moral questions. Even planning that keeps open that option has been questioned on moral and religious grounds. In considering such concerns, a judgment must be made as to whether forgoing that option would make a nuclear war more or less likely and whether abandoning the capability for retaliation or allowing it to erode substantially would increase the prospects for a world tyranny that is unlikely to be reversible. One must weigh the immorality of the many civilian deaths that would result from a retaliatory attack aimed at Soviet political leaders, their military forces, and economic resources against the immorality of leaving world rule in the hands of the group that launches such an attack on the United States—if that is the likely result of deciding not to retaliate against targets that would entail massive civilian casualties. Individuals and institutions outside government may be able to escape these genuine ethical dilemmas by advocating unilateral abandonment of retaliatory nuclear strategies and capabilities, but in my judgment, U.S. officials responsible for national security cannot risk undermining deterrence.

A second reaction to the destructiveness of nuclear war has also existed for decades and has once again become intellectually and politically influential. This is the position that a threat produced by technology can be alleviated by a combination of determination and additional technology—that nuclear weapons are simply another form of warfare and that an effective military counter can be found to every form of warfare. The flaw in this approach is that a millionfold increase (the difference between tons and megatons) is extremely difficult to overcome, even with the best combination of technology and determination. If a single weapon can destroy a city of hundreds of thousands, only a perfect defense will suffice. The extreme destructiveness of nuclear weapons is magnified by the concentration and fragility of urban industrial society. To this must be added the availability to the attacker of the tactic of concentrating its forces to saturate and overwhelm any possible defense, even if any individual defensive weapon can defeat an individual attacking weapon. In these circumstances, the prospects for a technical solution to the problem of preserving modern society in the face of an actual thermonuclear war—whether that solution calls for laser-antiballistic missile systems in space, elaborate civil defense schemes, or combinations of these with counterforce capability (that is, ways of destroying enemy weapons before they are launched)—seem to me very poor. The effort to attain such technical solutions can itself be quite dangerous if it creates an illusion that a solution has been achieved or is likely to be.

This must all seem a rather grim picture. It is. But the fact remains that nuclear weapons have not been used since World War II. In that sense, deterrence of nuclear war has worked. Given the world political situation for at least the rest of this century, nuclear weapons stockpiles will not be abandoned. Thus, the United States has no choice but to continue to depend on deterrence to prevent its destruction. At the same time, the task will be more difficult. During the 1980s and 1990s, the United States and the Soviet Union will have roughly equal strategic nuclear forces. The Soviet Union will be able to respond to any U.S. buildup of capabilities and thereby deny the United States the prospect of regaining superiority. Some elements of the nuclear forces on both sides will become increasingly vulnerable unless both technology and force levels are effectively constrained in arms control agreements.

REQUIREMENTS FOR DETERRENCE

Kinds of Deterrence

For nearly thirty years U.S. strategic planners, defense theoreticians, and civilian and military national security officials have sought to define the requirements for deterrence, to determine "how much is enough." No generally agreed-upon answer has been reached, and the question will continue to be controversial in coming decades. Is there some absolute level of damage that deters a rational opponent from starting a strategic nuclear war? (One level, chosen by U.S. military planners in the 1960s and often taken as a standard, is 50 percent of industry destroyed and 50 percent of the urban population killed, an effect that could be expected under most circumstances from 400 appropriately targeted 1-megaton explosions.) Is it also necessary to present a credible capacity to inflict lesser, bearable damage in retaliation for lesser attacks? Does the balance of strategic forces play an important role in deterrence? If so, which are the important components of the balance: the actual balance, or the perceptions of that balance held variously by the Soviet Union, U.S. allies, Third World countries, or the U.S. public and its leaders? Is the possibility of massive damage in a strategic exchange, rather than its certainty, a sufficient deterrent? If the important thing is that the initiator of strategic war can be certain that it will be destroyed in retaliation, what are the relative values of various degrees of assurance, and of assurance of various kinds and levels of damage, as a deterrent?

Answering these questions is difficult for several reasons. The degree of assurance that a particular level of damage could be inflicted by some given U.S. force depends on objective, technical questions of capacity and on subjective political and psychological factors of will and credibility. Technical judgments must be based on assessments of Soviet capabilities of destroying U.S. strategic forces before they are launched or defending against them afterward. These assessments depend on the scenario assumed, including such factors as the extent of warning, the state of alert, and decisions made during the actual event. Population casualties would depend on the size and effectiveness of the Soviet passive defense efforts (shelters and evacuation). There are substantial differences of judgment about each of these technical factors. Still greater are the differences over the subjective elements. Given that U.S. forces could be used to produce certain results, would they be so used? U.S. threats to "kill us both" may not be credible as a response to actions that would do great harm but fall short of destroying the United States as a society. The credibility of total retaliation depends on political and psychological factors and could vary greatly with scenarios and personalities.

There is a second class of differing judgments. A retaliatory capability sufficient to deter an attack out of the blue during a time of peace might not be enough to do so in an enormously more strained situation. The effectiveness of deterrence will also depend on what the political decision makers consider the likely consequences of not launching a strategic attack in a crisis. These consequences could be either military—a preemptive (i.e., first-strike) nuclear attack by the other side, or a nonnuclear defeat in a critical geographical area—or political. The balance of strategic forces can be expected to affect behavior differently in a political confrontation that could lead to a conventional war, in a conventional war that a superpower was losing and was unwilling to lose, in a nuclear escalation, or even in jockeying for political and psychological advantage in adversarial but not yet confrontational situations. U.S. strategic superiority in the 1950s, for example, probably did help to deter both a Soviet conventional attack on Western Europe and Soviet political intimidation based on their superiority in conventional military forces. Finally, deterrence of the Soviet Union depends in major part on Soviet perceptions, decision-making processes, behavior, intentions, and goals and on U.S. self-confidence and determination. But policymakers, scholars, and other experts differ considerably about the nature of the Soviet leadership and potential behavior. No wonder there is so wide a range of views about what is needed to deter strategic war, about the role of the strategic balance in strategic deterrence, and about the effect of the strategic balance on political and military matters other than strategic war.

Nevertheless, policymakers must make judgments of what is required to deter a strategic nuclear attack. In my view, deterrence is provided by a combination of the certainty of substantial damage in a retaliatory attack, the expectation of an even higher level of damage, and the possibility of a still higher level of damage.

Much controversy centers on whether a chance of total destruction and a clear technical capability to inflict it is sufficient for deterrence. A strategic war aimed at urban industrial targets, or even the side effects of a countermilitary strategic attack on civilian populations and urban industrial areas, would have enormously greater effects than those experienced over a comparably short time in any previous war. Thus it is not surprising that most people who have studied the problem have concluded that a certainty of the level of destruction resulting from a retaliatory strike of even only a few hundred one-megaton explosions will suffice to deter an attack on urban industrial targets. Almost all of those who have been connected with such considerations at the highest level of responsibility (Presidents and Vice-Presidents of the United States, Secretaries of State, Secretaries of Defense—including myself—and National Security Advisers) share that view. But I do not share the view that there are no other conceivable attacks the United States must be able to deter or that the credibility of an all-out attack on Soviet cities is high enough, alone, to deter other nuclear attacks on the United States or its allies. Forces above the level needed for assured destruction, calculated on the basis of the expected level of Soviet offensive and defensive weapons, are required to ensure a higher level of certainty in retaliation against urban and industrial centers; to deter and respond, if necessary, to nuclear attacks of other kinds—on U.S. military targets, on U.S. allies; to reduce potential future vulnerabilities; and to ensure an acceptable balance of strategic forces.

Soviet Views of Deterrence

The deterrence that the United States seeks is deterrence of Soviet actions, so a major issue is the nature of Soviet views—about nuclear war and ways of fighting it, about deterrence, about defense—and the implication of such Soviet strategic views for U.S. strategic nuclear force requirements. Must the United States have the same strategy and doctrine as the Soviets, whatever that might be? If so, will that create a requirement to increase U.S. forces substantially?

Decision makers in the Soviet Union may well be expected to hold (if not to display publicly) a variety of views about such matters as nuclear war and the nature of deterrence, as do civilian and military officials and scholars in the United States. The range of opinions need not by any means be the same among the two sets of decision makers. If Soviet political leaders, for example, held the view that a Soviet Union with 100 million survivors (including themselves) could be said to have "won" a strategic nuclear war over a United States with 50 million survivors, that clearly would have to affect U.S. strategy, doctrine, and forces. But there is no convincing evidence that such a view prevails among Soviet decision makers. Soviet military leaders, even more than military leaders elsewhere, must feel the pressure to be able to say—against the weight of the evidence—that they can defend the motherland, even in the thermonuclear age. And Soviet ideologues have a dogmatic reluctance to accept that a technical invention, however powerful, can upset the progress of history toward the triumph of socialism, as elaborated by Karl Marx.

But in recent years even Soviet military thinkers have included in their writings, and in their private conversations, a strain of doctrine that accepts the inevitable—that there would be no winners in a massive strategic nuclear exchange. Soviet political leaders are apparently more convinced of this than the military leaders. Nevertheless, U.S. planning must always allow for the possibility that the availability of enough Soviet strategic offensive and defensive capability could, in a time of crisis that had already grown into military conflict between the United States and the Soviet Union, be turned by a clever briefer into an argument for strategic attack as the best among a set of bad options. In their strategy and doctrine, the Soviets do contemplate the possibility of a somewhat protracted nuclear war. They give less attention and credence to the possibility of a limited nuclear war and express some ambiguity about the ability to survive or win a major nuclear exchange.

Soviet military thinking appears to be that the way to deter the United States is to establish superior strategic capability, not merely to be able to destroy some large percentage of U.S. population and industry. Soviet doctrine calls for the ability to wipe out enemy military forces and command-and-control structures as well as urban and industrial targets, and to do all of these more or less simultaneously. What is needed to deter the Soviets, in light of these strategies and doctrines, is a clear declaratory policy that in a strategic war, at any level of intensity they might choose, the Soviet leaders would lose more of what they considered valuable than they would gain by the damage inflicted on the United States. U.S. strategic forces must be of a nature and size to back up that declaratory policy. The United States needs a capability to attack each of the classes of Soviet targets selectively, but not necessarily to wipe out each class completely. By targeting Soviet conventional forces, for example, the United States would seek to prevent the Soviet Union from concluding that it would have the ability to dominate a postwar situation both in Europe and on the Sino-Soviet border.

Such an approach does not require the United States to replicate Soviet doctrine and strategy or to match the Soviet Union in every category of weapon or even in any given measure of strategic nuclear capability. It does require that the United States be certain it is able to destroy Soviet targets of various kinds at different levels of escalation. It also requires much more target destruction capability than would a simple strategy of targeting only urban and industrial areas. But even at lower numbers of warheads or megatonnage than now exist, the United States and the Soviet Union are both able to strike a large list of targets, including many more military than significant urban and industrial targets, with a high degree of certainty. The destruction of hardened military targets requires greater accuracy rather than larger numbers of warheads. Thus concerns about Soviet views of deterrence and nuclear strategy need not lead to the creation of unlimited U.S. forces. Pressure to increase the size of those forces is more likely to arise from concerns about avoiding adverse perceptions of the strategic balance.

Limiting Damage

A related question is the role of damage-limiting capabilities (civil defense, antiballistic missiles). Do they reinforce or undermine deterrence?

Some planners maintain that the ability to move large numbers of people into prepared shelters, or to evacuate them to places where they are less likely to be killed in an attack, and to have supplies of food and equipment to enable them to begin rebuilding a society has an advantage beyond that of increasing the number of survivors. They assert that it has a deterrent or even a coercive effect on the other side. Thus they advocate such a policy for the United States and are apprehensive about its effects in the Soviet Union. They believe an evacuation of Soviet citizens from cities or into shelters at a time of crisis would intimidate the United States, especially if the United States did not have corresponding capability. Other observers argue that, by making nuclear war seem more survivable, a civil defense capability on either side has the effect of increasing the probability of nuclear war. My own judgment is that neither passive nor active defenses would help the United States or the Soviet Union survive an all-out strategic exchange as organized societies in a recognizable form, as long as each side takes the necessary—and quite manageable—steps to ensure that its retaliatory capability is preserved.

But what might a military briefer be able to persuade a political decision maker in the Soviet Union to think about this question? Decision makers in both the United States and the Soviet Union have been cautious and conservative in such matters and would be especially so when it came to a decision to risk the nation's existence by launching a strategic nuclear war. But such a question would never even arise except in circumstances in which the alternatives were all dangerous and damaging. With an unknown future leadership, new military deployments, and a confrontation to retreat from which might spell political extinction, a particularly persuasive faction might be able to convince political decision makers that the damage from retaliation would be less than the damage from inaction. This would be particularly true if it seemed that there would be much less damage to one's country after striking first than from striking only in retaliation.

For this reason, such measures as antiballistic missile defense of urban industrial areas and massive civil defense programs may well destabilize the situation. They might reduce the likely number of deaths in case of a thermonuclear war, but they might also stimulate a responsive buildup of the other side's offensive forces that would more than overcome their damage-limiting effect—especially because damage-limiting measures are less likely to work than the countering offensive steps. They may then, in the end, result in more casualties in a thermonuclear war than if they had not been undertaken.

Deterring Attacks on U.S. Allies

Do U.S. strategic nuclear forces deter aggression other than attacks against the United States? If so, what kinds of strategic forces and balances are required?

In the 1950s, the basis of U.S. strategy was that U.S. predominance in strategic nuclear capability would deter not only Soviet nuclear attack on the United States but also Soviet nuclear and conventional attack in Europe. This was known as "extended deterrence." Secretary of State John Foster Dulles specifically threatened to respond to any Soviet aggression with a "massive retaliation at a time and place of our own choosing." President Eisenhower used the threat of nuclear weapons in 1953 to push the negotiations at Panmunjom toward a Korean armistice. U.S. strategic nuclear forces were not, however, able to deter Soviet military intervention in Eastern Europe or provide the means of carrying out the Eisenhower administration's campaign promise of "liberating" those countries from Soviet power.

Early in the 1960s, the Kennedy administration concluded that the threat of strategic war would not restrain Soviet promotion of communist revolutions in Third World countries or even, given sufficient Soviet confidence, a Soviet attack on Western Europe. During the Cuban missile crisis of 1962, the continued U.S. advantage in the strategic balance probably played some role in the calculations on both sides. But the expected unacceptable destruction on both sides in a nuclear war played a much greater role in keeping both sides from starting any war that could have escalated into a nuclear war. In that crisis, perhaps the closest approximation so far of the kind of superpower confrontation that might take place in the 1980s, the most influential factor of all was the great preponderance in conventional capability around Cuba that the United States had for several steps up the ladder of force escalation.

Recurrent crises in Berlin and doubts about relying principally on a nuclear deterrent to protect Western Europe from nonnuclear attack in the face of mutual U.S.-USSR vulnerability to strategic war led the United States to a new approach, which subsequently became NATO doctrine. This was to build up a conventional military capability in Western Europe that would provide the basis of a "flexible strategy" to make impossible a quick Soviet overrunning of Western Europe with conventional military forces. The allies had concluded that beyond some level of strategic nuclear forces on the two sides (a level that had surely been exceeded), marginal or even significant differences in strategic capability do not produce enough differences in the damage that would be suffered in a strategic war to deter conventional military action.

Deterrence of conventional military action depends on what the local political situation is, how critical the issue or area involved is to the respective interests of the two superpowers, which side is trying to upset the existing political situation, what balance of conventional forces can be brought to bear, whether escalation to tactical and then strategic nuclear war is considered a real and frightening possibility, and what escalatory steps are available to the two sides on the scene or elsewhere. Particularly important among these escalatory steps is the ability to reach the point at which the next step to be taken by the other side will involve it in what is perceived as a major escalation of its risk. The balance of strategic forces of the two sides is likely to condition political relations both between the superpowers and with other nations who may be involved. But both the inherent uncertainties of predicting the detailed outcome of a thermonuclear war and the high degree of certainty that it would result in the destruction of both the superpowers as functioning societies lead to a single conclusion—that differences in analysts' estimates of fatalities in a strategic war of two or even three times are unlikely to play so large a role in the evolution of such a crisis as the simple fact of the immense destructiveness of thermonuclear war.

Why bother, then, about the strategic balance? Because in circumstances of confrontation and crisis, or if conventional warfare between the superpowers has already broken out, decisions might be made that would seem quite irrational under more normal circumstances. If over the years the certainty of U.S. retaliatory strength had been eroded by a reduction in the ability of U.S. strategic forces to survive an attack or in their ability to penetrate Soviet defenses, or if the U.S. command-and-control structure is not seen as certain to execute such retaliation should a strategic war begin, these conditions would have two effects during a crisis.

First, the Soviets might actually decide to make a preemptive strike. The alternatives to preempting might seem to the Soviet leaders to be as damaging or even more damaging, and more important, *likely* in the absence of preemption by them. Still, such a decision remains unlikely, even under such extreme circumstances. But a second, more likely occurrence would be an erosion of the determination of U.S. decision makers, helped along by an avalanche of pressure from within the United States and from allies. Such pressure was substantial even during the Cuban missile crisis, when both the strategic balance and the local conventional balance were relatively favorable to the United States. Soviet perceptions of such a lack of determination could lead to the worst result for everyone: a Soviet miscalculation that the United States would not respond, when in fact the United States would—and does—so that a Soviet action sets off an all-out nuclear war.

The nuclear force characteristics, geography, history, technological development, and internal politics of the United States and the Soviet Union are significantly different, so it will never be possible to focus on a single measure of the strategic balance. A reasonable consensus within the United States about the nature of the balance, and statements about it by responsible officials, will often be more important than specific details of the various balances. U.S. national security officials (myself included) have faced a dilemma about how to speak of such matters. When the balance has been moving adversely, it is important to redress it. That makes it necessary to express some concern in official statements. Yet if the concern is mistranslated as a judgment about the present balance or an overstatement of the trend, it could lead to unwarranted conclusions about the weakness of U.S. capabilities and thus damage the U.S. political position. It could even conceivably erode Soviet inhibitions about reckless military moves.

Deterrence ultimately depends on a rough balance of strategic capability between the two sides. Neither side will accept inferiority of numbers or of capabilities. More weapons in one's own arsenal and a better balance from one's point of view will always be seen as the best deterrent, and disparities in particular criteria of measurement between the two sides will always be enough to fuel a demand for new systems and greater numbers. Thus in the absence of arms limitation agreements, the buildup of strategic weapons systems is likely to continue on both sides.

STRATEGIC NUCLEAR CAPABILITIES: THE TRIAD

A single 50-kiloton to 1-megaton nuclear explosion over a city will kill several hundred thousand people. The United States and the Soviet Union each have more than 6,000 such warheads, and the vehicles to deliver them, in their strategic stockpiles. Thus each has much more than enough capability to destroy all the large and medium-sized cities in the other's country. This fact has led to the development of the misleading concept of "overkill."

Reasons for Diversity

Why are so many warheads, ballistic missiles, cruise missiles, bombers, launchers, and submarines needed to deter an attack, or even to fight a strategic nuclear war? Why the diversity, why the numbers?

One answer is that deterrence of a nuclear attack depends critically on the certainty that much of the retaliatory force will survive an attack on it, that it will be effectively dispatched to retaliate, that it will penetrate such defenses as may be established to intercept it, and that it will find its targets and destroy them. Not nearly so important for ensuring deterrence is the possibility of a much higher level of retaliation, or the precise number of retaliatory warheads expected to reach their targets or of casualties they can be expected to inflict. A diversified strategic force is maintained to ensure an extremely high degree of certainty, both for the United States and for its potential adversary, that unacceptable damage will be inflicted in an all-out strategic nuclear conflict.

In establishing a clear capability to respond after any kind of attack, the U.S. triad of strategic nuclear forces requires the Soviets, if they plan a preemptive strike, to attack each of the components in a different way and to provide various kinds of active defenses.

Submarine-launched ballistic missiles (SLBMs) can be attacked before or during their launch only if the positions of the submarines that carry them can be determined with some degree of accuracy. Land-based ballistic missiles, or the shelters that house them, must be attacked with a high degree of accuracy (because these shelters can withstand a relatively near miss) and with more than one warhead per shelter to account for failures of reliability[1] in the attack. "Air-breathers"—the bomber force and the cruise missiles it carries—can be launched from their bases on warning of an attack and recalled, unlike the ballistic missiles. An attack on them must therefore rely on either destroying or confusing the warning system before the bombers can take off or else on a barrage attack to cover large geographical areas around their bases (many hundreds of thousands or even millions of square miles) with enough nuclear explosions to create overpressure that would destroy the bombers fifteen to thirty minutes after they have taken off. Each of these responses requires different technologies, different forces, and a considerable amount of development and deployment time to have a chance of success. Thus, provided that perceived vulnerabilities in any of them are dealt with in a timely manner, the diversity of U.S. forces provides insurance against the possibility that all three or even two of the legs of the triad could be put into substantial jeopardy at the same time.

The technologies and the development and deployment require-ments for systems to defend against such air-breathing weapons as bombers and cruise missiles differ substantially from those for ballistic missile defense systems to be used against submarine-launched ballistic missiles and intercontinental ballistic missiles (ICBMs). Moreover, the times required for the deployment of each of those systems are substantial (up to ten years), and the costs are high (tens of billions of dollars). Thus, active defenses have been made a difficult and relatively unrewarding way for the Soviets to negate U.S. retaliatory capability. And the geographic and technical requirements even within each of the ballistic and air-breathing classes create additional dif-ficulties for the defense. ICBM trajectories are different from those

---

[1]This is an example of the thousands of sometimes debatable mathematical calculations that lie behind decisions on military force structure. If the reliability and accuracy of a single warhead are such that it has a 10 percent probability of destroying a missile shelter (or any other target), then it would take 22 (not 9) to reach a 90 percent probability of destroying it. In effect that makes the attempt impractical. If the single warhead gives an 80 percent probability of destruction, then two will give a 96 percent probability—unless they interfere with each other.

of SLBMs. High-altitude and low-altitude air-breathing offensive weapons require different air defense designs.

These difficulties have not prevented the Soviets from attempting to create an air defense of considerable capability. This has in turn forced U.S. strategic planners to make considerable modifications in employment doctrine and in equipment for U.S. strategic forces. The B-52, for example, was originally designed to fly at high altitudes; now it is programmed to fly at low altitudes, and substantial electronic equipment for countermeasures has also been introduced into it. Overall, the result has been that the Soviets have had to spend four to five times as much on air defense as the United States has spent on its air-breathing strategic offensive forces. Yet at any time it has been a reasonable expectation that even without a prior U.S. ballistic missile strike most of the U.S. alert bomber force would succeed in penetrating. With new developments in strategic offensive air-breathing forces, a similar prognosis exists for the future. Given the extremely destructive effects of nuclear weapons, such a penetration rate will mean that the defense has failed, even after having spent several times as much as the offense.

A second reason for diversity in offensive forces is to ensure that any decision to retaliate would be communicated. Submarines are the most difficult force to communicate with and the force in which the cooperation of the largest number of individuals is required to effect a launch. These two factors explain why there is not on submarines, as there is on ICBMs and on bombers, a physical bar to a launching that can be unlocked only by the correct combination. That coded combination is transmitted in the message directing the launch sent from higher headquarters.

Diversity of forces is obviously useful. But is there something magical about a triad of strategic forces (ICBMs, SLBMs, and air-breathing bombers and cruise missiles) that requires the United States to hold firmly to all three forces? If the United States could with complete certainty meet a fixed level of capability far into the future, including the ability to survive expected preemptive attacks and penetrate expected defenses when Soviet forces will be directed at reducing both those abilities, then it could rely on only two components—perhaps even one. A larger, less diversified force could substitute for a smaller, more diversified force, but that is not a prescription for saving money. And diversification is a better hedge against uncertainty than force size. A dyad of bombers carrying many more cruise missiles and SLBMs is a plausible alternative deterrent force. But the restoration of a land-based ICBM with a reasonable chance of surviving an attack is a more reliable and less expensive hedge against the possibility of a future Soviet threat that should be presumed to include the capability of attacking the areas where bomber bases and submarines are deployed with barrages of thousands of ICBM warheads, guided by improved methods of locating their targets.

It is tempting to conclude that all the United States has to do is decide what strategic capability is required and declare that all forces beyond that level are unnecessary and wasteful. But there are too many uncertainties about the future size and capability of Soviet forces targeted to destroy U.S. retaliatory forces before they are launched or to intercept them before they reach their targets. Thus, decisions about kinds and numbers of such forces become judgments of some difficulty. This is obvious for conventional forces, but it is also true for strategic forces.

What is the proper balance among the various components of the strategic forces, and what should be the total force capability?

Submarine-launched Ballistic Missiles

Ballistic missiles launched from under water by nuclear submarines remain the U.S. strategic force least vulnerable to destruction before launch. This situation is almost certain to continue through the 1980s. The relative safety of SLBMs arises from the fact that an attempt to destroy a submarine, or to destroy its ballistic missiles during the early stages of flight, requires that the submarine or the missile be targeted. But it is difficult to locate a slow-moving, quiet nuclear submarine beneath the millions of square miles of ocean surface made available to it by the long range (2,500 to 4,800 nautical miles) of the current and future generations of submarine-launched ballistic missiles. SLBMs are inherently less accurate than land-launched ballistic missiles because of the uncertainties about the submarine's location and velocity. This effect can be substantially reduced by using star locations or communication with satellites to update the missile position and velocity in midcourse, and then making guidance corrections. But the additional complexity and possible vulnerability thus introduced make it preferable to do the job with a self-contained inertial system. Some time during the first half of the 1990s, U.S. SLBMs will probably be accurate enough to destroy fixed targets, even when those targets are hardened to resist the effects of nearby nuclear explosions—effects expressed in terms of overpressures of several thousand pounds per square inch. The Trident D-5 missile, scheduled to enter the force by then, has such an objective.

The ocean's lack of transparency to electromagnetic waves, and the consequent difficulty of locating a submarine, also make communications with submarines less certain than with other strategic systems; but if prompt communication is not required, adequate assurance is available.

There are some rather fanciful schemes for destroying SLBMs. One consists of detecting launches from space and intercepting the missiles with space-launched interceptors as they leave the atmosphere. The technical difficulties and astronomical costs of such a system (also proposed for defense against ICBMs) make it infeasible for this century, and perhaps for any. Another suggestion has been to cover the oceans, on a grid of squares with 100-mile sides, with trawlers capable of detecting and intercepting the SLBMs during their powered phase with long-range surface-to-air missiles. The trawlers could also launch antisubmarine missiles to destroy the submarine after its position has been given away by the launch of its first few SLBMs. A little arithmetic shows that covering the oceans this way would require well over a thousand such vessels. Their costs and their vulnerability suggest that this would be a losing game.

This situation may suggest to some that the United States and the Soviet Union could rely completely on their SLBM forces for deterrence. The difficulty with a defense policy and program based on such an assumption is that submarines do create signs of their presence or passage. Some of the technologies used to detect and locate submarines might be developed and deployed to change the picture substantially in the 1990s without relying on such far-fetched notions as space interceptors or trawler forces. Improvements in data processing and acoustic techniques may enable surveillance to locate submarines, even relatively quiet and slow-moving ones, to a degree of accuracy that would make submarine survival much more questionable than it is now. If a submarine can be located within a 10-mile radius, a few 1-megaton bombs have a good chance of destroying it along with its 200-warhead cargo. That sort of an exchange ratio would make SLBMs a poor retaliatory force. The present situation is far from this. With about a 75-mile uncertainty of location, it takes about as many warheads to destroy the submarine as the submarine carries.

But the very possibility of improved techniques for locating submarines, even if it is rather remote, serves as a caution against relying entirely on SLBMs or allowing either bombers or ICBMs to become and remain vulnerable over an extended period (beyond the late 1980s, say). To do so would be to invite the Soviets to concentrate the bulk of their technological and manufacturing efforts on producing and deploying an effective anti-SLBM system in the hope of gaining a decisive advantage in the strategic balance. If they could devote thousands of warheads to the task, their capabilities of locating U.S. submarines would not have to be outstanding. But as long as the Soviets are forced to spend $50 billion to $100 billion on air-defense systems in order to have a chance of destroying our bombers and cruise missiles, and another $50 billion or $100 billion on systems designed to counter land-based ICBMs, they are much less likely to have the resources to pursue the possible approaches to submarine location and destruction.

Land-based Intercontinental Ballistic Missiles

Today land-based ICBMs form the backbone of Soviet strategic power, as they have since the early 1960s. Soviet ICBM accuracies improved substantially during the 1970s, and their numbers of separately targetable ICBM warheads increased fivefold. Now, in the 1980s, they can have reasonable confidence of destroying nearly all U.S. Minuteman silos. Is the vulnerability of fixed ICBM silos a real problem? It is, despite claims that the Soviets could not execute a disarming attack because of bias errors in targeting caused by such factors as uncertainty in our knowledge of the earth's gravity field. Some Minutemen might survive; but a random one-tenth or one-twentieth of the existing force would not be an effective force, especially with the concomitant destruction of command-and-control and communication facilities.

Given the vulnerability of U.S. land-based silos, the United States could respond in a number of different ways. It would be possible to adopt a doctrine that the Minuteman ICBM force would be launched when warning was received from infrared observation satellites that a Soviet missile attack had been launched. The difficulty of basing war plans on such a doctrine is that the time for decision would be so short, and the information available so limited, that the decision on nuclear war would in effect have to be left to a computer. This would not be acceptable. There are, to be sure, circumstances—such as a gradual escalation of tension and hostilities—under which all the decision makers would be in good communication and well informed. For this case, it seems sensible to build up the quality and redundancy of the warning sensors and associated communication and data processing facilities to ensure that under a Soviet attack, the President could decide to launch the ICBM force at certain predetermined Soviet targets. Such an option creates an increased question in Soviet minds about their own assurance of being able to wipe out the missiles in fixed land-based silos before they are launched. But reliance on such an approach to ensure the survival of the land-based missile force has two serious problems. First, there is a dangerous asymmetry: at the present time the Soviet ICBM force is not at similar risk because the U.S. ICBM force does not have enough reentry vehicles of high accuracy to pose a like threat to the larger number of Soviet ICBM silos. Second, the use of a hair-trigger mechanism to launch a massive thermonuclear strike represents a dangerous instability.

Another alternative is to abandon the idea of a land-based ICBM force in the triad and to base any large new ICBM force at sea or on an aircraft. Whatever domestic political advantages these basing modes might have, they would not maintain the diversity and invulnerability of U.S. strategic forces in the face of projected Soviet deployments and advances in technology. Whatever the missile involved, it can survive an attack only if the platform from which it is launched can. Submarines would be vulnerable to improved or new methods of locating their position. Surface ships are considerably easier to locate. Aircraft are vulnerable to attack on the ground, to barrage attacks in the air, and to long-range active defenses. There are ways to counter such vulnerability, but any attack that succeeded against strip-alert bombers would also be able to succeed against strip-alert missile carriers. A continuous airborne alert would be a very expensive way to ensure the survival of a very small force.

For the United States to rely on vulnerable land-based ICBMs or to abandon them while the Soviet ICBM force remains much less vulnerable would be a peacetime military defeat of major magnitude and an international political defeat as well. For such an abandonment to take place under the pressure of Soviet ICBM deployment, and even more for it to occur as the result of a lack of political leadership in the U.S. Government in the face of popular and largely local pressure, may send a signal to the world that although it is possible to preserve a strong strategic deterrent capability in the face of a massive Soviet strategic buildup, the United States lacks the skill, the judgment, or the determination to do the job.

The United States devoted considerable effort during the second half of the 1970s to finding a land-based mode of deployment that would ensure the survival of the ICBM force in the face of an attack by the Soviet Union, with its growing preemptive abilities. Of the dozens of deployment modes examined, multiple hardened protective shelters (twenty or more per missile) among which 200 MX solid-propellant missiles, each capable of carrying ten warheads, could be moved as needed appeared—and still appears—to be the best approach from the military and technical perspective. This approach ensures that the Soviets would have to target all shelters to attack the missile force. Soviet attempts to detect which shelters contain missiles can be thwarted in various ways. The surest, using horizontal shelters, is to arrange for the missiles to be movable among shelters in a time shorter than the flight time of Soviet ICBMs.

The environmental costs and problems of such a system are significant, but both should have been manageable. Congressional approval of this deployment mode in 1980 suggested that the political problems might also be manageable, although statements made during the 1980 campaign and in 1981 by top officials of the Reagan administration greatly magnified local and national political opposition. In the fall of 1981 the Reagan administration decided to produce MX missiles and to deploy them in fixed silos—at least initially. They deferred a decision on a basing system better able to survive an attack.

Subsequently, Congress objected to that proposal, and the administration turned to the so-called Closely Spaced Basing (CSB), or Densepack, approach. According to this plan, fixed silos would be hardened so that a single 1-megaton blast going off between two silos spaced as close as 2,000 feet apart could not destroy them. The intent would be to prevent a successful attack by other warheads on nearby silos for some minutes or hours after the first explosion. Accurate reentry and detonation of the subsequent warheads would be prevented by the blast, the dust cloud, and the radiation from the earlier ones, in an effect called "fratricide." The details of the blast and other phenomena, and therefore both the extent of such fratricide and the ability of the silos to survive, are very difficult to calculate and cannot be tested. That makes the claimed ability of the basing systems to survive an attack uncertain, but it could also make an attacker uncertain about his ability to destroy such a system by a preemptive attack. Incoming reentry vehicles are more vulnerable than hardened silos. Unfortunately, the MX missiles are themselves still more vulnerable during the several minutes of their launch and powered flight and could be forced to remain in their silos, "pinned down" by the incoming Soviet attack. MX missiles could also be pinned down if the United States employed an antiballistic missile (ABM) defense of the closely spaced silos. Whether fratricide has a more destructive effect on the attack than pindown has on the residual MX force is a difficult question. So also is the question of the effect of the fireball on MX silo doors and the feasibility of launching the missiles through the doors and surrounding debris after they have survived an attack.

More important, the Soviets could institute tactical and design countermeasures over the next five to ten years to overcome the effects of fratricide. They could program the attacking reentry vehicles to arrive and detonate at their respective aim points simultaneously. They could deploy accurate reentry vehicles capable of surviving ground impact and then detonating simultaneously after arrival. They could employ much larger (25-megaton) warheads to destroy several silos at once. Thus, there is not high confidence that a Closely Spaced Basing deployment of MX missiles would be able to survive a well-planned attack by a force only a small fraction of the size of the present Soviet ICBM force but with appropriately rearranged payloads.

If combined with multiple protective shelters (MPS—"deceptive basing"), the Densepack approach would be less vulnerable. But if the silos are to be hardened, the Densepack plan would require vertical shelters. That would make rapid shuttling between shelters impossible. It would also make verification of numbers of missiles deployed more difficult, though not impossible. The Densepack plan would have the great advantage of allowing the United States to fit 4,600 shelters with 200 missiles into an area as small as 460 square miles. Thus the missile fields could be limited to the confines of two existing military bases. The cost of such a system might be comparable to that of the original MPS system, depending on the cost of so resistant a shelter. But without an MPS feature, the Densepack basing system poses a major, perhaps insuperable, problem in that it may violate the SALT II provision that allows mobile missiles but no new fixed silos. Moreover, the local political forces stirred up in earlier stages of the MX basing debate might be powerful enough to make any deployment, even Densepack deployment, difficult.

My own judgment is that Densepack without an MPS feature is likely to be vulnerable to destruction by a properly executed attack of only a few hundred 1-megaton Soviet warheads, or even fewer larger ones; thus it is not a good military or technical solution. An ABM overlay would not improve the outlook enough to be worth the cost of abandoning the ABM treaty. But Densepack including an MPS feature is likely to be capable of surviving a large attack and might have been politically acceptable if it had been adopted soon enough by the Reagan administration.

In the absence of some version of an MPS or deceptive basing system, the most sensible solution may well be to replace some Minuteman missiles either with MX missiles in the mid-1980s or with a version of the Trident II (D-5) missile at the end of the 1980s, deploying the replacement missile in existing Minuteman silos. The choice between D-5 and MX would depend on such factors as the relative costs and the value of earlier deployment. This approach would allow the United States to retain land-based missiles and accept their continued vulnerability, but Soviet ICBMs would also be vulnerable. In my view this is a substantially inferior substitute for the original MPS system, or even for Densepack with an MPS feature, but it is a minimally acceptable fallback.

Does the United States need substantial numbers of high-accuracy ICBM warheads? The threat to U.S. ICBMs from such a force in the Soviet Union is dismissed by some of the same commentators who accommodatingly put themselves in the position of the Soviet Union and see such a force—the MX or the Trident II—in the hands of the United States as terribly threatening. They argue that because the Soviets have more of their capability in land-based ICBMs, large numbers of accurate ICBM warheads threaten them more. But both the United States and the Soviet Union have SLBM forces that are likely to survive a preemptive strike. Moreover, the Soviet bomber force, though relatively small, could be brought to a level of alert that would allow the Soviet bombers to be launched on warning and thus to survive. When it comes to penetrating antiaircraft defenses, the Soviets have very much less of a problem than the United States, simply because the United States has no substantial air defense. If the Soviets were concerned that the threat to their land-based ICBMs was disproportionate, they would need only to cut the size of their individual ICBM missiles in half. That would allow them to distribute their strategic forces more uniformly among the various types of forces, make them relatively less vulnerable to a single kind of threat, and still leave them with double the ICBM payload of the United States.

In addition to diversifying retaliatory forces to improve overall chances of survival and penetration, ICBMs provide prompt and accurate capability against military targets. They have the command-and-control system that is best suited to survive. It could make sense in an arms control environment for both sides to phase out their ICBMs, but there is little merit in the argument that it is better for the USSR to be able to threaten U.S. land-based ICBM forces without the United States being able to threaten theirs than it is for each side's ICBM force to be able to threaten the other.

One more argument deserves attention among the MX issues. Some experts contend that the Soviets can always build enough accurate ICBM reentry vehicles to wipe out any number of hard shelters the United States may build. In principle this is true. In principle, though, the United States can also keep building shelters. The cost-exchange ratio works out to be fairly close, probably favoring the shelter-builders. The suggestion that the Soviets can overwhelm a deployment of MX missiles in multiple protective shelters is a good argument for strategic arms limitations, though it is not always intended as such by those who make it. It is an especially good argument for the SALT II limitations on accurate multiple independently targeted reentry vehicles (MIRVs) on ICBMs to about 6,000 for each country during the 1980s.

But another factor must be understood. If the Soviets were to embark on a course of acquiring the ability to overwhelm a multiple shelter deployment, that would be a clear rejection of arms control. This in turn would make it sensible for the United States to overlay the multiple shelter system with a hard-point antiballistic defense, an action that should otherwise be avoided because of its possible negative effects on arms control in general and on the mutually agreed 1972 ban on ABM defenses. Should arms control be jettisoned, however, because of an all-out Soviet ICBM reentry vehicle program, this reason would no longer have weight, and a relatively inexpensive ABM overlay (costing perhaps 20 percent of the cost of the MX deployment itself) would raise by another two to four times the number of Soviet reentry vehicles required to saturate the system. Raising the Soviet entry price from 200 to 600 warheads (as would be the case for a deployment of 100 MXs *without* multiple protective shelters) is not that significant; raising it from 5,000 or 10,000 to 15,000 or 30,000 is quite another matter. Thus an ABM overlay is worth little without MPS.

The Soviets can build the same number of reentry vehicles (RVs) in the absence of a U.S. MX-MPS system as they can in its presence. These RVs would then be available for barrage attacks on U.S. bombers and their bases. Ten thousand 1-megaton RVs could cover nearly 1 million square miles of the United States with an overpressure of several pounds per square inch, enough to destroy any aircraft in the area and incidentally to destroy most of the population in that area at the same time. Or they could be used to destroy all the submarines within twenty-five 100-mile-radius circles, a capability that would greatly ease the problem of submarine location in a Soviet preemptive attack.

Thus, though a dyad of forces is a conceivable strategic approach for the United States, it cannot be safely supported by programs planned by the Carter or Reagan administrations simply by subtracting the land-based ICBMs. Major additions would have to be made to the sea-based and air-breathing components. Even then, vulnerability to new Soviet deployments and technological developments would be more likely to become a serious problem than it would with a more diverse force.

Air-breathing (Aircraft) Systems

Bombers and long-range cruise missiles (which are unmanned aircraft) would take six to twelve hours to arrive at their targets. But they can be sent toward the target without an irrevocable commitment. This allows them to be launched on warning and thus increases their ability to survive an attack, provided the Soviets cannot launch a barrage attack so large as to destroy the aircraft even fifteen to thirty minutes after they have taken off.

The quantity, sophistication, and scope of Soviet air defense systems, now and increasingly during the 1980s, will dictate that penetrating bombers not fly directly over their targets and drop gravity bombs, but rather launch short-range attack missiles (SRAMs) that penetrate air-defense systems at high velocity. Thus the distinction between the penetrating bomber and the cruise missile carrier is one of distance. The penetrating bomber's air-to-surface missile has a 50-kilometer (30-mile) to 100-kilometer (60-mile) range, sufficient to outrange Soviet surface-to-air interceptor missiles. The long-range cruise missile has a 2,000-kilometer (1,200-mile) to 3,000-kilometer (1,800-mile) range, sufficient to allow the carrier that launches it to avoid Soviet interceptor aircraft. (These cruise missiles could be launched from aircraft. Alternatively, cruise missiles could be built in two-stage designs and launched directly from the continental United States, with a range of 8,000 kilometers or more.) The accuracy of these air-to-surface missiles can be expected to fall into the range of a few hundred feet or less during the 1980s. This is sufficient to destroy even the hardest targets unless they are buried far below the surface, in which case their connection with the surface would be destroyed, effectively sealing them off for days or even weeks.

Evaluating the capability of penetration of either the penetrating bomber or the cruise missile is difficult and complex. Countermeasures lead to counter-countermeasures. The B-52 now depends largely for its ability to penetrate defenses on flying at low altitude and on its electronic countermeasures, which blind or deceive ground-based or airborne radars. During the second half of the 1980s the B-52 will not have a high assurance of penetrating those Soviet air defenses, even using electronic countermeasures. An updated B-1 would have a better chance against the combination of Soviet surface-to-air missiles and fighter interceptors guided by airborne warning radar aircraft. It could not, however, be counted on to penetrate Soviet air defenses into and through the 1990s.

Two other air-breathing systems can. One is the long-range cruise missile. It can fly considerably closer to the ground than a manned aircraft, because some collisions of unmanned cruise missiles with obstacles can be accepted. It is smaller and thus more difficult to detect than a bomber. It can and will be built in large numbers, to saturate the defense systems. These features combine to give it much more assurance of being able to penetrate than a manned B-1 bomber. The second is the Advanced Technology Bomber (ATB)—a manned bomber that would employ "stealth" technology, already proved on a smaller scale, to make itself enormously difficult for Soviet radar systems to detect and track. As always, Soviet countermeasures against these systems are possible, but each would involve a huge additional investment—perhaps $100 billion—at the end of which the Soviet capability of intercepting most of the attack would still be questionable. The Soviet systems that can be used against the B-1 are precisely the ones they have been developing and deploying over the past ten years and plan to deploy over the next ten years.

The nature of Soviet defenses against air-breathing systems would have to be quite different from those against ballistic missiles. To escape detection, air-breathers rely on the curvature of the earth or on "signatures" that are nearly invisible to radar, optical search, or other detection systems. Ballistic missile systems cannot use the earth's curvature at all, and it is much harder to reduce their detectability than that of aircraft. It thus makes sense for the United States, in ensuring its own retaliatory capability, to subject the Soviet defenses to stress by including a substantial number of air-breathing systems as well as ballistic missiles in its strategic forces.

The question is what (if anything) should replace the B-52s. An appropriate combination would be to stop using the B-52s as penetrating bombers toward the end of the 1980s and convert some of them to cruise missile carriers. Some have already been converted, and cruise missiles deployed on them, during 1982. By the late 1980s or early 1990s, a successor to the B-52 as a penetrating bomber will probably be needed. An ATB "stealth" bomber could be introduced into the force in operational numbers just a few years after the B-1. The ATB is still in design and wind-tunnel tests, while the B-1 has flown for years (albeit in a configuration different from the one now proposed for production). The contractor and subcontractor structure for producing a new version of the B-1, however, was not (as of 1981) in much better condition than the contractor and subcontractor structure for the production of the ATB.

Moreover, current Soviet air defenses, and the ones to be deployed for the late 1980s and thereafter, were designed with the B-1 in mind. B-1 penetration in the 1990s would depend on an uncertain contest between its electronic countermeasures and Soviet counter-

countermeasures. An entirely new Soviet defense system would have to be devised for use against the "stealth" bomber. In either case, the Soviets will have to deploy the currently planned system to defend against cruise missiles launched from B-52s and from successor cruise missile carriers through the 1990s.

These factors make a "stealth" bomber a better choice than the B-1 bomber for the rest of this century. Some argue that the B-1 bomber could be used for launching cruise missiles or for conventional strikes against less well-defended areas outside the Soviet Union when it is no longer able to penetrate Soviet air defenses. This is hardly a justification for the expenditure of tens of billions of dollars. The B-1 is overdesigned as a cruise missile carrier and far more expensive than necessary for that purpose, notwithstanding its greater resistance to a nuclear barrage attack than that of the B-52s. It is worth tens of billions of dollars to deter the Soviets by being able to penetrate their defenses with a high level of assurance, but it hardly seems worth the same amount to be able to bomb the Bulgarians with impunity.

The correct approach for the United States is to maintain a balance among the various forces in the triad at a reasonable cost and to phase in the various new components in a way that preserves the ability of the strategic forces as a whole to survive an attack and penetrate Soviet defenses. No precise criteria exist, however, or can be defined, to determine the proper overall size of the force or the appropriate balance among the elements of the triad. Assumptions and even calculations about future technology, future Soviet decisions, "reactive threats," and the effects of some particular future tactical situation are too uncertain. The determination of "how much is enough" will always be influenced by budgetary limitations and by competition from nonstrategic military needs. In the end, the decisions will be made weapons system by weapons system.

Hard-Target Capability

In the 1980s and 1990s, the United States will have some capability against hardened Soviet missile silos and command posts. The Soviet Union already has the capability to destroy such hardened targets in the United States. The needed accuracy has been an almost inevitable result of technological advance. It would have taken strong and specific policy decisions for the forces of the Soviet Union and the United States not to have achieved such accuracy. Does the United States require a certain minimum "hard-target kill" capability? And must this be prompt—that is, able to arrive in thirty minutes on a ballistic missile rather than in ten hours on a cruise missile?

The United States must maintain some hard-target capability both to ensure strong deterrence (deterrence of a nuclear attack even in situations of extreme crisis with high stakes) and to ensure perception of a U.S.-Soviet strategic balance by being able to put at risk many hard targets of value to the Soviet leaders. But to serve those purposes that capability need not be exactly equal to Soviet hard-target capability. To this end, 1,000 to 2,000 warheads with prompt hard-target capability would be sufficient. The purely military advantages of prompt capability over delayed capability are modest, but they include a rapid response in kind to a Soviet attack on U.S. missile silos and a more effective ability to attack a Soviet political leadership that is being shuttled among hardened command posts.

Crisis Management

What are the implications of projected developments in U.S. and Soviet strategic nuclear forces for crisis stability, that is, for dealing with pressures to escalate to nuclear war in time of crisis? As strategic nuclear forces on both sides become more vulnerable, political decision makers will be able to calculate differences in short-term outcome between striking first and striking second, as shown by various balances after an exchange, e.g., remaining warheads or population fatalities. In a crisis, what difference will such calculations make? Even differences of a factor of two will probably have little effect. The damage to population and industry is sure to be so great that the prospect of halving it should not weigh heavily against the certainty that striking first would initiate a thermonuclear exchange. But if the difference between striking first and striking second were believed to be that between 100 million deaths and 10 million, that could affect potential decisions. Given a reasonable force structure, command-and-control systems, and target planning on the part of the United States, such disparities should not develop. On narrower measures, such as the number of land-based ICBMs surviving, large disparities are possible depending on who strikes first and on the characteristics of weapons systems, such as whether the ICBMs of one or both sides are vulnerable. But a decision to strike first would not be based principally on any one such ratio of surviving forces.

A Program for Strategic Offensive
Forces for the 1980s and 1990s

A reasonable allocation for the development and acquisition of strategic systems would average about $15 billion (in 1981 dollars) a year over the next decade. This would be less than 7 percent of expected total defense budgets during that period and about the same (in constant dollars) as the cost from 1955 through 1965 of developing and acquiring the forces that would be replaced.[2] The following programs appear sensible and should be possible by spending 7 percent of the U.S. defense budget over the next ten years on their development and deployment.

1. Deploying MX missiles based in multiple protective shelters. It would make sense to begin with only 100 missiles in 2,300 shelters. The system could later be expanded to double that size, or an ABM overlay could be considered if the Soviets launch an all-out arms race. Those decisions can be made later in the 1980s when Soviet force reactions and the course of arms limitation negotiations are clearer than they are now. The Administration would need to find ways to overcome local political objections in Nevada and Utah to MX basing in multiple shelters. One way may be to deploy the MX on military bases and to introduce an economic program to ameliorate the effects of a sudden and temporary influx of construction activity.

2. Maintaining the B-52 force for use as penetrating bombers and cruise missile launchers through about 1986, then phasing out their penetrating role and increasing their role as cruise missile launchers while phasing in an ATB "stealth" bomber beginning about 1990.

3. Introducing a larger submarine-launched missile (the D-5), to be retrofitted into Trident submarines beginning in about 1991 or 1992. Sixteen such submarines would constitute as large a force as the United States should now plan, and eleven are already funded. If the D-5 missile is delayed for technical or funding reasons, a modification should be introduced into the Trident I (C-4) missiles to give them substantially greater accuracy.

With these programs, the United States would have a truly formidable strategic nuclear force, with considerable resiliency even under pessimistic assumptions about future Soviet deployments and technological advances. If both sides can agree to arms limitations, the numbers could be smaller, and indeed some of these programs might not be necessary. But even if substantial reductions in the overall number of strategic warheads cannot be negotiated—which would be a tragedy—this force (16 Trident submarines each with 24

---

[2]The total cost of the strategic forces, strategic command-and-control and communications systems, and a reasonable allocation of the overhead cost of operating the military establishment has run to about 15 percent of the defense budget. This includes strategic warning and defensive systems, which now take only 1 or 2 percent of the defense budget. These figures include operating as well as acquisition costs. The ratios of operating to acquisition costs are very different for the different components of the strategic force.

SLBMs; 100–200 MXs; 2,000 cruise missiles; and 100 "stealth" bombers) would bring the total alert strategic forces to approximately the number of alert U.S. strategic warheads in the present force. The difference, and the justification for an investment of $150 billion (1981 dollars) over the decade, is a continued, indeed higher, assurance—in the face of continued Soviet force modernization—of the ability to survive a preemptive attack, penetrate prospective defenses, and destroy the full range of potential targets.

DEFENSIVE AND DAMAGE LIMITING SYSTEMS

If deterrence fails, an all-out strategic war is likely to kill about 100 million people on each side promptly. Under those circumstances, does it make sense to institute a civil defense program to try to save—30 million or 40 million who might otherwise have been killed—the difference, say, between 80 million and 120 million? When the question is put in those terms the answer would be yes.

But no civil defense program likely to be accepted or taken seriously in either the United States or the Soviet Union would be able to save a recognizable society, or in the case of the Soviet Union, to save the power of the leadership, which may be equally important to the Soviet leaders. The prospects for evacuating millions of people from cities in hours or even days, or for moving them into blast shelters, seem poor. The prospects for their survival afterward seem even poorer. Too many things are likely to go wrong. The people of the United States exhibited a substantial interest in the late 1950s and early 1960s in survival through shelter, but later in the 1960s it became clear that the public would not support the changes in political organization and in life-styles that come with a massive civil defense program. On the Soviet side that life-style is more familiar, but the actual capabilities of the Soviet program appear to be quite limited, despite the much larger number of people who have civil defense responsibilities.

Nevertheless, deterrence might fail, and some modest amount of money to increase the number of survivors of an all-out strategic war, at whatever wretched level of existence, may be worth spending. A U.S. program of $100 million to $150 million a year should not be seen by the Soviets as a threat to their deterrent capability and thus cause for a compensating (or overcompensating) force buildup. Still less should U.S. leaders regard such a civil defense program as giving us coercive strength in a crisis.

As for active defense of populations against missiles or bombers, neither is cost effective. For a given investment, the offense will be able to overwhelm the active defense of urban industrial targets. Some modest level of air defense is necessary to ensure control of the nation's air space in peacetime. It may also be useful to retain a somewhat larger capability in order to intercept a small bomber attack. But most of the investment should go into early warning systems, for both bomber and missile attacks. Such systems should include a capability to assess the *nature* of the attack as well as its size. An antiballistic missile defense of land-based retaliatory systems or of the command structure, beyond an ABM overlay on an ICBM based in multiple shelters, might also be built without creating the impression of urban industrial defense. But such a distinction would be hard to observe in practice. The Soviets would presumably expand their ABM defenses in accord with any loosening of limits in the ABM Treaty. U.S. analysts would be concerned that it might have urban defense capabilities or the potential for breakout even if it was deployed to protect strategic forces. Such steps, therefore, always run the risks associated with massive air and ABM defenses—they could lead to the initiation of nuclear war on the basis of a tragic miscalculation of the ability of the defensive systems to protect urban-industrial targets.

COMMAND-AND-CONTROL AND COMMUNICATIONS (C³)

The most vulnerable parts of the U.S. strategic forces are the command-and-control and communications (C³) systems on which it relies for assurance that the information about the onset and evolution of a strategic war would be correct and would be properly communicated to the decision-making authorities, that the decisions about the U.S. military response would be made by duly constituted authority, and that those decisions would be carried out. Such a system should be robust enough that there is little temptation for the adversary to launch a relatively small strike at it alone to prevent retaliation or to see it as incapable of supporting any but a spasm response to an attack.

The degree of flexibility required depends on how many different strategic options must be available and for how long. This in turn depends on the doctrine adopted for deterring and, if necessary, carrying out a nuclear war. In the simplest case, where the only response contemplated is all-out thermonuclear retaliation on military and urban industrial targets, no great sophistication is needed. What would be of concern, in this as in other cases, is the possibility of a decapitation attack that cuts off the Presidential authority constitutionally required to decide on and direct a response. There is an elaborate combination of ground-based and airborne support and transmission facilities to ensure that the "go" code, directing military units in the field to strike the chosen targets, is given. There is also a great variety of ground-based, air-based, rocket-based, and satellite-based relay systems to ensure that the message is received. But a submarine-launched missile could wipe out Washington with no more than ten minutes' warning, perhaps less. It is inappropriate to go into the details of the arrangements that have been made for such contingencies and thus suggest to the Soviets how to get around those arrangements. But one criterion for such arrangements ought properly to be that a decapitating attack should have the effect of making the response an all-out, unrestrained one.

At all times there is at least one Strategic Air Command aircraft (called "Looking Glass") airborne with the necessary transmission facilities. In times of tension, this aircraft would be backed up by additional airborne and ground-based command centers. It would make sense under such circumstances for a Presidential successor, particularly the Vice-President, to be airborne in the National Emergency Airborne Command Post (NEACP).

According to Soviet doctrine, a massive attack on U.S. retaliatory capability would be accompanied by an attempt to blanket the command-and-control systems in order to prevent or minimize U.S. retaliation. But such a Soviet tactic would probably be viewed by its initiators as a gamble on improving the outcome for them rather than the principal way of avoiding retaliation. Neither side can make predictions with any confidence about the factors that would govern the outcome of this type of gamble. To reduce Soviet confidence in the effectiveness of such a tactic still further, the United States needs to make substantial and expensive increases in the extent, redundancy, and survivability of its command-and-control system. These would include additional NEACP aircraft, with hardened communications, and mobile land-based and perhaps sea-based (even submarine-based) alternative command posts. Fixed, hardened, land-based command posts, unless built in very large numbers, are not likely enough to survive to be worth their cost. Confidence in command-and-control systems also requires continued attention to practice exercises.

NUCLEAR DOCTRINE AND NUCLEAR WAR PLANS

There is no way of judging with any confidence what the process of fighting a nuclear war would be like. The magnitude of the destruction, the confusion, the psychological pressures on decision makers, the difficulty of making judgments about what was actually happening, and the problems in reestablishing any sort of civil or military order would all be incomparably greater than any that have ever been experienced by political and military leaders in past conflicts.

A strategic war that involved a massive attack on urban industrial areas would be unimaginably catastrophic. Many serious thinkers about the subject have concluded, partly for this reason and partly because they believe that talking about any gradations in such a catastrophe increases the likelihood that it will happen, that the United States should have no plans for anything less than a total use of its strategic force against all kinds of Soviet targets. Some of this school maintain that the United States should have only one plan if a nuclear attack of any magnitude is launched against the United States by the Soviet Union under any circumstances—to retaliate by an all-out attack on Soviet urban and industrial areas.

There is a good chance that any U.S.-Soviet nuclear exchange would escalate out of control. The possibility of such a total disaster is a significant element in overall deterrence. But it would be highly irresponsible to say that, because we cannot predict how such a war would happen, the United States should make no plans for how it will be fought. Imagine a military planner or political official who had to tell a President who had asked for options in responding to an actual strategic attack that there were no such plans because such a war had been judged inconceivable or unimaginable. Should a nuclear war begin, it is the responsibility of the political and military authorities to try to limit its damaging effects.

It is hard to believe that serious thinkers would really want the United States to respond massively and indiscriminately without considering the nature of the attack being responded to. If the Soviet Union were for some reason to launch an attack that included fifty nuclear weapons and killed 1 million Americans, would adherents of such a doctrine (if they survived) advise the President to launch an all-out attack that would kill 100 million Soviets and bring a Soviet response that would kill an equal number of Americans?

It is argued, correctly, that such a scenario is improbable. But so is every particular scenario for a thermonuclear war. One can only hope that all of them taken together are also sufficiently improbable. But military planners must provide plans for all eventualities that are sufficiently serious, and reasonably possible, even if they are improbable. The tensions and potential disasters that could make a nuclear attack look like a serious choice for a Soviet decision maker would arise in situations of enormous strain and distortion. Under such circumstances, the United States would not want its strategic nuclear force capabilities or doctrine to suggest to the Soviets that there could be levels of strategic warfare at which they might gain an advantage. For that reason, over the two decades during which the Soviet Union moved from a position of clear strategic nuclear inferiority to one variously characterized as parity, essential equivalence, or incipient superiority, U.S. strategic doctrine evolved from massive retaliation to graduated response to a countervailing strategy. In fact, effective deterrence is improved by a convincing ability to respond at all levels. General recognition that the United States has capabilities and plans not only for an all-out spasm response but for more limited, victory-denying responses as well could be a factor in making Soviet leaders step back from an attack.

In the late 1970s, the United States examined its strategic nuclear force capabilities, doctrines, and plans specifically in light of what was known about Soviet forces, doctrine, and plans. There was some concern that the Soviet leaders appeared to contemplate at least the possibility of a relatively prolonged exchange if war came. There was also concern that decision makers in some Soviet circles appeared to take seriously the possibility of victory in such a war. And there was rather strong evidence that, though the Soviets fully recognize the terrible destructive potential of nuclear weapons, they do not believe that the only possibility likely enough to plan for is an all-out nuclear exchange.

As a result, President Carter in 1980 promulgated the countervailing strategy, according to which the United States seeks to maintain military (including nuclear) forces, contingency plans, and command-and-control capabilities to convince Soviet leaders that they cannot secure victory, however they may define it, at any stage of a potential war. That is, the United States seeks a situation in which the Soviets would always lose more than they could reasonably expect to gain from either beginning or escalating a military conflict.

This is easier to ensure for nuclear war than for conventional war. For some kinds of conventional war, the United States would either have to build up a massively superior overall conventional military capability or make credible the incredible threat that any such conventional attack would quickly lead to a mutually suicidal all-out strategic nuclear war.

The countervailing strategy is less of a departure from previous doctrine than is often claimed. It keeps deterrence at the core of U.S. policy. And it implies no illusion that nuclear war once begun would be likely to stop short of an all-out exchange. But it does acknowledge that such a limited war *could* happen, and it seeks to convince the Soviets that if a limited nuclear attack by them somehow failed to escalate into an all-out nuclear exchange, they would not have gained from their aggression.

Operationally, the countervailing strategy requires that plans and capabilities be structured to emphasize U.S. ability to employ strategic nuclear forces selectively as well as in all-out retaliation for massive attacks. This means having the necessary forces and evolving the detailed plans to ensure that Soviet leaders know that if they choose some intermediate level of nuclear aggression, the United States will exact an unacceptably high price in things that the Soviet leaders appear to value most, using large and selective but still less than maximal nuclear responses. The targets of such an attack could be military forces, both nuclear and conventional; the industrial capability to sustain a war; political and military leadership and control structures; and industrial capacity.

Such targeting plans raise a legitimate concern as to whether they create an unlimited requirement for strategic forces, especially if the Soviets add to their own strategic forces for the same reasons. The United States has had plans to attack a variety of Soviet targets since the early 1950s, and budget constraints have always acted to limit the United States to a capability to strike some, but not all, Soviet targets. The number of U.S. targeting options will probably continue to grow, but only modestly. This is the result not principally of the adoption of flexible targeting options but rather of the existence of more classes of Soviet nuclear targets and the need to put at risk additional assets valued by the Soviet leaders.

The plans to carry out the countervailing strategy could require increases in accuracy to attack hard targets, and they will certainly require improvements in command-and-control. The evolution from the criteria in National Security Study Memorandum 242 in 1974 (which calls for targeting plans, including options to threaten Soviet military targets, based on available weapons systems) to those of Presidential Directive 59 of 1980 (which makes flexibility in targeting options a factor in systems acquisition) could also provide a justification for an expansion of U.S. counterforce capability. But in fact, competition for resources for other purposes, conventional and nuclear, has in the past limited that demand. The number of U.S. strategic warheads has remained roughly constant during the past few years, and the previous increase was more the result of concerns about survival and penetration of U.S. forces than of a longer target list. U.S. military planners can be expected to continue the pattern, now three decades old, of deriving force levels and characteristics from perceived needs for retaliatory capability (though the characteristics are also influenced by technological advances) and then creating targeting options for use under various circumstances.

CONCLUSIONS: THE BALANCE AND ARMS CONTROL

Since the mid-1960s, the strategic balance has altered (not continuously, but overall) in a direction less favorable to the United States. There have been and will continue to be interminable arguments about the exact balance of U.S. and Soviet strategic capabilities. There is no single criterion, and it is difficult to make a precise comparison at any one time. It is considerably easier to make a judgment about the trend, which was adverse for the United States from about the mid-1960s through the mid-1970s. This trend has made a difference in perceptions clearly detrimental to the United States in the Third World, among U.S. allies, and with the American people. It is harder to judge, but it is also likely that this trend has affected the perceptions of the leaders of the Soviet Union, although probably they do not consider themselves to have achieved strategic superiority.

Military strength is a central factor in the outcome of a military conflict. The *perception* of military strength can be a critical element in a political confrontation. Perceptions of a military advantage, or even of a trend in relative military capability that reflects a likely future balance, affect the political behavior of potential adversaries and of third parties in contemplating what actions to take in a crisis. The Soviet willingness to indulge in expansionary policies along their borders and in the Third World may in part be the result of a shift in the strategic nuclear balance.

For this reason, as well as to ensure deterrence of nuclear war, the United States must continue to modernize its strategic forces. But the modernization of these weapons will not in itself guarantee that the United States will attain its related national security goals of minimizing the chance of a strategic nuclear conflict and avoiding a situation in which the strategic nuclear posture of the United States is, or is perceived to be, inferior to that of the Soviet Union. The United States must have an associated arms control and diplomatic posture; the unending and unlimited competition likely in their absence clearly carries major risks to U.S. security and indeed to U.S. survival. On the other hand, an arms control and diplomatic program stands no chance of success in the absence of an adequate strategic arms program, because unless the United States has both the appearance and the reality of sufficient strength in strategic matters, neither U.S. allies nor the Soviet Union will be prepared to take those diplomatic and arms control approaches seriously. And any cessation of U.S.

efforts in the arms competition that is not accompanied by limitations on Soviet actions would be even more risky to U.S. security and survival than unlimited or resource-limited competition on both sides. Thus, both these approaches together will be needed, and even that may not be enough.

A national security program encompassing both approaches should have as its goal strategic stability, that is, a situation in which neither side can achieve significant gains by a preemptive attack and in which deployment of particular new technologies or weapons systems will not substantially alter the relative strategic positions, at least in the short run. In such a situation, each side would have the strategic forces that it regarded as adequate to deter the other, but it would lack the forces that might make it think it could coerce the other. It is unlikely that meaningful superiority can be achieved against a determined opponent; the Soviet Union is certainly such an opponent, and the United States had better be. There are real dangers that the attempt to achieve superiority will lead to a continued escalation of arms deployment, of rhetoric, and of ill feeling and introduce insta- bilities into the strategic relationship. But if superiority is an idle goal, inferiority is still a possible outcome—if U.S. will or judgment or technological ability is inadequate. The United States cannot afford inferiority.

An important element in the diplomatic and arms control approach is the process of negotiating strategic arms limitations and reductions. Too often, both critics and advocates of strategic arms limitation agreements have expected too much of them. It is not too much to hope that further agreements will, like the SALT II Treaty, contain some actual reductions. This would be in line with the Reagan administration's renaming them—before they recommenced—as START, Strategic Arms Reduction Talks. And in the long run the United States should aim for substantial reductions. But it is too much to expect that any arms control agreements, including SALT— or START—will in the real world live up to our idealized hopes. The proper standard by which a strategic arms agreement should be judged is whether it produces a more favorable and more stable situation for the United States than would be the case without it. Each side can be expected to seek to limit the existing or prospective weapons of the other that most concern it. But it is possible for strategic arms limitations agreements to improve the security of both sides beyond what they would be without such agreements. Unless they meet that criterion strategic arms limitations agreements either are not possible or will not endure.

From the U.S. point of view, limits on the fractionation of payloads (numbers of warheads per missile), especially on ICBMs, are desirable. Otherwise, the trend toward larger numbers of MIRVed warheads will increase the threat to land-based ICBM systems and tend to destabilize the strategic balance by its possible effect on the ability of the other components of the triad to survive an attack. Limits on the total number of warheads and launchers (or missiles), on payloads, on the number of new systems that can be developed in a particular period, and on testing rates can all be useful and, if properly balanced, can improve security and stability on both sides. Reductions of the systems on each side that may appear to threaten the ability of the other's forces to survive an attack can be even more effective to this end. The SALT II Treaty contained a number of such provisions useful to the United States without significantly inhibiting the programs the United States would need to respond to Soviet forces held to the agreed size. It is important for U.S. security that those agreed limitations be preserved, whether by a continued voluntary observance on both sides or, preferably, by incorporating them into a SALT III or a START I Treaty that further limits and reduces strategic forces.

6

The United States, Europe, and the NATO Alliance

During and since World War II, the security of Western Europe has been the top priority of U.S. foreign and military policy. World War II provoked a bitter debate on this issue. Some would have given primacy to the Pacific war. Others believed that an Allied victory in Europe would ensure the subsequent defeat of Japan, while Allied concentration on the Pacific could allow Hitler to consolidate his victories in Europe and ensure permanent German domination. President Roosevelt decided on the Europe-first strategy. Hindsight supports the correctness of his decision.

The industrial productivity and skilled work force of Western Europe, and U.S. political, cultural, and historical ties with that region, continue to make Western Europe central to U.S. foreign policy. After World War II, political leaders from both the center-right parties and the social democratic parties in Europe, and Republicans and Democrats in the United States, saw major threats to democratic government from the Soviet Union and from substantial communist parties in some Western European countries. The Marshall Plan and the North Atlantic Treaty alliance—NATO is its military organization—were devised in the late 1940s and early 1950s. They were aimed at restoring the economies of the Western European nations, preserving their democratic institutions, integrating the new Federal Republic of Germany (FRG—West Germany) into the European and Atlantic communities, and creating a partnership between Western Europe and the United States. Europe remained pivotal in U.S. geostrategic thinking throughout the 1950s, 1960s, and 1970s, even though the United States during that period fought two major land wars in Asia.

THE STAKES

Western Europe recovered quickly after World War II, both politically and economically. France and Italy staved off internal political drives by their communist parties. West Germany established a stable democratic political structure and entered into the economic and military arrangements of the West. During the 1970s, the establishment of new forms of government in Portugal and Spain (which became a NATO member in 1982) completed the democratization of Western Europe. Greece and Turkey, both NATO members, have undergone periods of military rule but have thereafter returned to the free electoral process. Turkey experienced a military coup in 1980 for the second time since World War II and took steps toward restoration of the democratic political process in 1982.

All of Western Europe experienced unprecedented economic growth from 1948 to 1973. This growth was the result of hard work, unusually free world trade, U.S. investment in Europe and U.S. markets for European goods, and such intra-European cooperation as the European Economic Community (EEC). As a result of this progress, Western Europe, with a population of 350 million and a GNP greater than that of the United States and Canada combined, remains the weightiest single regional center of world production and trade.

The Atlantic alliance has also been a success. Despite the French departure from its military command structure in the 1960s, and deepening rifts in its ranks, the alliance remains an effective political and military instrument for the defense of Western Europe.

Western Europe has not developed as a political entity, and its political fragmentation and economic, linguistic, and social heterogeneity—features it does not share with Japan or the United States—have greatly limited its ability to bring its weight to bear internationally. These characteristics ensure that the functioning of Western Europe's partnership with the United States is likely to remain geographically limited and somewhat one-sided. But preventing Western Europe from falling under Soviet domination and control, by political, economic, or even military means, has been the single most important regional aim of U.S. foreign policy for almost four decades and is likely to remain so during the rest of this century.

The Soviets have a corresponding focus on Europe. Next to the defense of the Soviet homeland itself and the preservation there of the system by which they rule, Soviet leaders have, from the final days of World War II, placed their highest emphasis on dominating Eastern Europe. They see it as a buffer against another military attack from the west of the kind Russia has experienced so many times in the past. Eastern Europe also serves as a salient thrusting into the West to threaten *it*, especially to intimidate West Germany while keeping it separated from East Germany (the German Democratic Republic). These functions are served by the Warsaw Pact, organized by the Soviet Union in response to the formation of NATO, in order to tie the Eastern European countries into a military command totally dominated by the Soviets.

The Soviet empire in Eastern Europe also provides them, through the Council for Mutual Economic Assistance (COMECON), with a trading area they can dominate entirely. Eastern Europe undoubtedly once represented to its Soviet rulers an opportunity to use military and political domination to extract economic gain. Immediately after the war the transfer of equipment and machinery, especially from East Germany, did serve that purpose. The population of the Soviet-dominated countries of Eastern Europe is almost a third of the population of the Soviet Union itself, and their per capita GNPs are in most cases somewhat greater. They constitute a key part of the Soviet empire, in a near-colonial sense. The higher standard of living in some parts of Eastern Europe than in the Soviet Union suggests the situation in which the nomadic empires of the fifth through the fifteenth centuries dominated the more urbanized areas from the steppes, rather than the colonialism of the nineteenth century, in which larger and more established countries dominated less industrialized lands. The Soviets now probably recognize that Eastern Europe is an economic drain rather than a benefit, but they still value it as a physical and ideological buffer. Whatever its value, it is doubtful that they see any way to ease their rule there.

Thus Europe, east and west, has been central to U.S.-Soviet competition since World War II. Eastern Europe is the one area of the world outside its own borders of which it has always been true that the Soviet Union was prepared to take high risks of war, even with the United States, in order to preserve its control. It has used its own troops to preserve that domination when its client regimes were threatened from within—in East Germany in 1953, in Hungary in 1956, in Czechoslovakia in 1968, and in Poland in 1970—and it will probably do so again.

The rise of the Solidarity labor movement in Poland in 1980, the economic and political problems that generated it and that it in turn aggravated and the disruption and division in the Polish Communist Party presented the Soviet Union with a difficult problem: to reverse an unacceptable situation without provoking major and damaging economic and political retaliation from the West. The skillful solution the Soviets and the Polish military government reached in the winter of 1981–1982, using Polish security forces to impose martial law and crush Solidarity, and the fragmented Western response suggest that Eastern Europe remains vital in Soviet eyes and that unrest will not automatically tilt the political and military balance toward the West. But political unrest and economic stagnation in Eastern Europe will continue under Soviet domination.

In turn, the United States has made it clear since the late 1940s that it would be prepared to go to war with the Soviet Union in order to prevent the Soviets from conquering Western Europe. To this end, the United States has built up a succession of nuclear shields, tripwires, and forward defenses, all involving U.S. nuclear and conventional forces. There is much less tension, and smaller forces are deployed, at the Bering Strait, where the United States and the Soviet Union face each other only 50 miles apart, than in Europe—1,500 miles from Moscow and 3,500 miles from Washington. This clearly indicates where both countries consider the stakes to be the highest.

THE POLITICAL FACTORS, EAST AND WEST

The populations in the Soviet Union's Eastern European satellites are generally anti-Soviet, though in varying degrees. The Soviets could view only the Bulgarian and perhaps the East German military (but not the East German people) with any confidence in a military conflict that displayed discouraging deviations from a prior plan. Bitter memories persist, of unrest, revolt, and Soviet intervention to suppress workers' movements and of more massive suppression of deviant governmental or party behavior. More distant historical animosities toward the Russian Empire also affect Soviet relations with Poland, Hungary, and East Germany. Moveover, there is substantial resentment among the Eastern European populations toward their own "new class" of rulers, seen usually as Soviet puppets, often corrupt and almost always inefficient and ineffective in economic matters. Expectations that arose from détente and increased Western credits have been disappointed. Hard times, economic and political, have followed.

The combination of anti-Soviet and antiregime attitudes means that in the hypothetical case of a sudden magical disappearance of Soviet military power, or the threat of it, from Eastern Europe, none or almost none of the present communist regimes would last a month, or even a week. This is not a pleasant situation for the Soviets to have on their borders and in their immediate neighborhood. Nor does it provide the best possible lines of communication for military action against the West. On the other hand, Soviet concern for the stability of such regimes provides a strong reason for the Soviets to keep some modest military forces in the Eastern European countries. Twenty divisions in East Germany and five in Czechoslovakia, with massive tactical air power, are, however, much more than can be attributed to any such need.

Western Europe has evolved and changed substantially since the 1950s. The welfare state has become practically universal. The new generation remembers neither the lesson that World War II taught their parents about the risks of inadequate military preparation nor the deep if sometimes overdramatic concerns about the Soviet Union that existed in the late 1940s and the 1950s. The antinuclear movement of the 1950s and 1960s has now been revived, in some cases coupled with neutralism and a degree of pacifism. This movement is to some extent encouraged by the churches, in a phenomenon reminiscent of the mid-1930s. Moreover, antinuclear groups have lately been joined by a middle-class, middle-aged, moderate group that fears that the U.S.-Soviet antagonism could lead to a nuclear war in Europe. These new, or rather, revived intellectual attitudes have some basis in reality, albeit a distorted one. It is true that if a war took place in Europe it would probably escalate to the point of nuclear destruction of both Eastern and Western Europe—and of the United States and the Soviet Union. The real issue, however, is the way to prevent such a war from beginning, or from escalating once it has begun. The advocates of "better Red than dead" appear to assume that those are the only alternatives; they seem not to have taken to heart the lesson of Cambodia—that accepting the former condition may well not save you from the latter.

The economic stagnation of the late 1970s that followed the unprecedented improvement in standards of living in Western Europe during the 1950s and 1960s threatens to continue or worsen in the 1980s. The resulting heightened competition for resources within government budgets tends to erode both the will and the capacity to increase military strength. Moreover, in considering their relations with the Soviet Union and the value of increased military strength, Western European countries—and especially West Germany—tend to be quite reluctant to risk what they perceive as the benefits of détente.

Over the last few years, Western European concern about Soviet expansionism and military strength has revived. This concern, however, has generally been much less than in the United States and has provoked a different response. Great Britain, at least under Prime Minister Margaret Thatcher, appears most willing to build up its military forces insofar as its economy will allow and to apply economic pressure to the Soviets—partly because, of the major Western European countries, it has the least economic interaction with the Soviet Union. West Germany has made improvements in its military posture during much of the 1970s, but it sees itself as benefiting substantially from détente. Harassment in Berlin has lessened, cultural and family interactions are allowed across the border between the two Germanys, many ethnic Germans have been permitted to emigrate from the Soviet Union and the rest of the Soviet bloc, and economic relations with the Eastern European countries, particularly with East Germany, have increased. All the countries of Western Europe emphasize diplomacy and negotiation in response to Soviet military buildup and expansionism far more than has any U.S. administration since Richard Nixon's. These differences with the United States have shown up sharply in the respective U.S. and Western European responses to the December 1981 repression in Poland. Even Great Britain refused to allow its manufacturers to obey U.S. Government restrictions imposed in 1982 on the sale of parts destined for the Soviet gas pipeline.

A separate and disturbing view has arisen in most of the smaller NATO countries. Believing that the large countries will in any event protect them—the United States because it considers their security important to itself, West Germany because it lies closest to the Soviet Union—many see little need for any action but to bask in the benefits of this protective concern. There are exceptions. Norway, which shares a border with the Soviet Union, is one. But the general trend is troublesome. A few years ago a small NATO country conveyed through its Defense Minister the information that it would not be raising its defense budget that year by 3 percent in real terms, as all members of the alliance had agreed to make every effort to do, because it could not possibly afford such an added expense in light of its poor economic condition. Simultaneously, an *increase* in its annual social welfare programs equal to the *entire* defense budget was being debated in its parliament—and most of that increase was adopted. At the time that nation had nearly the highest per capita GNP of any NATO country.

The current stagnation of Western and specifically of European economies comes after a fifteen-year period during which growth was substantially greater in Western Europe than in the United States and the Europeans overtook the United States in total GNP. They have thus collectively become of equal weight with the United States in one of the major measures of world power, and this causes them correctly to conclude that they ought to have more say in alliance affairs. They are gradually, though unevenly, coming to appreciate that their say will be commensurate with their actual efforts on behalf of the alliance rather than with their capacity to make such efforts.

This enormous European economic growth has, moreover, made Europe much more dependent on oil from the Persian Gulf and the Middle East than it was twenty years ago. But the European nations have not yet concluded that this gives them a military responsibility for the security of that area. Europe's economic growth has made it, if anything, an even more tempting target for military or political domination by the Soviet Union. A successful Soviet coercion of Western Europe through military pressure or political intimidation might, for example, lead to the negotiation of $100 billion in long-term, interest-free credits from Western European financial institutions to the Soviet Union. (Given the tendency during the past decade of some European governments and private financial institutions to subsidize trade with the Soviet bloc, however, one may wonder whether much coercion would be required even now to produce such a deal.)

On the other hand, the prosperity of Western Europe, despite its economic problems, aggravates Eastern European resentment of their own governments and their subservience to the Soviet Union. In short, the economic environment is a complicating factor of multiple dimensions, some of them reducing Western European wariness of the Soviet Union, but in the long run giving Western Europe enormous strength, should it choose to make use of that strength to improve its own security.

In summary, each superpower sees its highest security priority— aside from its own survival—in Europe. Western Europe alone, if it could be considered as a unified entity, would have industrial strength comparable to that of the United States and double that of the Soviet Union and a population substantially larger than either. This economic strength and its greater contribution to its own defense since the 1950s have increased the freedom of Western Europe to act independently both at home and in other parts of the world. Interests that Western European countries perceive as being in conflict with those of the United States—in trade with the Soviets and the rest of Eastern Europe, in perception of the Soviet military and political threat, in attitudes toward the Middle East, the Persian Gulf, and other Third World areas—have caused major new strains in the Atlantic alliance. So too has a strengthened sense among Western Europeans that they could be wiped out in a nuclear war by a U.S.

or Soviet decision. This is in part the result of the loss of a perceived U.S. strategic nuclear superiority, in the shadow of which the Europeans felt safer.

Frictions within the alliance about responsibilities, burden sharing, and behavior outside the geographical boundaries of the alliance are not new. The French were concerned in the 1960s about what de Gaulle saw as U.S. hegemony; the United States objected to the British and French invasion of Suez in 1956; and the Europeans disagreed with U.S. policies in Vietnam in the 1960s and 1970s. Now the political-military balance appears uncertain because of the growth of Soviet military strength. Hopes for Western European political unity have receded, if not faded entirely. The European economic situation is stagnating at best, and Western Europe is more dependent than before on Third World resources and markets. These factors combine with a generational change in attitude to produce public protests challenging even modest governmental commitments to the alliance and governmental policies toward the United States and the Soviet Union. But there are basic strengths in Western Europe and in the alliance that strong political leadership should be able to use to surmount or outlast these problems.

Eastern European problems are even worse—deteriorating economic conditions, agricultural disasters (except in Hungary), and political systems with no legitimacy in the eyes of their populations. Free elections are nonexistent, and street protests have been unable to effect basic systemic change. This situation is likely to persist unless the economic system breaks down entirely or the Soviets involve Eastern Europe in a disastrous foreign adventure.

HISTORY OF U.S. AND SOVIET FORCES IN EUROPE

Both U.S. and Soviet forces in Europe originated as combat forces against the Axis powers and then became occupation forces—for the United States in Germany and Austria, for the Soviet Union in those countries and many others. Soon thereafter, the United States substantially demobilized its military forces. Though apprehensions arose even then about Soviet actions in Eastern Europe and intentions toward Western Europe, the United States viewed its nuclear monopoly as enough to deter Soviet action. But the perceived threats to Greece and Turkey in 1947, in Greece from insurgency and in Turkey from without, sharpened concerns in the United States and Europe. (Greece and Turkey are far from Western Europe, and most of Turkey's land mass is in Asia, but their historical ties with the rest of Europe and their strategic location in the eastern Mediterranean make them of critical importance to Western Europe and to the United States.) The overthrow of the democratic government in Czechoslovakia and the blockade of Berlin—both in 1948—raised those concerns to a new height, and Americans began to believe that a Soviet military attack on Western Europe was possible despite the U.S. nuclear monopoly.

There followed the organization of NATO, the subsequent inclusion in it of West Germany, the beginnings of rearmament in Western European countries (albeit at a very low level), and the reintroduction of U.S. combat forces into Europe. Throughout the 1950s the Soviets built up their forces (principally in East Germany), gradually improved their equipment, and configured both for offensive operations across the East-West line. During the 1950s the United States began to introduce substantial numbers of tactical nuclear weapons into its forces in Europe and to provide nuclear weapons for use under U.S. control by European forces. All of this was seen as a way of offsetting the Soviet predominance in numbers and strength of conventional forces as the Soviets built up their strategic nuclear forces.

Crises came and went: the various unsuccessful revolts in Eastern Europe, Khrushchev's missile-rattling in the late 1950s, the Berlin crises, and the construction of the Berlin Wall. The forces on both sides continued to grow and be modernized. During the Vietnam War, U.S. forces in Europe declined in size; equipment aged and combat stocks were reduced. Western Europeans, without the excuse of a war on another continent, still did little to improve their own forces until the late 1960s. The Soviets embarked on a massive reinforcement and reequipment program in the mid-1960s, integrated into their plans for combat in Western Europe the five Soviet divisions that crushed Czechoslovakia in 1968, and reequipped and modernized the non-Soviet Warsaw Pact forces during the 1970s.

REQUIREMENTS FOR CONVENTIONAL MILITARY FORCES

What balance of conventional forces is required to deter attack or intimidation by the Soviets in Western Europe credibly? What are the components, scenarios, and criteria to be considered in reaching such a judgment?

Force Levels

The appropriate comparison of conventional military forces is not between U.S. and Soviet forces but between those of NATO and those of the Warsaw Pact. In number of troops under arms, NATO and Warsaw Pact forces do not differ greatly on the central front (that is, the area on either side of the borders dividing West Germany from East Germany and Czechoslovakia). The number is about 1.2 million in ground and air forces on the Warsaw Pact side and about 1 million on the NATO side. If French forces are added on the NATO side and Soviet forces in the three Western Military Districts of the USSR on the other, again a rough balance exists. But in striking power, firepower, and number of divisions, the Warsaw Pact has an advantage of two or even three to one.

These comparisons must, however, be seen in light of differences between NATO and the Warsaw Pact with respect to the ratio of combat and support troops and to the replacement of combat casualties. In general, the NATO forces have more troops assigned to support and service tasks, including engineer, transport, and communications units. This is a deliberate choice following from the NATO doctrine that sustaining capability and support allows a more flexible and effective defense. NATO also plans to replace combat casualties within units, as opposed to the Soviet approach of replacing entire units with successive waves of reinforcements. Which of these is the more sensible approach is a matter of judgment. The United States has shifted back and forth in its ratio of support units to combat units. Between 1973 and 1976, for example, the U.S. Army increased by three the number of active combat divisions, using personnel spaces made available by reducing support functions or transferring them to reserve forces. But subsequently, the Army leadership has pressed strongly for the restoration of those support functions to active forces.

The central issue in the balance of forces on the European central front is how rapidly NATO forces in West Germany can be reinforced should the Soviets begin to mobilize in a crisis. From the NATO point of view, the ratios of forces would not be severely adverse in a Warsaw Pact attack with forces as they exist in peacetime. The ratios get worse as the Soviets mobilize. Various scenarios have been posited, including a Soviet attack with three "fronts" (a Soviet term for what is roughly the equivalent of a NATO army group, perhaps twenty divisions) after about fifteen days of Soviet mobilization or with five "fronts" after about twenty-two days. These are formidable forces, too great for the NATO forces to withstand unless they are reinforced by mobilization of Western European reserve forces and by the transport of additional divisions from Great Britain and the United States.

This is the reason substantial efforts were made during the 1970s to increase the speed with which reinforcements could arrive from the United States. Increased speed was made possible by prepositioning division sets of equipment in West Germany and other European countries so U.S. troops could be flown over and matched with the equipment in a short time—a week or two. This could be done because the United States and other NATO countries have an enormous civil air fleet of jumbo jets that can move several hundred thousand troops in a few weeks. Equipment prepositioning is required because the United States does not have the cargo aircraft capacity to move equipment for these troops rapidly, especially such large equipment as heavy battle tanks. Equipment and supply requirements range from five tons up to twenty tons per soldier, depending on definitions of initial equipment, on supply and resupply, and on the mix of infantry and armored forces. By the mid-1980s the United States is aiming to be able to move five and one-third divisions to Europe to match up with prepositioned equipment within two weeks after a decision is made to do so.

Two additional divisions within the U.S. Army (the 82nd Airborne and the 101st Airmobile) are available on very short notice. They can be used for sudden but minor contingencies to which they can be lifted by air along with their equipment. (The United States now has the airlift capabilities to do that for one division.) They could also join the divisions, committed for U.S. reinforcement in Europe, that have equipment prepositioned there. U.S. reinforcements would visibly demonstrate U.S. willingness to defend Europe in a crisis or when the Warsaw Pact begins to mobilize, as U.S. stationed forces provide strong evidence of political determination in peacetime.

U.S. Army divisions in the United States (other than these two) are at a lower state of readiness than those deployed overseas in West Germany or South Korea. It is appropriate that their readiness be lower because they are used in part as a training base as well as for reinforcement. Moreover, there is no point in their being ready before they can be transported to the scene of combat. As airlift and sealift capability increases, it becomes logical to increase the peacetime readiness of forces in the United States so they can be brought to full readiness by the time the lift transportation to the combat zone becomes available.

Once a crisis develops or the Warsaw Pact begins to mobilize, NATO's prospects will depend on how quickly political leaders make the decision to increase NATO readiness and begin reinforcement. Whether that would in fact happen quickly enough depends not only on the quality of the intelligence about Warsaw Pact mobilization—which will be sufficiently good—but also on the political state of the alliance, including the degree to which the political authorities trust their military intelligence.

Reserves

The role of reserves in any European scenario depends on assumptions about the potential length of a nonnuclear war, the capabilities of the Warsaw Pact reserves, and the support functions the reserves are intended to perform for the regular forces that will be used as the first reinforcements. The Soviet Union has very large reserves, though the extent of the military stockpiles available to sustain them is not known. If a two-year or three-year war is envisaged, then it could be important to have massive reserves ready to be deployed within a period as short as six months. But it is highly improbable that such massive U.S.-Soviet combat would go on for six months, let alone two or three years, without an escalation to all-out nuclear war.

Training

It is difficult to compare the training of NATO and Warsaw Pact forces, for the quality is highly variable on both sides. For the great bulk of their forces the Soviets use two-year draftees, who get most of their training in combat units. Despite the many denunciations of the quality of the U.S. soldier in the all-volunteer army, no one has offered evidence that he or she is on the average inferior in education, training, or motivation to the Soviet soldier, either at the lowest ranks or among noncommissioned officers. Indeed, there is considerable evidence that the U.S. soldier has at least as good an education as his or her Soviet counterpart, more training, and more initiative. The Soviet alcohol problem is probably more serious than the U.S. drug problem. The tendency to move U.S. military people around from one unit to another more often has probably resulted in less smooth operation than the Soviets have often achieved, especially where sure and confident operation of sophisticated equipment is required, as in tank crews. Of the other allied forces on the central front, those of West Germany and Great Britain (and France, outside the NATO military structure) operate at a high level of training, but the others are variable. Non-Soviet Warsaw Pact forces are comparable in training to their Soviet counterparts, but there is inevitably a real question about how well the non-Soviet forces will cooperate with the Soviets in an actual conflict.

Equipment

Soviet ground force equipment is generally equal in quality to that of the United States and in some cases superior. If the balance is drawn between NATO and Warsaw Pact forces in general, the quality of ground force equipment is about even. This is probably a better way to draw the balance, because NATO forces from Europe would make up about 90 percent (75 percent on the Central Front) of the initial ground forces and non-Soviets would probably be about 50 percent of the Warsaw Pact forces. On the other hand, Warsaw Pact forces have more than 20,000 tanks, compared to 10,000 on the NATO side. The disparity in numbers of artillery pieces is even greater.

But the comparison of numbers of tanks, for example, is not really the appropriate one. At least as important is the tank strength on the Warsaw Pact side as opposed to the antitank capability on the NATO side. And the antitank capability on the NATO side remains superior, although the Soviets have begun to catch up in recent years. During the past five years, NATO has added thousands of antitank launchers and tens of thousands of antitank weapons to its arsenal.

On the NATO side, attack aircraft are designed to substitute in part for artillery and armor. The overall tactical aircraft balance after reinforcement is numerically about equal on the two sides, but NATO forces—and especially U.S. tactical aircraft—tend to be attack or dual-purpose aircraft rather than pure air defense aircraft. There are some exceptions, such as the F-15 air combat aircraft.

Examples can be given of past campaigns in which the use of attack aircraft worked as a substitute for ground firepower and of others in which it did not. It was notably successful for the German Air Force early in World War II in short campaigns. To some extent, the allied (and especially U.S.) concentration on attack aircraft creates an unfavorable ratio for air-to-air combat. Warsaw Pact forces have about twice as many pure air-to-air aircraft as NATO. The higher quality of NATO aircraft should, as a rule, compensate for this difference. The best U.S. tactical aircraft are probably by and large still several years ahead of their Soviet counterparts, although that technological lead has shrunk significantly over the past decade.

But this advantage in air-to-air combat can be effective for U.S. and other NATO forces only if they can use their longer-range and more effective air-to-air missiles, whether infrared-homing or radar-directed. To do so confidently in complex air combat situations requires an electronic system to distinguish friend from foe. If the pilot must wait for visual identification, the superior numbers on the other side could carry the day, even if the individual opposing aircraft have inferior aerodynamic or weapons capability. Agreements on such command-and-control hardware and procedures are especially difficult for an alliance of sovereign countries to reach. The NATO Air Forces have the capability to identify friendly aircraft by signal (IFF—

Identification Friend or Foe), but they must now adopt a doctrine that any aircraft that fails to identify itself electronically as friendly, for whatever reason, will be attacked in wartime. On such procedures depends victory in the air battle.

Command-and-Control, Communications, and Intelligence

The complicated interaction of the command-and-control, communications, and intelligence functions of the various NATO countries is one of the greatest causes for concern about the ability of the alliance to function in wartime. Because logistics has always been a national rather than an alliance function within NATO, the individual countries make procurement decisions. That in turn limits the ability of the various military forces to communicate and operate with each other. It would be unrealistic to expect the Soviets, in the event of an attack on Western Europe, not to take advantage of this vulnerability or of those that derive from the need for the NATO forces to shift from national command to NATO command in wartime. For the Warsaw Pact forces, equipment is interoperable and command is highly integrated. This is because the Soviets clearly run the Warsaw Pact structure unilaterally. The dominance they maintain over Eastern Europe allows them these military advantages, but that dominance is the very factor that produces so much resentment, periodic rebellion, and unrest among their Eastern European allies. This then raises questions about the reliability of most Eastern European military forces that counterbalance the vulnerability created by fragmentation in NATO.

The NATO Flanks

The situation on NATO's flanks differs from that on the central front. In the north, neither the Soviet Union nor NATO has many forces stationed immediately on the Norwegian-Soviet border, but the Soviets have considerably more military power—land, sea, and air—within a few hundred miles, on the Kola Peninsula. In the event of a war the Soviets could be expected to seize northern Norway in order to provide a safe base for their own naval operations in the Norwegian Sea and a position from which they could more effectively threaten the supply routes between North America and Europe with surface, subsurface, and long-range naval air attacks. To prevent this, U.S., Canadian, and Norwegian reinforcements are planned to be moved rapidly into northern Norway. Carrier battle groups would need to be deployed as far forward into the Norwegian Sea as is consistent with their survival. That deployment would depend in large measure on the balance of land-based air power from each side able to operate in the region. The Norwegians are making considerable progress in improving their ability to receive such reinforcements rapidly, in the event of warning of a possible Soviet move. The ability of Denmark, on the other side of the Baltic straits, to hold out until similar reinforcements can arrive—or to receive them when they do—is, however, considerably less promising.

On the southern flank, perhaps the most serious problem is the political one posed by the recent trend toward neutralism in Greece and by the long-standing but recently exacerbated stresses between Greece and Turkey. These have made joint military planning practically impossible in the eastern Mediterranean and in Thrace. Soviet land-based air power has a significant edge in the region, unless U.S. land-based air power can be brought in rapidly to reinforce the one or two carrier battle groups in the Mediterranean. In wartime those might well have to be held in the western Mediterranean unless the balance of land-based air power can be improved in the eastern Mediterranean. The Turkish straits would be the most valuable prize in such a conflict, because of the effect that control of them would have on military operations in Europe and in the Mediterranean. Capturing the straits or forcing a way through them, however, could be made difficult for the Soviet Union if even a modest early reinforcement could be made by NATO or if Turkish forces were redeployed to the area in advance and supplied with modern equipment.

THE BALANCE OF CONVENTIONAL MILITARY FORCES

In assessing the overall balance of conventional forces in Europe, it is difficult to believe that present allied forces could sustain a successful defense of a forward line near the German border, or even substantially within it, against an all-out Warsaw Pact attack for as long as several months. There is also nothing the Soviets could lose in the short run outside Europe that would be as valuable to them as the conquest of Western Europe. But it is also highly doubtful that a massive conventional war in Europe could last more than a few weeks without escalating to a nuclear war, first tactical and then strategic. Moreover, if a Warsaw Pact attack failed to achieve victory in even so short a time as thirty to sixty days, the stability of the Warsaw Pact, both militarily and politically, would come into considerable doubt. Indeed, destabilizing repercussions from even a temporarily stalled attack would be possible even in the Soviet Union. This combination of deterrents is a powerful one, provided that NATO nations show determination and unity in a crisis, are prepared to take the political decision to mobilize in a timely manner, have a visible capability to fight conventionally for a reasonable period (say a month or more) to prevent the Soviets from quickly overrunning Western Europe, and make clear the high risk of escalation to nuclear war in any attack on Western Europe.

Specifically, NATO needs a conventional military capability to prevent a quick conventional Soviet victory by stabilizing for at least thirty days a line near the inner German border. NATO cannot confidently expect to do this now. Although the Soviets are probably not certain of being able to drive to the Rhine, the North Sea, and the English Channel in that time, their confidence of doing so probably exceeds the NATO countries' of being able to stop them. That leaves NATO with an uncomfortable reliance on the threat of nuclear escalation. To reduce this military risk and the potential for Soviet intimidation, NATO must increase its levels of prepositioned equipment, improve the interoperability of its command-and-control systems and the readiness of its forces, and expand its reinforcement capabilities. NATO need not make major changes in its force levels. The great bulk of NATO resources should be directed toward improving immediate combat capabilities. The next priority is to increase the sustainability of NATO (not just U.S.) forces to thirty and then to sixty days. Diverting resources to improve the capability of fighting a conventional war for two or three years would almost certainly be a mistake.

The key to the military balance is not merely the overall force ratios in the area between the Baltic and Switzerland, but the ability of the invading Warsaw Pact forces to outmass the allied defensive forces at the three or four geographically dictated breakthrough corridors. At present the thin linear defense in NATO's center region would, once penetrated, be very difficult to restore. Thus NATO needs not only external reinforcement but also more reserve infantry units to defend in depth a complex of urbanized areas, forests with roads through them, and invasion corridors. These units would supplement the heavy mobile divisions needed to move along the front, both to shore up defenses and to prepare for counterattack.

The NATO military position on the central front could also be improved by the construction of a heavy line of fixed fortifications, not to substitute for but to complement the in-depth defenses, heavy mobile forces, and light reserve infantry. But fortifications are no panacea. They can be overflown by airborne attack or flanked by sea or by land. Still, in a complementary role the fortified lines can force an attacker to increase still further the concentration of forces in attempting a breakthrough—especially if these fortifications are themselves deployed in depth. That can give more tactical warning to the defender and also provide more time for mobile forces to back up the fortified line. Unfortunately, the political objections in West Germany to emphasizing the physical division at the inner German border, the financial costs of such a line, and the potential economic and political disruptions in the border region have operated in conjunction with military doubts to deny such proposals full consideration.

French forces, part of the alliance though not of its military organization, would also have to play a substantially greater role to increase the credibility of a conventional defense. The two French divisions now stationed in West Germany and the two just behind the border would be joined by others in the role of reinforcements and reserves. French ground lines of communications should be prepared for emergency logistic use by reinforcements from outside the continent. The decisions to use French forces and territory would have to be made by the French government. The development of French attitudes toward a potential Soviet attack has in recent years allowed for more confidence that such a decision would be made. But without adequate plans, preparations, and exercises, such a decision would probably fail in its intended effects, both defensive and deterrent.

Many of these needed improvements are called for in the NATO Long-Term Defense Program adopted in 1978 by the heads of government of the NATO countries. But the prospects for success remain unclear. Many military leaders, opting for worst-case scenarios, call for growth in military budgets beyond the resources likely to be available given political realities. Finance ministers in Europe sometimes pick the best-case scenario and thus argue for low growth in or even reductions in defense spending. Heads of governments sometimes combine the worst-case scenarios with economic constraints and public reluctance in order to come up with a reason for giving up the military competition. Only occasionally do they support major but achievable defense growth as a part of an overall alliance security policy that includes economic, political, diplomatic, and military measures to reduce military risk.

The complexities of conventional military defense and political imperatives in Western Europe make even such a symbolic goal as a 3 percent annual real growth in defense spending a useful fallback in the absence of agreement on a detailed and comprehensive program. At least it produces a basis for real improvement, although the extent will depend on subsequent specific decisions. It spreads the responsibility for decisions through the alliance and creates external pressures to balance the domestic pressures for other uses of resources.

THE ROLES OF U.S. AND WESTERN
EUROPEAN CONVENTIONAL FORCES

What role should U.S. conventional forces play in deterring Soviet aggression in Europe? Should the United States seek more flexibility in its commitment of forces to Europe in light of changing threats elsewhere and changing perceptions of the threat in Western Europe? What contributions should the Western Europeans make, both individually and collectively? Should various divisions of responsibility be made? What are the possibilities for rationalization, standardization, and interoperability of equipment?

One function of U.S. conventional military forces in Europe has always been to make a visible statement that a Soviet attack would run the risk of a response by U.S. theater and, in turn, strategic nuclear weapons. But the advent of strategic parity has raised concerns in Western Europe that the United States might accept the overrunning of Europe and the death or capture of 300,000 U.S. troops without making a nuclear response. Thus the NATO forces, including U.S. forces, must also be evaluated according to their ability to deter or fight a conventional war.

What effect do U.S. forces in Europe have on the ability of NATO to hold Warsaw Pact forces for weeks at some militarily and politically defensible line? In peacetime, the United States provides only about 10 percent of the ground forces in Europe and a somewhat larger share—perhaps 15 percent—of the ground firepower (armored division equivalents). On the central front, U.S. divisions constitute about 20 percent of the total number of divisions before mobilization (excluding French forces; about 17 percent counting the French forces). U.S. tactical airpower is about 25 percent of the allied peacetime total on the central front. Reinforcement plans call for the ground forces provided by the United States to double during the first three weeks of an allied mobilization and for U.S. air forces to rise to about 50 percent of the allied total during the first ten days. These U.S. capabilities are significant percentages of the total allied strength, and they greatly improve the likelihood that a Warsaw Pact attack could be contained to some degree and for some period.

At the same time, there is little point in the United States's planning protracted conventional force strategies and equipping its forces to fight for, say, thirty days unless the Western Europeans are prepared to do the same. Today, for example, U.S. ammunition stocks exceed those of the other NATO forces. Moreover, in light of the plausible or even likely need for the United States to be able to project military force to protect vital alliance interests elsewhere, especially in Southwest Asia, it makes sense for the United States to introduce more flexibility in its commitments to NATO for reinforcements. Most important, the United States is much more likely to maintain its commitments and forces in defense of a Western Europe that is seen as prepared to maintain its own defense efforts. The degree to which the United States makes provisions for reinforcements in Europe rather than elsewhere—by prepositioning additional equipment beyond the present levels and by orienting airlift and sealift planning and equipment—should depend strongly on Western European estimates of the Soviet military threat against Western Europe as measured by European political and military responses. The unwillingness of some Western Europeans even to acknowledge the existence of a major military threat from the Soviet Union hardly encourages the United States to spend added billions to preposition more division sets of equipment in Europe or to plan for added airlift and sealift to Europe. At present Western European defense levels, no prepositioning beyond the five to six division sets currently in place or in process would be appropriate.

Differences of view about sharing burdens among alliance members have been sharpened by the growth of Western European economic weight relative to that of the United States and the intensification of security issues vital to both in other parts of the world, especially in Southwest Asia. The process of agreeing on shares of defense expenditures and of political and security commitments in various European and non-European regions cannot be carried out by rational deduction from first principles; it is a matter of political compromise. But some factors seem obvious. It is much easier to start from present contributions and commitments and, agreeing that greater efforts are needed from all, share the increases. A rational division of labor suggests that the United States should continue to provide almost all of the intercontinental nuclear deterrent forces and the bulk of the theater and battlefield nuclear forces for the alliance. Correspondingly, the comparison of U.S. forces for distant power projection—including long-range airlift and sealift, long-range land-based tactical air forces, and aircraft carrier battle groups—with those of the other allies suggests that the United States must assume most of the responsibility for defending access to the oil that is so much more vital to Western Europe and Japan than to the United States itself. Still, some European participation is essential for political reasons.

Western Europeans are already making major contributions to the effectiveness of U.S. forces in Europe through host nation support, which includes such functions as providing local fuel supplies, equipment maintenance, and base structure. West Germany has recently agreed to contribute personnel for this purpose. They can do more, including but not limited to providing medical support, transportation, and communication, and they can do it more efficiently than the United States would be able to from more than 3,000 miles away.

Calls for withdrawing U.S. troops from Europe on the grounds of the failure of Western Europeans to contribute adequately to their own defense miss several points. First, though the Western European defense budgets are smaller as a percentage of their GNPs than that of the United States, conscription in the continental members of NATO makes their effective defense budgets somewhat higher, by replacing the cost to the defense budget with an opportunity cost levied on the civilian economy. The European allies appropriately provide the great majority of alliance troops on the continent. Second, relocating U.S. troops from Europe to the United States would require base construction at a cost of more than $15 billion. This relocation would probably not change operating costs very much, though it would improve the balance of payments. Some advocate disbanding such withdrawn forces. That proposal in effect leaves Western Europe to fend for itself and ignores both the region's importance to the United States and the strategic value of deterring and defending against attack through a forward defense thousands of miles away. Moreover, U.S. troops in Europe are much closer to Southwest Asia than they would be if stationed in the United States, though their redeployment to Southwest Asia in a crisis must be prearranged with the European allies, who would have to compensate in their own planning for such diversions of stationed forces or reinforcements.

The fundamental issue raised in discussions of sharing burdens and in proposals for U.S. troop withdrawal is that of the existence of the NATO alliance itself. The security of Western Europe cannot be more important to the United States than it is to the Western Europeans themselves; but it is—next to the security of the United States itself—the most important security interest of the United States. If Europe is not to be defended, for example, the United States has little reason to defend access to oil from the Persian Gulf states. The people of the United States may or may not like it, but the United States and its European allies share not only cultural, political, and economic ties but also a mutual security dependence for which neither has any realistic substitute. Once that fact is realized and accepted, the detailed issues of sharing responsibilities can be painfully wrestled with until an agreement is reached.

Western European efforts for defense would be much more cost effective if the functions of the various national forces were rationally divided rather than duplicated. West Germany and France, because of their geography and population, provide most of the ground forces and the corresponding tactical air power. Unless the Scandinavian and Benelux countries provide more significant locally based and forward-based ground forces respectively, their commitment to the defense of their own territories will continue to be seen as dubious. Those countries and Canada can also provide specialized naval and air forces for antisubmarine warfare and air defense. France and Great Britain are appropriate providers of major naval and air power, including some possible deployments east of Suez. Italy and Spain can play a corresponding role, appropriate to their capabilities, in the Mediterranean and anchor the line to the south, as Greece and Turkey ought to do in the southeast if and when they can resolve or ignore their differences. The United States must provide the great bulk of sea-based air and amphibious forces for the alliance, though NATO's other trading nations should also contribute civil reserve airlift and sealift forces.

Great Britain and France face particularly important choices of resource allocation. Both have political and military or strategic reasons for maintaining nuclear deterrent capabilities. But it would be damaging, both for those nations and for the alliance, if a large fraction of either's military budget were to be spent on nuclear forces. They can at reasonable cost maintain a minimum deterrent (in de Gaulle's words, one that "would tear off an arm"). In the face of Soviet capabilities, that is about all that either can maintain. The conventional forces that would be severely slighted by unrealistic British and French nuclear aspirations include the naval forces of both nations, especially valuable because they can be used outside NATO's geographical boundaries. In the case of France, they also include a ground force that is the West's second-largest on the central front, a force that needs to be further planned for, positioned, and trained as an echelon that would come into play immediately behind NATO's forward defense forces. The British Army of the Rhine, well-trained but marginally equipped, is a necessary and valuable sign of Great Britain's commitment, even if from a purely military point of view it might rank behind the Royal Navy in priority for the overall alliance. Canada, whose GNP is fifth-largest in the alliance and which participates as one of the Group of Seven in the economic summits of the industrialized democracies, should provide a modest strengthening of conventional forces along similar lines to that of Great Britain.

Unless a major improvement in the coordination of development and procurement is effected within the alliance, an inefficiency of perhaps 30 to 40 percent will persist in these activities. To a degree, such improvement will depend on the alliance nations' agreeing to a common military doctrine and tactics, but much can be done even in the present state. More political, economic, industrial, and bureaucratic resistance exists to standardizing equipment and making it interoperable among the military forces of the various nations. But even though it will take great effort over a decade, the results would be worth the trouble. Research and development (R&D) savings would be great. Production cost savings would also be significant, although it would be politically necessary to run both Western European and North American production lines and to maintain the price competition that such a division makes possible. Most important, with the NATO allies using common systems for command-and-control, communications, and logistics, the Soviets would no longer be able to exploit gaps between national systems.

NUCLEAR FORCES

Can U.S. nuclear forces still play a role in deterring Soviet aggression and intimidation in Europe? Is a strategy of flexible response that includes the possibility of the first use of nuclear weapons still viable? Should the United States streamline its nuclear posture in Europe?

One of the major deterrents to a Soviet conventional attack on Western Europe is the likelihood that such a conflict will escalate to a nuclear war. NATO doctrine calls for an initial conventional defense and, if that fails, the use of theater nuclear weapons, both to disrupt the conventional attack and to give a signal that escalation to general nuclear war is likely unless the attack is halted. A breakthrough on a military front is likely to lead the commanders in that area to call for the use of short-range nuclear weapons; that is likely to lead to pressures on both sides to move to longer-range nuclear weapons to disrupt the operations of the enemy in the rear, which in turn could well lead to strikes by the superpowers on each others' homelands. The existence of this continuous nuclear "powder train" acts to increase the power of deterrence.

The concern that Soviet conventional superiority, accompanied by superiority in long-range nuclear weapons, could affect the willingness of the United States to use nuclear weapons in response to a Soviet attack on Europe is somewhat theoretical. But so is everything that is connected with the idea of nuclear war. Perceptions do count in these matters. Should the Soviets be seen as superior at every level up to that of strategic war, that could be a powerful political influence on a U.S. president, especially in a time of crisis. This may have been one reason West German Chancellor Helmut Schmidt raised the question of the "Eurostrategic balance" in 1977. Such a concern did form the basis of the modernization of theater nuclear forces agreed to in December 1979 by the NATO foreign and defense ministers.

Use of any long-range theater nuclear weapons, even though they would probably be aimed principally at military targets, would be a desperate response to a desperate situation. But the presence of such weapons in Europe implies a greater likelihood of their use in response to an attack on Europe, especially a nuclear attack, and thus has an extra deterrent effect beyond that provided by U.S. strategic forces. Moreover, NATO's long-range theater nuclear force program seeks to avoid any major gaps in the various kinds of nuclear forces in Europe. As a substitute for the new Pershing II and cruise missiles, NATO could rely on cruise missiles launched from U.S. nuclear attack submarines (SSNs). These would have the virtue of providing less of a target for protests by European antinuclear groups, but they suffer the political disadvantage of providing no visible evidence of U.S. commitment. The Western Europeans would have no way of knowing that the submarines were near enough to be useful. There would also be a military disadvantage: If the SSNs were doing their job of antisubmarine warfare, they would *not* be near enough.

Thus, the December 1979 NATO decision on modernization and arms control for intermediate-range nuclear forces (INF), along with the commitment to a 3-percent annual real growth in defense budgets in NATO countries and the specific improvements called for in the NATO long-term defense program, constitutes the principal visible symbol of NATO's political will and determination to do what is necessary to provide for its own defense. Failure to carry these out would demonstrate NATO's weakness dramatically and would have grave political as well as serious military consequences.

Battlefield nuclear weapons were introduced in the 1950s to offset Soviet conventional superiority. Their introduction forced a revision in Soviet tactics away from massive concentrations on a narrow front, designed to break through allied defenses, and toward greater dispersal; and their presence ensures that this dispersal will continue. Soviet deployment of battlefield nuclear weapons poses considerable problems for the ability of NATO military forces to survive as well. These threats and the fear of escalation may deter both sides from immediate use of nuclear weapons. But the presence of large numbers of battlefield nuclear weapons on the Western side is no longer so much of an advantage to NATO as it once was. The launchers are highly mobile, but the proximity of their fixed ammunition storage sites to the front makes them quite vulnerable, even to sudden conventional attack. The wide distribution of tactical nuclear weapons requires that the elaborate communication networks that have been set up to ensure control of their use be activated early in a conventional conflict in Europe. Such a step could then lead the Soviets to a preemptive attack. All U.S. battlefield weapons are mechanically controlled, so that they cannot be exploded on the order of a low-level commander even if he thinks his troops and the weapons are about to be overrun. But if they are likely to be overrun, the pressure on senior officials to release the battlefield nuclear weapons for use will be strong. To the degree that this situation establishes a "powder train" that makes escalation more likely, it increases the credibility of the nuclear deterrent. It is dangerous, however, to rely on those pressures as a cardinal element in military planning. Moreover, short-range nuclear forces are an unsatisfactory substitute for adequate conventional military force.

For these reasons, and because of widespread antinuclear sentiment in Europe, the number and characteristics of battlefield nuclear weapons should be reviewed. Changes can be made without abandoning the deterrent effects of tactical nuclear weapons. Perhaps U.S. and NATO purposes can be served just as well if most or even all nuclear weapons with 15-to-30-kilometer (9-to-18-mile) ranges are replaced by delivery systems aimed at the same targets but having 300-to-400 kilometer (180-to-240-mile) ranges. Those weapons could be based much further back, could not be so quickly overrun, and could be controlled more easily. These virtues would have to be weighed against the possible greater Soviet ease of locating and destroying such weapons and a diminished responsiveness to local battlefield situations, which might reduce Soviet fears of concentrating their forces locally. But a thinning-out of battlefield nuclear weapons would have political advantages as a response to European concerns about destruction of civilian targets in a battlefield nuclear war, and it might be presented as part of a program to increase allied conventional forces as well as to modernize intermediate-range nuclear forces.

Raising the nuclear threshold substantially is a desirable goal. Incorporating into allied forces large numbers of advanced nonnuclear munitions capable of covering wide areas and of being delivered by missiles or aircraft to respond to the second wave of a Soviet attack would help raise the threshold. So would the addition of more allied forces. The total cost might raise European defense budgets by 5 percent a year in real terms over the next five years, instead of the previously agreed (but not implemented) 3 percent. It is not clear that Western European governments would be willing to pay that price, however much they might wish to raise the nuclear threshold.

CONCLUSIONS

The Soviets are not likely to attack Western Europe under present circumstances. The high likelihood of escalation to theater and to strategic nuclear war, the uncertainty that they could overrun Western Europe quickly, the substantial possibility that failure to achieve such a quick victory would be followed by massive defections of non-Soviet Warsaw Pact forces or even disintegration in Eastern Europe, and the availability of less risky options for possible Soviet gains all suggest that it would be uncharacteristic of even a much more reckless group than the present aged and conservative Soviet leaders to risk such an adventure.

But in the future, with new Soviet leaders as likely to be more adventurous as to turn inward, conditions could arise under which the Soviets could be tempted to some sort of adventure in Western Europe. If NATO's ties were substantially loosened, the Soviets might conclude that an attack on one would not necessarily be regarded as an attack on all. Or the Soviets might seek to take advantage of some economic catastrophe and the internal conflict and even violence it could create in Western Europe. Economic and political difficulties in the Soviet empire—the only remaining empire in the world—might cause a massive explosion of unrest in Eastern Europe that could spill over into or encourage conflict between the Warsaw Pact and NATO. Even under these circumstances, the Soviet Union might choose a limited thrust to cut off and take over some key objective in Western Europe. For whatever reason, any attack—if successful—would shock the political and military structure of NATO and shift the world balance decisively in favor of the Soviets. Even if a frantic NATO rearmament effort then began, Soviet political and military pressure might well preempt it.

The probability of such a combination of circumstances is already low, but it is worth a great deal to the United States and its allies to keep it so. To that end, a restoration of a sense of shared goals and a closer political consensus are needed. Perhaps the latter could grow out of a regularization of the seven-power summit meetings, together with reorientation of those meetings toward political and even military consultation. Such an outcome will require as well a willingness to accept occasional domestic disadvantage in order to strengthen the alliance. The alliance also needs to reexamine present and possible future Soviet objectives and capabilities and to evaluate the other economic and political problems of the world to provide a basis for redefining alliance goals, priorities, and resources.

The issue for U.S. policy toward Europe is not whether the alliance will survive, though it may come to that if relations are mismanaged badly enough. Rather the issue today is how to manage these central relations in the face of enormous world changes. U.S. leadership of the alliance cannot be so overt or unilateral as it was in earlier decades. Nor can the United States bear so large a share of the economic, political, and military burdens. But the United States must still lead. No other nation among the industrialized democracies can. The levels of skill, responsibility, and maturity required are even higher than before. Attaining such levels will entail a reversal of the trends of the last two decades. But the record is not all bad. The century and the opportunity are not yet lost.

7

U.S. Security Interests in East Asia

Europe is the external region whose security has been of steadiest and greatest interest to the United States since the beginning of World War II. Southwest Asia is the area whose vital importance has been most suddenly revealed. But it is in East Asia that U.S. relationships have shifted most sharply. Those changes, and the wars that grew out of them, produced the most severe effects on American society and domestic politics. Since 1950 the United States has twice sent up to ten division equivalents to engage in combat on the Asian mainland. Now the United States has fewer forces in the Far East than at any time since World War II. One of those wars ended in a military stalemate but political victory; the other was a defeat by both measures. Nearly thirty years after the end of the first, and a decade after the end of the second, the political-military balance in 1980 in the Pacific appeared more favorable to U.S. security interests than at any time since the communist revolution in China in 1949. Moreover, the prospects for trade, economic development, and political relations with all the countries of East Asia except the Soviet Union and Vietnam are bright. Still, there are military, political, and economic problems that will require skillful handling if U.S. interests are to be protected. Those problems have grown more troublesome in the early 1980s.

What is the preeminent U.S. national security interest in East Asia? It is that U.S. relations with as many as possible of the countries in the region be politically friendly and of mutual economic benefit, to avoid economic disruption and minimize the chance that the United States will be drawn into a third post–World War II military conflict there. Stable political conditions, avoidance of Soviet predominance in the region and control of its resources, and above all, the continuation of Japan's successful economic development and liberal political structure are central to these U.S. interests.

Many of the countries in the region have begun to follow the trail of economic success blazed by Japan. Few others have gone as far along the path of democracy. Preserving the Japanese example, and fostering its emulation elsewhere in East Asia, including encouraging evolution toward greater human rights and toward more amicable relations with the industrialized democracies, are the most important goals of U.S. national security policy in the region. Any program to achieve those ends must include economic and military as well as political and diplomatic elements. Success in East Asia could have a major impact on other countries in the Third World.

THE IMPORTANCE OF EAST ASIA

The evolution of the lands of East Asia that rim the Pacific is the unsung success story of U.S. foreign policy since World War II. Western Europe had been, along with the United States, the most economically advanced part of the world before World War II. East Asia, except for Japan, had been backward and colonial—and before World War II even Japan, though a formidable military power, had an economy only a tenth the size of that of the United States. Now Japan's is the second-largest national economy in world trade. It is second or third in GNP, depending on how one measures the Soviet output. The economic growth of the rest of noncommunist East Asia— the Republic of Korea (South Korea), Hong Kong, Taiwan, and the member countries of the Association of Southeast Asian Nations (ASEAN) (Indonesia, Thailand, the Philippines, Malaysia, and Singapore)—is perhaps even more startling. Many of these nations have relatively little in the way of raw materials, but through their human resources, foreign capital, and hard work, the peoples of East Asia have created an economy that exceeds that of the Soviet bloc and rivals those of North America and Western Europe. East Asia (including Oceania) has now equaled and may have surpassed Western Europe as a trading partner of the United States. The combined imports and exports between the region and the United States were about $114 billion in 1980—about the same as the figures for Western Europe and the United States.

The economic and political character of Australia and New Zealand makes them part of the industrialized West. They have mutual security commitments with the United States and are associated with Great Britain as part of the Commonwealth. Their present and potential military facilities and their natural resources augment their importance to U.S. security interests in the Far East. Geographically and through trade, however, they are closely tied to East Asia, which is to them the "Near North" rather than the "Far East."

East Asia also contains the People's Republic of China (PRC), with a quarter of the world's population. China is a world power, though far from a superpower. Its prospects for achieving substantial world economic weight lie well in the future, but they are real. China is too populous to adopt in its economic dealings with the world the Japanese, South Korean, or Singaporean approach of becoming a manufacturing processor of raw materials and an exporter of medium- or high-technology goods. A nation with a population of 5 million or even 100 million can perform such specialized functions in a world of 4 billion, but not a nation of 1 billion people. The capital for rapid and major growth cannot be raised from internal savings or gained—on a scale corresponding to such a huge population—from outside. But China's enormous natural resources and its industrious population make it a possible long-term prospect for internal development on a continental scale, as has been achieved in the United States and the Soviet Union. For example, if China could sustain a per capita GNP growth of 5 percent a year, it would have an economy approaching $1 trillion (1982 dollars) by the year 2000. Should this happen, China would still be a poor country ($1,000 per year per capita GNP), but it would become a superpower indeed. In the meantime, it plays a minor international economic role, a significant international diplomatic role, and a major geostrategic role. Specifically, its geographical situation, its substantial military capability, and its severe historical, ideological, and political differences with the Soviet Union combine to tie down on the Sino-Soviet border approximately 25 percent of Soviet ground and air forces.

The United States holds certain clear security and economic interests in common with most of the countries of the region: with Japan, the second-largest industrialized democracy, in promoting and maintaining both its industrial might and its democracy; with the PRC, in opposing Soviet expansion; with South Korea, in deterring a North Korean attack; and with all of these and the ASEAN nations, in maintaining or establishing trading partnerships. But at the same time, the United States has interests that diverge from those of the various East Asian governments—and not just the unfriendly ones of Vietnam, North Korea, and the Soviet Union. Japan is a major economic competitor.

The PRC's attitudes toward Taiwan and toward Southeast Asia differ markedly from those of the United States. South Korean political instability could contribute to involving the United States in a conflict on the Korean peninsula. But so far, the United States's adversaries are clearly a much greater threat to the stability of the region than its friends.

Soviet interests in the region center on the PRC and Japan. The Soviets view the PRC as an ideological, political, and military threat, ungrateful for the Soviet industrial and military help of the 1950s, pressing claims to Soviet territories in Central Asia and the Far East for historical and demographic reasons (though except in Manchuria, the borderlands do not have a high population density on either side). The Soviets view Japan as a potential source of capital and technology. They seek to keep the PRC militarily weak and to encourage anti-Chinese attitudes in China's other neighbors—the nations of Indochina, those of the Indian subcontinent, North Korea, and the ASEAN nations. The Soviets hope that Deng Xiaoping's successors can be encouraged by intimidation or promises to be more friendly to them and less friendly to the United States. The Soviets want a militarily weak Japan, less aligned with the United States and the other industrialized democracies. Throughout the area they would like to see U.S. influence decreased. Their relations with the more remote countries of the region are directed at keeping them militarily weak, encouraging them to cooperate economically with the Soviet Union, and separating them from Japan, the PRC, and especially the United States.

In East Asia as elsewhere, there has been a major Soviet military buildup. Before 1965, the Soviet military forces were directed primarily at establishing a capability against the U.S. forces in the Far East and against Japan. The Soviet Pacific fleet was structured to defend Soviet territory and carry out coastal operations. Thereafter, the Soviet Pacific fleet and other Soviet naval forces began to acquire the capability to operate on the open ocean, with periods of deployment from its bases growing longer. To a substantial degree the Sea of Okhotsk and even the Sea of Japan—in which U.S. surface vessels had been dominant—became the preserve of Soviet surface forces, bolstered and protected by Soviet long-range naval air power operating from Petropavlovsk, Vladivostok, and Belaya.

The Soviets during the late 1960s and 1970s added about twenty-five divisions and 1,000 bomber, fighter, and attack aircraft to the twenty divisions and 200-odd tactical aircraft deployed in 1965 on the Chinese border. They have subsequently modernized and mechanized those ground forces and deployed many of their newest aircraft, including the Backfire bomber. During the middle and late 1970s, the Soviets also deployed substantial ground, helicopter support, and tactical air capabilities in the northern territories, the small islands immediately northeast of Hokkaido, which they took from Japan after World War II. This force amounts altogether to about one division and corresponding support. By itself it could not serve as a major invasion force, but it could begin operations suddenly and divert Japanese attention from more massive air and amphibious operations that the Soviets might launch—and are capable of launching—across the Sea of Japan. They have in the past few years placed about a hundred SS-20 missiles in the Far East and Central Asia, where they can reach targets in China, Japan, and Southeast Asia. Soviet nuclear forces could devastate all of East Asia. Soviet conventional forces could mount a major invasion of the PRC, a significant assault on the Japanese islands, and an interdiction campaign against sea lines of communication in the western Pacific.

Moreover, the continued economic development within the Soviet Union will largely depend on natural resources to be found in Asia, including the Far East. The virgin agricultural lands; the major new oil, gas, and mineral deposits in Siberia; the Central Asian regions where Soviet population is growing most rapidly—all are closer geographically to Peking than to Moscow. The development of Soviet Asia will both support further increased military capability there and create a "defensive" need for it, at least in the eyes of Soviet leaders.

North Korea is the most militarized regime in the world, and one of the most closed. Taken together with its economic failures and a potential struggle over succession, these factors make it an unpredictable flash point. Hanoi, having conquered South Vietnam, has had great difficulty integrating it into a unified Vietnamese state. It has completely failed to solve the economic problems of what was once Indochina, even while it successfully pressed for hegemony over the other parts—Laos and Cambodia—through political manipulation and military conquest. The massive Chinese incursion into northern Vietnam in 1979—undertaken in part to reduce Vietnamese pressure on Thailand and on the forces of China's ally in Cambodia, Pol Pot—contributed in turn to the Vietnamese willingness to allow Soviet use of facilities at Cam Ranh Bay. In Southeast Asia, Vietnam now begins to look like a miniature replica of the Soviet Union, militarily impressive, but ideologically unappealing and economically deficient.

For Japan, South Korea, or the ASEAN nations to fall under Soviet influence would be very damaging to U.S. security, though probably not as catastrophic as if the same thing were to happen in Western

Europe. For the PRC either to fall under Soviet influence or to return to the relationship it had with the Soviets during the 1950s would be an extremely serious and adverse change for the United States. It would allow the Soviets to reallocate a large percentage of their forces to threaten Western Europe or Southwest Asia still further. Putting together these two, admittedly worst-case, scenarios for Soviet success in the PRC and in the other East Asian countries shows that the geostrategic stakes in East Asia are high indeed.

THE HISTORICAL SETTING

The past half century in East Asian history has had three major turning points. The first is the end of the era of white (European and U.S.) domination. Japanese occupation and the ouster of the colonial powers during World War II left a legacy of nationalism throughout East Asia. New nations, with new aspirations and tensions, appeared: North and South Korea, with their ideological split; Indonesia, with its territorial claims on some of its neighbors; Vietnam, with its hegemonism.

The second is the U.S. occupation of Japan. It left an impressive legacy, but some features of that legacy now inhibit U.S. security goals. The economic miracle, for which the Japanese deserve the principal credit, was encouraged by the economic and political climate of the MacArthur proconsulship and protected by the U.S. security umbrella. It was strongly stimulated by U.S. use of Japan as the rear base during the Korean War and by the huge purchases of Japanese goods and services by the U.S. military at the time. Indeed, the Korean War in a real sense marks the beginning of Japan's rise to the status of economic superpower. The Vietnam War provided a similar, though proportionally much less important, stimulus. And the openness of the U.S. market to Japanese products was a vital factor in Japanese economic progress.

On the other hand, the role of the United States as a protective "elder brother" in security matters and the deliberate Japanese decision not to sustain a military capability at all commensurate with its economic strength have left Japan essentially without a military security policy except reliance on the United States. That decision was encouraged, indeed imposed, by the United States in the early days after World War II and accepted by the United States later on, but it is now proving troublesome. Japanese foreign policy—excluding foreign economic policy—is also essentially rudimentary.

The third major turning point in East Asia's history since the 1930s was the communist revolution in China in 1949. Its major effects on world events were, first, a major and bitter Chinese conflict with the United States and, later, a major and even more ideologically severe conflict between the PRC and the USSR, which began in the late 1950s and early 1960s but was inadequately understood by U.S. policymakers until the end of the 1960s. This second conflict has not expressed itself in a large-scale war like the one the United States and China fought in Korea, which left scars that have not fully healed even after thirty years. But the bitterness of ideological quarrels between Marxist-Leninist cousins, and the tension created across a militarized border thousands of miles long, are in the long run probably more lasting than the bitterness and tension arising from a single sharp military conflict of a few years' duration. Relations between the United States and China over the last century or even two centuries have in general been friendly, while those between Russia and China have always been characterized by enmity, territorial aggrandizement, and attempts at economic domination.

China's internal economic growth has been inhibited not only by its external quarrels but by its domestic political difficulties. The communist revolution in China probably eased the worst extremes of poverty and famine and unified the country. It also created turmoil, disruption, and intellectual stagnation that have plagued the PRC ever since. The Great Leap Forward and the Cultural Revolution in particular inhibited economic progress for decades and created problems that ensure that for the rest of this century growth will be modest at best. Nevertheless, the ultimate economic potential of the PRC remains great.

Since World War II, the United States has fought two ground wars in East Asia. The first, in the early 1950s, expressed the U.S. commitment to Northeast Asia and recognized South Korea as a key to Japanese security. In the second, the U.S. stake in Vietnam appears in retrospect to have been much too small to justify the cost of U.S. involvement. The policies that guided U.S. conduct seem to have been based on a misunderstanding of the relationship of the PRC to the Soviet Union, to the United States, and to Southeast Asia itself. Moreover, policymakers at the time clearly overestimated the U.S. ability to influence events in a situation in which the South Vietnamese government lacked adequate indigenous political support. But since history does not reveal its alternatives, we will never know what difficulties would have followed had the United States allowed the South Vietnamese regime to collapse in the mid-1960s. In any event, the U.S. commitment to the security of East Asia has been proven in blood and resources over three decades.

THE CURRENT CONVENTIONAL MILITARY BALANCE

What balance of military forces should the United States maintain in East Asia? Measuring the conventional military balance and establishing criteria for it are considerably more complex for East Asia than for Europe. The distances involved—from Northeast Asia, the Kuriles, and the Aleutians to Southeast Asia, the equator, and the eastern approaches to the Indian Ocean—are greater. And there is an even more complex cast of nations, with varying political and military relationships.

The United States has active military relationships with Japan, South Korea, and the Philippines. The ASEAN nations fall into the friendly category but offer varying degrees of military cooperation with the United States. The PRC is not a U.S. ally, but it is clearly hostile to the USSR, and a limited security relationship is evolving with the United States. Soviet allies include the Mongolian People's Republic (which would affect a USSR-PRC struggle) and Vietnam and its conquered states in Indochina (though the latter may subtract from rather than add to Vietnam's military strength). A third potential Soviet ally in some conflicts is North Korea. The balance must, therefore, be considered in various geographical and functional segments.

The basis of U.S. military and political relations with Japan is the U.S.-Japanese Security Treaty of 1960, which commits the United States to the defense of Japan. The obligation is not reciprocal. If the United States were to become engaged in a conflict in Korea, or elswhere with the Soviets, the Japanese Government could take any of several courses. It could use its own forces in combat on the U.S. side; it could refrain from doing so but allow U.S. forces to use bases in Japan; or it could deny U.S. forces the use of Japanese facilities in support of its combat operations—or even entirely. The Japanese choice would be determined by the nature of the conflict and their perception of their stake in it and by their assessment of the military and political balance. If they were attacked, they would be expected to fight themselves. Certainly the United States would not fight in defense of Japan if the Japanese themselves did not. If South Korea were attacked from the north, Japan could be expected to cooperate but not participate in combat. In a war between the United States and the Soviet Union confined to Europe or to the sea, Japan might, depending on the origin and circumstances, declare neutrality. Inability to use Japanese facilities would severely hamper U.S. ability to project military force into Northeast Asia and the western Pacific.

The United States currently has bases in Japan (including Okinawa), the Philippines, and South Korea. These are essential for the projection of U.S. military power. They also serve as evidence of the U.S. commitment to the security of East Asia. The base structure is adequate for present needs, but if threats to sea lines of communication in the Indian Ocean and the western Pacific increase, the Indonesian Straits and the Gulf of Thailand would then be critical way stations on the route to the eastern Indian Ocean, Diego Garcia, and the Persian Gulf. Present arrangements with Australia for use of facilities and military cooperation will increase in value. It would also be important to have access rights in some ASEAN countries (Thailand and Singapore, for example). At the same time, the United States must be careful not to offend local political sensibilities by seeking explicit treaty arrangements. Those countries may have as much to gain by such agreements as does the United States, or even more; but their domestic situations, their relations with their neighbors, and the inability of the United States to make an unlimited security commitment to them (or the unwisdom of making such a commitment) all argue for caution.

The Naval Balance

The course of a U.S.-Soviet naval war would be determined in large measure by how well the United States and Japan were able to close the straits that separate the Sea of Okhotsk and the Sea of Japan from the western Pacific. It would also depend on whether the Soviets had deployed their surface and subsurface navy through those straits before the conflict began. The Soviets could, for example, assign highest priority to defense of their own Pacific coastlines, the surrounding waters, and the Soviet ships in them and not attempt to close sea lines of communications between the United States and the western Pacific.

The Soviet Union has more surface ships and submarines available in the region than do the United States and its allies. These ships and submarines have formidable antiship cruise missiles. Soviet land-based naval aircraft, particularly the Backfire bomber armed with cruise missiles, pose a formidable threat—perhaps the most severe threat—to U.S. naval surface forces. But U.S. and Japanese land-based air power, especially with U.S. reinforcements using airborne warning and control aircraft (E-3s, or AWACS) to control the air battle, would stand a good chance of countering Soviet air capabilities over Japan and the Pacific. The two U.S. aircraft carrier battle groups usually deployed in the western Pacific could be augmented by one or two more in a war in the Far East. The single Soviet Pacific carrier, with small vertical take-off aircraft, provides nothing remotely comparable in attack capability. U.S. fixed and towed sonar array capability is not duplicated by Soviet systems; this helps give the United States superior antisubmarine capability everywhere except close to the Soviet coasts.

Geography and base structure combine with the balance of naval forces to favor Soviet naval forces in the Sea of Okhotsk and the Sea of Japan, around the Kuriles, and perhaps in the western Aleutians. But elsewhere in the Pacific these same factors favor allied naval forces. Thus U.S. and Japanese naval forces could be expected, over time and depending on other demands on the U.S. fleet, to gain dominance of the western Pacific outside the Japanese straits. But carrying out attacks on the Soviet coast would be difficult in view of the Soviet ability to use land-based air power over such combat zones.

Japan

Soviet capabilities against Japan are substantial, but the distances are so large that given the movement of U.S. air and sea power reinforcements to Japan at the first indications of Soviet action, the Soviets would have a difficult time launching large-scale amphibious operations against Japan. Japanese ground forces and stocks of land, sea, and air munitions, however, are marginal at best. In the absence of a buildup in those capabilities, therefore, a sustained Soviet attack—though unlikely—poses a substantial threat to the territorial integrity of Japan.

The speed and magnitude of U.S. reinforcement would obviously depend on the political and military situation elsewhere and on other demands on the central U.S. force reserves, as well as on airlift and sealift capacity. In particular, U.S. lift capabilities will limit any U.S. reinforcement through the 1980s. Depending on the circumstances, two or three divisions might be moved to Northeast Asia (Japan or South Korea) in a month to reinforce the two divisions already there (an Army division in South Korea and two-thirds of a Marine division in Okinawa). Two carrier battle groups could be moved across the Pacific in two or three weeks to join the one or two already there. Several wings of land-based fighter and attack aircraft could be deployed at about five-day intervals.

Both to deter any direct Soviet threat against their country and to insure against the possibility that U.S. military forces in or earmarked for Northeast Asia may be needed in other parts of the world during a crisis, the Japanese must make a series of military improvements. They need to increase their air defense capabilities and upgrade command-and-control, including the ability to operate more closely with U.S. forces. They should add several modern fighter wings; build up their stocks of combat and combat-support supplies (air and ground munitions, spare parts, and fuel) to be able to last for at least weeks rather than days; and expand their naval forces, in particular their surface escort, antisubmarine warfare, mining, and minesweeping capability.

Korea

The Korean Peninsula has traditionally been seen as a bridge between Japan and the mainland of Northeast Asia. The U.S. commitment to defend South Korea is intended not only to preserve South Korea's independence but also to protect Japan from possible aggression launched by way of that bridge and from the political pressures that would result from such a radical change on the Korean Peninsula.

The nature of the military and political threat to South Korea has changed over the past decade. From 1970 to 1977, North Korea increased the size of its ground forces by about 30 percent and almost doubled its tank and artillery inventory. It built up enough of a military stockpile for two or three months of combat and is able to make its own tanks, artillery, and antitank missiles. Because this was done gradually and because the level of secrecy is probably higher in North Korea than anywhere else in the world, U.S. intelligence did not become fully aware of this buildup until late in 1977. Why the North Koreans undertook these steps is not known. They may have concluded that they could not rely on either the PRC or the USSR for major assistance in case of an attack on South Korea. North Korean naval power, which includes several submarines, also remains much greater than that of South Korea. North Korean combat aircraft significantly outnumber those of South Korea, though the quality of the South Korean aircraft is superior. South Korea thus depends heavily on U.S. naval and air forces, as well as U.S. support of logistics, command-and-control, communications, and possibly on U.S. ground reinforcements in the event of a North Korean attack.

In assessing the military situation on the Korean Peninsula, it is important to note that North Korea maintains its military forces in a high degree of readiness and could launch an attack with little warning—perhaps only a few days. Compounding this problem is the location of Seoul, the South Korean capital, about 40 miles from the border. The Seoul region contains the central governmental apparatus and perhaps 30 to 40 percent of the population and industry of the country. Its loss would be crippling, even though the Korean War of the 1950s was fought to an acceptable conclusion after Seoul was twice captured. The devastation of South Korea as a result of those overrunnings, and the even greater relative industrial and demographic weight of the Seoul region in South Korea today, argue strongly that the main early goal for the United States and South Korea in a military conflict on the peninsula should be to prevent North Korean forces from reaching the capital. Moreover, North Korean doubt about its ability to do so would constitute a strong deterrent to such an attack.

If the North Koreans attacked, U.S. and South Korean forces on the scene, together with whatever South Korean forces could be mobilized within the warning time and during the early stages of combat, would have to stop the North Korean advance. U.S. reinforcements within those critical days would be limited to air and naval power, but these could still be significant. Under present circumstances, the initial outcome of a North Korean attack cannot be confidently predicted and would depend critically on the amount of warning.

If Seoul were not captured by North Korean forces early in a war, full mobilization of U.S. and South Korean reinforcements would be possible. South Korea would then have the edge in a protracted struggle. It has twice the population and more than twice the GNP of North Korea. Its economic and productive capacity would combine with U.S. reinforcements and materiel support to prevent a North Korean victory.

South Korea, during the long rule of President Park Chung Hee, quadrupled the size of its economy and created a modern and substantial military establishment. In their first Military Force Improvement Plan (in the early 1970s) and in the current one, the South Koreans have made substantial improvements in their military forces and have acquired some of the most advanced U.S. military equipment.

The United States currently has one ground force division and about a hundred tactical fighter and attack aircraft in South Korea. It could deploy several additional U.S. divisions over a period of two or three months and 200 fighter aircraft within about two weeks. But U.S. flexibility in deployments to other areas would be severely limited if these forces were engaged in combat in Korea. This indicates the need for a further South Korean ground force buildup, increasing the number of troops and the speed of their mobilization, adding to the stockpiles of such equipment as tanks, artillery, and antitank systems, and improving the capability of command-and-control systems and the measures to ensure their survival. It also makes it necessary for the South Koreans to strengthen defensive positions north of Seoul and to inaugurate countermeasures to airborne and seaborne assaults behind those defensive positions and to disruptions by North Korean special forces. A restoration of the balance that existed in 1970—in armored division equivalents and in other measures—should be the goal. That will take four or five years of continued growth in South Korean ground force capabilities—by 25 or 30 percent overall—and should be possible given that the South Korean economy is expected to continue to grow at a real rate of between 5 and 8 percent. Ground force buildup should take priority over the development of additional air and naval capabilities, which the United States can provide quickly in an emergency. The United States is appropriately the principal air and sea power in the U.S.–South Korean alliance.

Half of the U.S. ground forces were withdrawn from South Korea in the early 1970s. The plan to remove the remaining ground forces, begun in 1977, made some military sense given what was then known. But the discovery of the previously unrecognized North Korean buildup of 1970 to 1977 made it much more risky. Moreover, the withdrawal plan shook Japan's confidence in the United States, threatened domestic security in South Korea, and even raised concern in the PRC, which was and is nominally opposed to the U.S. military presence in South Korea. In 1978 the United States suspended the withdrawal of the remaining U.S. ground forces after a few thousand troops had been returned to the United States.

U.S. ground forces in South Korea provide a tripwire—that is, an assurance to both the South Koreans and the North Koreans that a North Korean attack will engage U.S. forces. Whether that assurance can be sufficiently provided without the presence of any U.S. ground forces is a central and difficult question. The answer will depend in large part on the political relations between the two countries and their degree of common purpose. One consideration would be the effect a complete ground force withdrawal would have on South Korea's desire to gain more political and military independence from the United States. Complete withdrawal of U.S. ground forces, even if U.S. air power and support personnel remained, could well persuade the South Koreans of a need to develop major air and naval forces, which would in turn diminish U.S. influence over their military actions. Whatever the judgments, such a withdrawal should occur only after a South Korean buildup and in a time of relative political and military stability on the peninsula. The worst course would be a sudden withdrawal in response to U.S. popular pressure at a time of and in response to instability or the danger of conflict in Korea.

What role do U.S. nuclear weapons play in deterring war in Korea? The possibility that they might be used if the North Koreans were overwhelmingly defeating the South Koreans, especially if U.S. ground forces were engaged, cannot be lost on North Korean leaders, who remember President Eisenhower's implicit threat to use them in 1953. Especially in the absence of strong support of North Korea by the USSR or the PRC, U.S. nuclear weapons help deter North Korea from attacking. They also provide reassurance to South Korea. The U.S. nuclear deterrent could, in military terms, be based offshore— with sea-based aircraft, long-range bombers, tactical bombers, or cruise missiles. Such basing would remove the chance that the weapons might be captured in a North Korean attack and would thus reduce the chance of early pressure for their use. The arguments for deployments in Europe do not, however, apply in Korea: The balance of conventional forces is closer than in Europe, and North Korea has no nuclear weapons of its own.

U.S. nuclear force presence and ground force presence are related. It can be argued that U.S. ground forces require nuclear deterrent protection, but in Korea that can surely be provided from offshore. Each type of force reinforces the deterrent effect of the other and the reassurance that the other provides to South Korea. If one force is removed, it becomes considerably riskier to remove the other. To give a nuclear deterrent political credibility, the United States might have to base at least a few nuclear weapons in South Korea, especially if its ground forces were removed. With U.S. ground forces present, it should be politically feasible to base outside South Korea such nuclear weapons as are needed to deter North Korean attack.

U.S. policies on arms sales to South Korea relate directly to U.S. intentions to maintain a military presence. The greater the U.S. presence and the corresponding political commitment, the more sustainable is a policy that limits the sales of advanced air and naval equipment. This in turn gives the USSR and PRC more opportunity to adopt a similar policy toward the North Koreans. On the other hand, the United States would be under greater pressure to provide advanced equipment if it asked the South Koreans to take over full responsibility for their own defense so that the United States could remove its military presence.

The People's Republic of China

A military balance that does not involve the United States directly but is extremely important is the one between the Soviet Union and the People's Republic of China. Though the PRC army, even the part of it that could be deployed to the PRC-USSR frontier, is at least twice as large as the number of Soviet troops available, the Soviet air and ground forces clearly outclass those of the PRC. About the same numbers of tanks and aircraft would be engaged on each side in the initial stages of a conflict, but the Soviet equipment is of more modern design by twenty years and correspondingly more capable. Assuming that the Soviets would be deterred from using either tactical or strategic nuclear weapons by the prospect of Chinese retaliation against Soviet urban-industrial centers in Siberia and perhaps in European Russia as well, they could still be expected to make major advances (of more than a hundred miles) in many places along the Sino-Soviet and Sino-Mongolian borders. Thereafter, the terrain would become more mountainous and the effect of lengthening supply lines could well begin to show. It might then become feasible for the Chinese to offer substantial frontal resistance and at least equally effective popular resistance behind the invaders' lines, as occurred in China and in the Soviet Union during World War II. Whether the corresponding major territorial conquests and the domination of many urban centers would constitute an achievement of Soviet objectives cannot be predicted. But given the Soviet experience in Afghanistan, it would be rash of the Soviets to conclude that the Chinese, thirty times more numerous and enormously better equipped than the Afghans, would prove easy to conquer.

The Chinese cannot be considered a first-class military power. Their performance against the Vietnamese in 1979, in what was an invasion rather than a defense of their own territory, must have disappointed the Chinese leaders. But the sheer size of the PRC armed forces, the quantity of their equipment, and the great distances involved in any military move through China should make them formidable defenders of their own territory. What they lack is modern equipment, training, and doctrine for joint service operations.

To equip PRC forces with modern equipment in quantities comparable to that possessed by the Soviet forces on their borders would cost $200 billion to $400 billion. There is no way that the Chinese themselves can produce such quantities of equipment over the next decade. The state of their technology is now such that they could not even fully develop 1980-vintage equipment by 1990. Moreover, no outside source is going to provide them with such quantities of equipment or the funds to buy it. It is sensible, therefore, for the PRC to take the approach that it has—to acquire advanced technology, perhaps as part of a package deal involving modest purchases, and then themselves develop and produce the equipment. But such an approach will take decades to bring their forces to a 1980s state of modernity.

Still, a substantial improvement toward a more modest goal— improving the PRC's capability to defend itself against armored and air attack—could be made through the development or procurement of more modern antitank and antiaircraft systems. Here an investment of $10 billion over six or seven years—less than 10 percent of present PRC defense costs—would make an enormous difference.

Other East Asian Countries

Vietnam is the preeminent local military power in Southeast Asia. Its military strength troubles its small and medium-sized neighbors even beyond the boundaries of Indochina. That and its political and military flirtation with the Soviet Union, particularly in providing bases, have drawn severe reactions from the PRC and the United States. Though Vietnam itself is unlikely to be able to project its military power effectively over Southeast Asian waters, it has been involved in nasty words and a few incidents with the PRC, the Philippines, and Western oil-rig operators over offshore islands and oil. Of more immediate concern are its incursions into Thailand in trying to seal off the Cambodian border and the possibility that its military power could affect the political stability of Thailand. That threat is limited to some extent by the PRC's ability to punish Vietnam, as it did in the brief, bloody, and only partially successful incursion of 1979.

The other countries of Southeast Asia, while not having discarded all previous animosities or frictions about territorial claims, offshore oil, and the like, seem in no early danger of armed conflict with each other. Indeed, in the ASEAN pact they have clearly embarked on an indigenous cooperative course, largely economic and political in nature, but involving security arrangements as well. Within the ASEAN nations, suspicions of the Chinese minorities in Malaysia and Indonesia make those nations relatively less hostile to Vietnam and more concerned about PRC interest and involvement in Southeast Asia.

The Two-Front Issue

The magnitude of the forces that the United States or the Soviet Union could bring to bear in East Asia would clearly depend on what forces might be required for combat elsewhere. In turn, any commitment in East Asia would affect the ability of the superpowers to carry out combat operations effectively elsewhere. The PRC, Vietnam, North Korea, South Korea, and Japan would commit forces, if at all, only in East Asia. Although the raw materials vital to Japan come from elsewhere, there is no near-term prospect that it would commit forces anywhere outside the Japanese islands and their surrounding waters.

A great deal has been made of the risk to the Soviet Union of a two-front war, and indeed the Soviets must be gravely concerned about this, especially given the difficulties they face in moving forces among potential fronts in Europe, in East Asia, and in Southwest Asia. But the United States and its allies would have a corresponding problem. Moreover, Europe, Southwest Asia, and East Asia are more distant from the United States than from the Soviet Union, which has the additional benefit of interior lines of communication. The United States, with its allies, could be expected to dominate the air and sea lines of communication between itself and these distant theaters because it devotes a large percentage of its military resources to naval and air combat and lift forces for that purpose.

At least as much as the Soviet Union, the United States must be concerned about the prospect of having major forces pinned down in one theater when conflict in another, perhaps more crucial one erupts. If the Soviets were planning adventures in Europe, in Southwest Asia, or in both, it would make sense for them to persuade the North Koreans to attack South Korea with the intention of drawing major U.S. air, naval, and perhaps ground forces into a conflict there for some months before launching their own attack on one of the other fronts. The Soviets may lack such influence, but the North Koreans might seize the opportunity to attack the South in a time of crisis or war elsewhere, even in the absence of explicit Soviet support. Depending on the timing, this might or might not pin down U.S. forces. As previously discussed, the U.S. ability to operate successfully in East Asian seas or on the Korean Peninsula depends greatly on the availability of Japanese bases for use by U.S. forces. Thus the balance of forces depends significantly on the lineup of other participants alongside the United States or the Soviet Union. Moreover, both the United States and the Soviets are exposed to potential pinning down by the prospect of a global conflict covering several theaters of combat. How can the United States best take advantage of this situation as part of a global strategy for limiting Soviet expansionism? A modest buildup of Japanese military strength, and the gradual modernization of Chinese forces, would help. Maintaining good U.S.-PRC-Japanese relations without goading the Soviets into adventurism is as important—and more difficult.

The problems of multifront war are further addressed in Chapter 10. On the basis of the factors already discussed, however, it is clear that the political relations among a large number of countries are important, perhaps decisive, elements in determining the overall balance in East Asia.

THE POLITICAL FRAMEWORK
FOR A MILITARY STRATEGY

Japan

Decisions by Japan on the nature of a future security policy will be conditioned by its relations with other nations in the region. In recent years, Japan's relations with the PRC have warmed, and those with the Soviet Union have become nearly frigid. Relations with the Chinese have been stimulated further by U.S.-PRC rapprochement; the Japanese want to stay at least as close to the PRC as the United States does. For a time it appeared that the Japanese would be in a position to profit greatly from the Chinese economic opening to the industrialized democracies, but this has been delayed by the PRC's lowered estimate of its economic capacity to engage in capital imports and new industrial developments.

For the souring of Japanese-Soviet relations, the Soviets have principally themselves to blame. Their disregard of Japanese sovereignty in their fleet movements, their refusal even to discuss the issue of the northern territories, and the implicit threat contained in their deployment of military forces there have all reinforced the traditional Japanese unfriendliness toward Russia.

Despite a series of economic and diplomatic shocks, Japanese leaders and the Japanese people continue to believe that Japan's security depends fundamentally on the U.S.-Japanese security relationship. The nuclear umbrella, the preservation of the military balance on the Korean Peninsula, continued access to the energy and raw materials on which the Japanese economy depends, and deterrence of the admittedly unlikely prospect of a Soviet attack on Japan— none of these can be effected by Japanese military capability alone, even if it were greatly increased. Moreover, though Japan's economic power is substantial and its political power significant, neither would weigh heavily enough in the balance against a foe that saw sufficient gain in a successful military domination of Japan.

The combination of great economic weight, considerable economic fragility as a result of dependence on external markets and raw materials, and small military strength cannot be a comfortable one for Japan. The U.S. security connection is a great strength to both countries, but at a time when the American public sees Japan most notably as an economic competitor, a careful reexamination of the requirements for Japan's security and a frank discussion of the sharing of the necessary functions by the United States and Japan are needed. A division appropriate for the 1950s, when the United States had ten times Japan's GNP, is neither realistic nor healthy for either country today, when that factor has shrunk to less than three and when the Soviet Union—much closer to Japan than is the United States—has achieved military strength comparable to that of the United States.

Only a tiny fraction of Japanese officials and opinion leaders believe in a Japan so substantially rearmed as to be able fully to defend itself. A somewhat larger group, but still a minority, is prepared to share the burdens with the United States on the basis of economic strength, population, and global interests. A group of comparable size is committed against any significant Japanese military capability and is inclined to neutralism. The inclination of the majority is to make only as much of a military contribution to the joint security of the United States and Japan as is required to ensure that the United States will maintain the security relationship. In line with this approach, successive Japanese governments have played an extremely passive role in foreign affairs. They have tended to limit their interests to what is necessary to preserve Japanese access to raw materials and markets and to define their policies toward the Middle East, southern Africa, Europe, and the Soviet Union accordingly. This is not an entirely inappropriate approach for a country whose principal interest in the rest of the world is economic.

This spectrum of views in Japan has little in common with U.S. perceptions of the security situation in East Asia or the world during the past five years, or even with the détente-oriented U.S. policies of the 1970s. Yet there is a basis for bringing U.S. and Japanese policies back together. The two countries must define their respective responsibilities, taking into account political realities as well as military requirements. An increase in the Japanese defense effort from approximately 1 percent of GNP to 6 percent as in the United States, or even to 3 or 4 percent as in the NATO countries, would stimulate great fears in East Asia, and perhaps in the United States, too. Chinese leaders have indicated that a doubling of Japanese force levels would not trouble them—but the Japanese, as their economic activities show, do not do things by halves. Thus there are good reasons for the United States and Japan not to share defense responsibilities equally, even in East Asia.

But to retain public support in the United States for its East Asian policy, a more equal division is required, with the Japanese concentrating on the functional and geographical areas that are most immediate to their own needs. This would include most—but not all—of the self-defense of the Japanese islands, air defense and antisubmarine warfare (ASW) capability, and control of the air and sea over and around Japan as well as along the nearest 1,000 miles of Japanese sea lines of communication. That would extend to the vicinity of Luzon in the northern Philippines and Guam. Japan should provide economic support, through trade and some aid, to South Korea, the ASEAN countries, and developing countries in the Middle East and Southwest Asia (Pakistan and Egypt, for example), and it should continue to increase its financial contribution in support of the U.S. military presence in Japan. The United States should contribute to the forces needed to deter or defend against a conventional attack on Japan. It should also take exclusive responsibility for the nuclear umbrella, provide forces in South Korea (where a Japanese military contribution would be politically counterproductive), and ensure the power projection forces required for security and stability in East Asia. Japanese assumption of this last role would be politically destabilizing both in Japan and in the rest of East Asia.

The United States and Japan must also be more sensitive to each other in their economic and political interactions. Over the past decade, new problems have erupted in U.S.-Japanese relations: unsubtle U.S. pressure on the Japanese for a massive increase in Japanese rearmament, rather than a more modest acceleration; the controversy about whether U.S. nuclear weapons have been stationed in Japan; and Japanese concern about a perceived decline in relative military capability and strength of will in the United States. The overall effect has been increasing disquiet and uncertainty in Japanese attitudes toward the United States since 1970. This trend requires special U.S. attention, lest it lead in time to a greater chance of Japanese neutrality in a conflict between the United States and the Soviet Union in Europe, Southwest Asia, or even some parts of the Far East. Because the perceived economic interests of the two nations often diverge markedly, and those conflicts have intensified markedly in recent years, a frank exposition and negotiation of economic issues is a prerequisite to the restoration of healthy relations.

More total military strength is needed in the western Pacific. The United States and Japan must decide jointly what additional strength is required and then jointly allocate the responsibilities for that strengthening. Japan's role is limited politically, even constitutionally, and to some degree economically as well. But all nations suffer economic and political constraints, and Japan has managed to build a substantial military establishment within its constitutional constraints. The Japanese, through their political process, must decide how much more they are willing to do and in what form to provide for their self-defense—that is, for the defense of Japanese territory and of the sea and air routes nearby. Japan should consider what it can do to reduce the prospect of military action that would cut off its trade or threaten its territory directly, and of political intimidation through the threat of such action. But in so deciding, Japan should not lightly assume that the United States will or even can supply whatever military strength is needed for everyone in the area, independent of Japanese actions, simply because Northeast Asian security is so important to the United States. The security of Northeast Asia, and specifically of Japan, *is* important to the United States, but it cannot be more important to the United States than it is to Japan. Inevitably, the U.S. impression of how important it is to Japan will be shaped by Japanese actions.

The People's Republic of China

The single largest new political factor in the Far East during the 1970s has been the gradual rapprochement between the United States and the PRC. Several factors contributed to this change. Turmoil in the PRC involved a series of ebbs and flows between ideologues and pragmatists, culminating in a victory for the pragmatists, who encouraged an approach to the industrialized democracies for an infusion of technology and capital. This approach, combined with an increasingly hostile attitude toward the USSR, caused the PRC's leaders to see their security interests in a different light, revising their policy of all-out hostility to both the United States and the USSR by easing PRC relations with the United States. On the U.S. side, a clearer perception of the dangers of Soviet expansionism coincided with a recognition that the Chinese had increasingly come to share that concern as their major one. The opportunity for change in U.S.-PRC relations created by the end of U.S. participation in the Vietnam War coincided with the Nixon administration's perception of declining U.S. strength and will and of a consequent need to find new ways to offset Soviet strength. This led to the opening of serious discussions and to the Shanghai Communiqué of 1972. The Carter administration took the major additional step of working out formal recognition and establishing diplomatic relations and followed this up with a set of discussions across the board—economic, technological, agricultural, and geostrategic—extending finally to a very modest and limited military relationship.

The China card is actually a full deck. At the top is peace between the United States and China—until the early 1970s relations between the two countries were anything but peaceful. In the middle is a whole spectrum of normal diplomatic, economic, commercial, and technical relations, extending down toward the various kinds of military cooperation at the bottom. That bottom contains additional cards, including discussions of the world strategic situation at the level of foreign or defense ministers; parallel diplomatic and strategic actions; exchanges of military scholars; transfers of fundamental technology that has both civilian and military applications; sales of military equipment other than weapons; sales of military components; sales of minor and major military weapons systems, including those more purely defensive and, later, those capable of substantial offensive use; subsidized sales or grants of weapons; and, at the very bottom, joint military planning and various informal and formal military alliances. The U.S.-PRC military relationship clearly has not gone very far into the bottom of the deck. And there are good reasons, from the U.S. and the Chinese points of view, why they should not. Nevertheless, the comparison of the present situation with that of ten years ago indicates a great change in security relations and defense dialogue.

U.S. policy in East Asia should seek gradually to strengthen these ties with the PRC without succumbing to the illusion that the PRC will become like the United States or like Japan. It should aim to contain Soviet military power, applied directly or through surrogates, without unnecessarily feeding Soviet obsessions about encirclement.

It should not become a simple expression of the state of U.S.-Soviet relations. Such a course would involve great risks. The Chinese could be tempted to adopt a similar attitude and, if they failed to get enough of what they wanted from their relationship with the United States, turn back toward the Soviet Union. A second and even more severe risk is that the Soviets would go beyond their present extreme, almost paranoid view of a U.S.-PRC alliance and conclude that a major joint military venture is planned against them. This could cause them to take some rash and dangerous actions that could be catastrophic for the entire world.

The proper attitude for the United States is to hold to its friendly relations with the PRC independent of the state of U.S.-Soviet relations. The United States should resist Soviet attempts to prevent anyone from transferring weapons or even technology to the PRC, an embargo the Soviets attempted to impose in 1978 and 1979 by putting strong pressure, in the form of threats, on the Western Europeans. But neither should the United States move the degree of its military relationship with the PRC up and down tactically in the deck described above according to whether the USSR behaves in what the United States sees as a more or less expansionist direction. For one thing, once a degree of military cooperation with the PRC is reached, to back off from it would damage U.S.-PRC relations. For another, the details of such a finely balanced approach would undoubtedly either be lost on or misunderstood by both the PRC and the USSR, to the detriment of the relations of both with the United States.

The best approach is to establish a firm policy of increasingly friendly relations with the PRC across the whole spectrum of political and economic cooperation, but to be quite cautious about the rate of increase in military relations. This policy should be made clear to the PRC. At the same time the USSR should be given to understand that over the long run the nature of U.S.-PRC military cooperation will depend on the way both nations perceive the degree and nature of Soviet expansionism. The United States should be particularly careful about beginning sales of weapons systems (as opposed to sales of nonweapons equipment or transfer of dual-use technology). At some point, weapons system sales may be in order. But such a step should not be taken unless it is clear that there is no realistic chance of more restrained behavior on the part of the Soviets.

The more extreme cards in the China deck are very threatening in the eyes of the Soviet Union. At the same time the United States has very few comparably powerful levers to deter Soviet moves that are truly dangerous to the industrialized democracies, such as a military venture in Southwest Asia. For both these reasons it is important to preserve the potential of the more threatening aspects of military cooperation with the PRC to deter more dangerous Soviet actions that are difficult to deter or counter directly on the spot.

The issue that threatens to upset relations between the PRC and the United States is not the degree of U.S. military cooperation with the PRC; it is Taiwan. This issue was papered over in the Shanghai Communiqué and again at normalization. The PRC sees arms sales to Taiwan as a denial of its sovereignty and a basis for the Taiwanese authorities to resist reunification. But more fundamentally, it fears a U.S. move toward a two-China policy. Such a policy would be unacceptable to the PRC. Moreover the remaining ties between the United States and Taiwan are an effective weapon in the hands of those in the PRC who are fighting the attempts by the current leadership to institutionalize the shift to pragmatism in domestic and foreign policy.

The United States has commitments to a peaceful settlement and to its friends on Taiwan, with whom a close relationship existed for so long. Those commitments set a limit to potential accommodations to the PRC position. It is not for the United States to force Taiwan to a settlement, by setting a deadline or by any other means. To do so would raise doubts about U.S. reliability elsewhere. The PRC's nine-point formula for reunification, set forth by Ye Jianying, is on its face too good an offer to refuse, but only if the PRC can first persuade the authorities on Taiwan that it would be carried out in a way they would find acceptable. The United States can and should, however, make it clear that a peaceful reunification would be welcome, and U.S. arms sales to Taiwan should be restrained. Such restraint is compatible with the fact that the environment in the Taiwan Strait is more peaceful than it has been since the late 1940s. Arms sales should be adequate for but limited to a level consistent with Taiwan's real self-defense needs. As the Chinese on both sides work out a settlement, those needs can be expected to decrease. Such a policy is consistent with the U.S.-PRC agreement of August 1982. The problem is a significant possibility that domestic ideological conflicts about Taiwan in the United States and in the PRC will cause a severe rift between the two nations, to the detriment of the security of both. The 1982 agreement, reached after cliff-hanging negotiations, just avoided a major rift, and the controversy left a sour taste on both sides.

Suspicions remain on both sides, and the Taiwan issue will not go away in the foreseeable future. As a result, China will periodically distance itself from the United States, identifying itself with the Third World and its positions. The Chinese moved in this direction in late 1982. Moreover, the PRC took the initiative in seeking to ease its relations with the USSR by dropping its demand that the Soviets admit the justice of Chinese border claims. The issues of the Soviet military buildup on that border, of the Soviet invasion of Afghanistan, and of Soviet support for Vietnam remain.

To summarize, most of the benefits arising from the improved relations between the United States and the PRC are attributable to internal attitudes and political dynamics in the PRC and to its relations with other countries. The massive national and ideological hostility between the PRC and the USSR ties down 25 to 30 percent of Soviet air and ground forces and splits extreme left-wing parties in Europe and Asia. Chinese preoccupation with internal problems has reduced what could otherwise be (and was) seen as a major threat to the noncommunist countries of East Asia. The reduction of that threat has permitted noncommunist East Asia's rapid economic growth and its more modest political evolution. But as the different situation in the 1950s and 1960s reminds us, these advantages depend on U.S.-PRC relations that are at least no worse than USSR-PRC relations. Even now, while the U.S.-PRC relation is helpful to the United States in some situations (as in Korea), it has more complex effects in others (Vietnam and Cambodia).

From an evolving U.S.-PRC relation, the United States should seek a situation in which the PRC continues to help limit Soviet expansion, without finding itself in a war with the Soviets; in which it acts as a stabilizing force and a positive economic power in East Asia; and in which it develops internally without evolving a politically or militarily expansionist posture in the region. To this end, the United States should concentrate on political and economic relations with the PRC. Parallel and even cooperative geostrategic and diplomatic actions should be pursued to assist joint political aims, where these exist. Military relations should be expanded cautiously in support of these other goals.

Korea

The prospects for peace on the Korean Peninsula over the next two decades depend strongly on an adequate military balance. North Korea, under Kim Il-sung a highly militarized and regimented state dedicated to reunification on its own terms, is likely to remain so under his successors. (In light of the likely succession arrangements, it may be considered the first monarchical communist state.) The North Korean evaluation of the effectiveness of subversion or invasion to achieve that end will be influenced by its perception of South Korean political stability and economic strength.

In South Korea, the future political situation remains uncertain. The South Korean military becomes more opposed to loosening the authoritarian patterns of its government when North Korean military capabilities become more threatening or when the United States appears more likely to withdraw its military support. In principle, the elements of a South Korean evolution toward economic strength, military security, and a government more acceptable to the economic and intellectual producers on whom an industrial society depends are all available. President Chun Doo Hwan took some steps in that direction in 1980 and 1981, and the economy has improved and the degree of tranquility has increased. But unrest and the corruption scandals in 1982, combined with past history, allow only modest optimism.

Southeast Asia

There have been remarkable economic gains in most of the ASEAN nations during the last fifteen years. Indonesia has enormous natural resources, but it also has difficult geographical and transportation problems, great linguistic and ethnic diversity, and governmental corruption. The Philippines have similar problems. Vietnamese expansion causes disquiet in the area. Soviet support of Vietnam both increases the threat and gives the Soviets a base for maritime operations in the southern Pacific and the Indian Ocean.

The ASEAN nations enjoy only modest political cohesion. The Indonesians and Malaysians are more concerned about the PRC's influence than the others, because of their substantial ethnic Chinese minorities. The Thais are particularly troubled by Vietnamese incursions across the Cambodian and Laotian borders into Thailand, deliberately designed to intimidate them. The United States has properly retained a relatively low profile in this area since the early 1970s, responding on a modest scale to requests for sales of military equipment and trying to restrain military action by all parties in the region. The possibilities of establishing diplomatic relations with Vietnam went glimmering in the late 1970s when the Vietnamese embarked on massive military aggression and on a persecution of ethnic Chinese and political and economic dissidents so intense that it drove almost a million refugees to desperate measures to escape.

The Balance of Political Factors

To summarize the political factors, the situation in East Asia contains substantial risks for the industrial democracies, especially for the United States. But it appears to pose even more problems for the Soviet Union. To a degree this is the reverse of the situation in Southwest Asia. In particular, cooperation among the United States, the PRC, and Japan is increasing. Substantial if spotty in political terms and ranging from minor (United States–China) to major (United States–Japan) in military terms, this cooperation certainly holds the potential in Soviet eyes for a major and dangerous alliance. To the Soviets, these three nations represent the world's still leading and adversary superpower, the USSR's competitor for the role of second-largest industrial power, and the world's most populous state, bordering the USSR's own most underpopulated and resource-rich territories. The prospect of such an alliance must truly be a nightmare for the Soviets, and the modest cooperative steps of 1975–1980 have in my judgment tilted the political-military balance against the Soviets to a degree that significantly exceeds the advantages accruing to them from their substantial military buildup in the region during the late 1960s and 1970s.

WHAT SHOULD U.S. POLICY BE?

During the early decades of the twenty-first century, East Asia could come to exceed Western Europe or North America in economic weight. The situation there is extraordinarily diverse and complex but relatively advantageous to the United States. U.S. policy should be to maintain that advantage.

Such a policy requires skillful diplomacy, especially in relations with the PRC, whose political and economic characteristics thirty years from now cannot be predicted. In the shorter run, continuing to safeguard the economic growth and development of Japan, South Korea, and the ASEAN nations by adequate security arrangements must remain a central feature of U.S. policy. The PRC's status as a partial counterbalance to Soviet strength in the region can be an important contributor to the preservation of the security of the pro-Western industrialized countries on the edge of East Asia, as long as it remains a natural outgrowth of Chinese attitudes and not something artificially induced by the United States.

It is in the interest of the United States to exert a stabilizing influence in East Asia, and the mutual political commitments and strategic relationships the United States has or is developing with Japan, South Korea, the PRC, and the ASEAN nations serve that end. Keeping substantial U.S. military forces and U.S.-operated base facilities in the region is a necessary condition to achieve that goal. The United States must maintain, modernize, and perhaps slightly increase its military force deployments in East Asia. Some redeployments or readjustments within the region may also be appropriate. But major increases would reduce the flexibility the United States needs to maintain in the form of a central reserve of forces that can be deployed in a crisis to whichever region is deemed most in need of them.

The importance of U.S. commitments in Europe and in Southwest Asia requires that Japan share the burdens of military security in the Far East fairly. That this can be accomplished during the 1980s still seems a reasonable expectation, despite the difficulties of recent years. The understanding of the Japanese leaders and people about their security needs has increased greatly over the last decade. Moreover, as a consequence of the enormous growth in the Japanese economy, the Japanese military budget has grown to be the seventh largest in the world without taking up a substantially increased percentage of Japan's GNP. But economic growth has slowed in Japan, as elsewhere. Simultaneously, the needs for military strength and for closer joint military planning, exercises, and cooperation between Japan and the United States have increased. The Japanese must make some new decisions if their own security and that of the other East Asian nations with which they trade heavily are to be preserved.

It is not feasible for Japan to play a global security role. Even a security role throughout East Asia is not appropriate during the 1980s because of constitutional and political strictures within Japan and historical and national attitudes in the other nations of the region.

But Japan can and should assume the principal role in the conventional self-defense of its own territories and a major share of the defense of its surrounding waters and air space, including its major sea lines of communication up to a distance of about a thousand miles from Honshu and Kyushu.

The best way for the United States to assist Japan in making the correct decision is through quiet and protracted discussions with the Japanese, on both official and unofficial levels, to arrive at an agreement about what has to be done overall for the region's security. At the appropriate stage in those discussions, it will become necessary to work out what constitutes a fair division of responsibilities between the United States and Japan. Any such determination will have to take into account political, constitutional, economic, and public opinion constraints on both sides.

8

U.S. Security Interests in Southwest Asia

Southwest Asia has been a region of great importance to the industrialized democracies—and specifically the United States—since World War II. Since the early 1970s U.S. interests and those of its allies have been vitally affected by events in this part of the world. The region includes Turkey and Egypt in the west (though part of Turkey's territory is in Europe and Egypt lies almost entirely in Africa). It extends to Pakistan and Afghanistan in the northeast. In geostrategic terms, it can be considered to encompass the Horn of Africa on the south and the Maghreb far to the west. Political and military factors and events in each part of the region affect the rest, but conditions in each country differ, so the United States must define a policy for each part as well as an overall policy for the region.

THE IMPORTANCE OF SOUTHWEST ASIA

U.S. interests were expressed in Southwest Asia during the late 1940s in the application of the Truman Doctrine to Turkey and in U.S. support for the creation of the state of Israel. Soon after the end of World War II, the United States and Great Britain pressured the Soviet Union to withdraw its military forces from northern Iran, where the Soviets had sought to extend their influence by supporting a client Azerbaijani regime. Subsequently the United States sponsored (though it did not join) the Central Treaty Organization (CENTO) alliance to provide a southern containment barrier against the Soviet

Union. That alliance lost most of its effect in 1958 with the Iraqi revolution; twenty years later the Iranian revolution finished it off.

In these early actions, the United States recognized the region as a geographical area of major strategic significance through which pass the routes connecting Europe, Africa, and Asia. But in the 1940s and through the 1950s, though the oil-producing capacity of the region was significant, it was by no means the principal source of oil in international trade. Only during the 1960s—and even more during the 1970s—did Western Europe, Japan, and the United States become so dependent on oil from Southwest Asia.

The full extent of the dangers that this posed became clear only through a series of events: the 1973 Arab-Israeli War and the subsequent Arab oil boycott and oil price increase; the Iranian revolution, which exposed the frailty of a U.S. policy dependent on Iran not only for oil but also for political and military resistance to Soviet expansionism; the second major oil price increase of 1978–1979; the Soviet invasion of Afghanistan in 1979, which showed Soviet willingness to use military force outside the borders of the Warsaw Pact nations; and the Iran-Iraq War that began in 1980.

The nature and degree of Western energy dependence are major facts of geopolitical life. It is notable that Western Europe and Japan rely on oil from the Persian Gulf states considerably more than does the United States. About 9 percent of total U.S. oil consumption comes from that region. The figures vary among the European countries, but Western Europe as a whole gets about 55 percent of its oil from the area, and Japan more than 60 percent. About half of the net oil exports in international trade come from the region.

What would happen if these oil exports dried up? For the United States, a reduction of 9 percent in oil consumption might be manageable, though it would certainly be painful. But even if the United States were to weather such a cutback, problems would remain. If oil exports from the Gulf states were to be withheld entirely from international trade, the rest of the oil that the United States imports (approximately 30 to 35 percent of its consumption) would be substantially disrupted. The demands of other importers dependent on the Persian Gulf exporters would affect both the availability and price of oil from other sources. The Europeans and the Japanese do not have even the choice of managing without Persian Gulf oil. An extended cutoff of oil from the Persian Gulf would be disastrous to them. Though the percentage of world oil supplied to importers by the Persian Gulf states has decreased as a result of the Iranian revolution and the Iran-Iraq War, they will remain so large a supplier through the 1980s that this dangerous situation will continue.

POTENTIAL THREATS

U.S. policy toward the Persian Gulf faces two nightmares. The first is a possible cutoff of exports as a result of internal actions or disruption from within the region. The second is a series of political and military measures that would give the Soviet Union control of the resources of the region.

Conflicts within or between the major oil-exporting states, or a major change in the internal political complexion in any of them—as occurred in Iran in 1978 and 1979—could cause a major reduction in oil exports. Depending on whether this happened in several of the smaller producers or one or more of the larger producers, the loss to the international supply of oil could run anywhere from a few million to 15 million barrels a day. An internal change could lead to reductions in a producing nation's oil exports to a level just sufficient to meet its foreign exchange needs. Some of the Persian Gulf states' exports have in the past been far larger than this, in part out of a recognition that too low a production rate or too high a price could cause economic catastrophe in the industrialized world, with negative repercussions on the Gulf states themselves. Radical regimes are unlikely to accept this line of reasoning; hence their tendency to reduce output to the level of foreign exchange need or, if they are disorganized enough, even below it. Major wars within the region could have even more severe effects. Regimes at war are likely to have their oil facilities destroyed or disrupted, with the result that production could be reduced to below the level of foreign exchange requirements, as has happened to both participants in the Iran-Iraq War.

A general Arab-Israeli military conflict would severely threaten overall levels of oil exports, and the disputes over the Palestinians tend to exacerbate tensions elsewhere in the region. But other wars are possible. Egypt fought in Yemen during the 1960s. Conflicts persist between the two Yemens. Iran and Iraq have fought bitterly in the early 1980s. That war, or Khomeini-style religious extremism, could spill over into other Persian Gulf states and shut down oil production. Various other ethnic, tribal, sectarian, and national splits exist within the Islamic nations.

The second, even more severe threat would involve a gradual or creeping Soviet political dominance over various parts of the region, with the Soviets exercising increasing control over decisions about oil exports and prices. The Soviet Union could send advisory missions to governments in the region, thus creating a significant Soviet presence. Or they could make incursions into border areas under the pretense of supporting indigenous ethnic or political movements and accompany these with major arms transfers and the assignment of military advisers. The most formidable military challenge, though the most unlikely, would be a massive and direct Soviet military attack aimed at conquest of part or all of the Persian Gulf region and control or destruction of the oil fields.

A Soviet military takeover would clearly be a mortal blow to reliable access for the industrialized democracies. And the legitimate interest of the industrialized democracies is that of *access* to the oil in the region, not *control* over it. The Soviets, like the industrialized democracies, have a legitimate interest in access to Southwest Asian oil and in its availability for purchase at market prices. Preemptive or concessionary access through predominant political and military influence would be another matter, illegitimate and gravely damaging to the other industrialized nations and to the developing nations as well.

Still another troublesome, though less catastrophic, possibility would be a program of economic collaboration by Persian Gulf states and other oil producers to raise real prices of oil at a rate that would damage the prosperity of the industrialized democracies and the oil-importing developing countries. Such action appears much less likely in the stagnating world economy of the early 1980s than it was in the 1970s. Its feasibility would depend both on the appropriate economic conditions and on a certain degree of political cohesion and stability in the Persian Gulf states. Despite the reduction in supply resulting from the Iran-Iraq War, 1981 and 1982 saw a glut of oil production and a fall in real prices. The recession in the West and conservation steps have made the immediate threat of price increases less worrisome. But economic growth of 3 percent a year would raise world consumption by 8 million barrels a day by the end of the 1980s, even if oil use per unit of economic output drops by 1 percent a year as a result of conservation and of displacement of oil by other fuels.

Some have maintained that a cutoff of oil from the Persian Gulf states to the industrialized democracies for political reasons, or even a large price increase and reduction in shipments, would constitute (indeed, has constituted) an act of war. This threat to the existence of the industrial democracies is said to justify military action against the Southwest Asian governments who take (or have taken) these actions. Both principle and pragmatism argue against this view. The dependence of the industrialized nations on oil is their own doing. Economic needs, whether for *Lebensraum* or for oil, cannot justify attacks on Poland or Pearl Harbor. Adventurism based on such justification would probably fail on the scene anyway, given the vulnerability of oil facilities to sabotage or destruction by the indigenous population. It would also give the Soviets the opportunity to launch a counterintervention, announcing themselves (and even being welcomed as) protectors of the Persian Gulf against Western imperialism.

Finally, the United States confronts the possibility that nuclear weapons will be introduced into Southwest Asia by present nuclear countries outside the area or through the development of indigenous nuclear capabilities. Israel is generally believed to be capable of quickly completing the process of nuclear weapons production. Pakistan appears to have under way a serious nuclear development program. Others are in much earlier stages. U.S. nuclear weapons should be able to deter nuclear threats to U.S. interests in the region, but the existence of indigenous nuclear capabilities would create enormous uncertainties and additional complexities.

ELEMENTS OF A POLITICAL
AND MILITARY STRATEGY

What should be the elements of political and military strategy to protect the interests of the United States and its allies in Southwest Asia, and what specific steps should be taken to implement such a strategy? With the United States taking the lead, such strategies have been designed for Western Europe and East Asia. These strategies have included military, political, economic, and cultural elements. In Southwest Asia, more than in the other regions, these elements tend to be in conflict.

Military: The Balance

The military balance in Southwest Asia will be important both in peace and in war. Even if the likelihood of a Soviet military attack is small, the military prospects in the event of such an invasion will influence peacetime political attitudes. The United States faces a number of obvious disadvantages in achieving a military balance. The Soviets (or at least the Soviet borders) are much closer to the region than is the United States. It is easier to shut down the oil production and export facilities than it is to preserve them, and the Soviets could do almost as much damage by destroying as by controlling them. The Soviets have large military bases in South Yemen and in Ethiopia, both relatively close to the Persian Gulf. And Soviet military equipment, with the influence and potential leverage that it implies, is present in a number of the major nonaligned states in the region, including Iraq and Syria.

Still, the advantages are not all on the Soviet side. The United States can (and now does) dominate the seas adjacent to the region. Indeed, U.S. naval power in the Arabian Sea outclasses anything the Soviets have there now or could realistically bring to bear. This naval power can also be supplemented by some French, British, and Australian naval units. The United States can probably count on military help from some countries in the region, acting in self-defense.

Another factor that could favor the United States and its allies is the location of Turkey athwart the Soviet invasion routes from the Caucasus to the Persian Gulf. The availability of enhanced eastern Turkish bases for Southwest Asian contingencies as well as improvements in Turkish military capabilities in eastern Turkey would have to give the Soviets pause. But the Turks are not inclined to participate in planning for Southwest Asian contingencies in the absence of both a U.S. and a NATO-wide commitment to their defense in the event of Soviet retaliation. Finally, there is considerable distance and difficult terrain—choke points, mountains, and few roads and railroads—between the Soviet borders and the Persian Gulf itself. It is more than 600 miles from the Soviet Transcaucasus to the Persian Gulf. If opposing forces could be interposed, and interdiction accomplished early, a Soviet advance could be severely slowed. The prospect of extended ground conflict with U.S. forces and of geographic expansion and intensification of the conflict would help to deter the Soviets from military aggression in Southwest Asia, as it does in Europe.

What military strategies are available to the United States for the defense of the oil fields in the Persian Gulf region? One is to hold a line along the Zagros Mountains in western and southwestern Iran. Another is to build an enclave around the oil fields. Each of these would require ground and air forces based in the region as well as naval surface vessels, submarines, and sea-based aircraft to protect the sea lines of communication. Another strategy, the so-called naval strategy for Southwest Asia, calls for the use of aircraft carriers and other surface ships (including battleships) with cruise missiles and naval guns to defend the oil fields. One problem with such a strategy is that the Persian Gulf is too confined to bring aircraft carriers into it prudently, in the face of the threat from land-based air power around its periphery. Even if that risk were accepted, an enclave (let alone a Zagros Mountain line hundreds of miles away) could not be supported without land-based air power and substantial ground forces.

What is the overall military balance in Southwest Asia? It is not favorable to the United States. U.S. military capability and potential there has been built up quickly since the late 1970s, but not nearly enough to produce prospective force ratios even as good as those that exist in Europe. It is doubtful that the U.S. forces rapidly deployable to a Zagros Mountain line any time before at least the late 1980s could hold back a determined Soviet attack there. This means that at least for a time the Soviets could see less military risk in an adventure in Southwest Asia than in Europe. And the prize would be nearly as great, because control of Persian Gulf oil would make it possible to dominate Western Europe and Japan.

The chances of early Soviet military action along these lines are nevertheless low. The risks to them, though not as high as those of an attack on Western Europe, are still considerable. Moreover, the Soviets probably see as less risky certain political moves that also offer them the prospect of a greatly improved position—perhaps even dominance—in Southwest Asia.

Military: Deterrence of a Soviet Invasion

Though a Soviet military invasion of Southwest Asia is one of the less probable adverse contingencies in the area, it is the most threatening. Both its inherent gravity and the likelihood that it would lead to or be associated with a war outside the region make deterrence of such an action a high priority of U.S. policy in the region and the central goal of U.S. military policy there.

Some have argued that Persian Gulf oil is so obviously vital to the industrialized democracies that the Soviet Union will be deterred by that very fact from a military move to acquire control, knowing that a Western response could in one way or another lead to thermonuclear war. The fact that the supply of oil is so vital is certainly one element of deterrence, and it reduces the probability of certain Soviet military actions. But it is notable that in Western Europe, where U.S. interests are at least as vital, the United States and its allies have been and remain unwilling to rely entirely on that fact for deterrence of Soviet attack. The United States deploys conventional and nuclear forces there to counter Soviet military power and to demonstrate its commitment to the defense of its vital interests. It also engages in an explicit political-military commitment in Europe in the form of the NATO alliance.

A vital U.S. interest in Southwest Asia must likewise be accompanied by political support and military strength there or nearby. Otherwise, the Soviets, by a quick military success in the region, could suddenly and shockingly change what they call the "correlation of forces" so much that the coherence of U.S. relationships there—and even throughout the world—might dissolve quickly. Then the United States and its allies would probably have to use military force to have any chance of dislodging the Soviet Union. Those steps would represent a substantial increase in the intensity and the danger of the situation.

In the absence of available actions in the region itself, the threat of major retaliation elsewhere is also not a very convincing deterrent to Soviet attack, let alone to political and military encroachment. The United States could respond to Soviet attack in the Persian Gulf by deliberate military action in areas of Soviet interest or vulnerability other than Europe—the Soviet fleet, Cuba, or the Soviet base in Aden. Having the capabilities for such an action and making the threat part of U.S. declaratory policy might enhance deterrence, but it is hard to believe that the loss of Cuba and the end of the economic drain that its $3 billion-a-year Soviet subsidy entails, or even the loss of the ability to operate civil and military surface ships on the high seas, would damage the Soviets anywhere near as much as the loss of free access to Persian Gulf oil would damage the industrialized democracies.

Deterrence will ultimately depend not only on Soviet perception of vital Western interests in the region and of an inherent risk of escalation of any conflict but also on the military and political balance in the region. The political balance will in turn be more favorable, the more the United States and its allies are able, and are seen to be able, to offset Soviet military capabilities. All these considerations argue for a U.S. military capability to hold off a Soviet attack, at least to the extent of being able to prevent a quick overrunning of the oil fields in the western Persian Gulf region. This concept of deterrence is similar to the one the United States holds in Western Europe, though the great political and military differences between the two regions make the appropriate detailed strategies different as well.

Despite U.S. attempts to build a strategic consensus, most of the inhabitants of Southwest Asia do not regard the East-West conflict as their principal security problem, nor do they have anything like the conventional forces required to oppose a Soviet military attack. The lack of indigenous capability means that a larger relative force contribution would be required of the United States, and perhaps of other Western countries, to establish acceptable ratios of forces with respect to the Soviet Union. And nuclear deterrence, in the form of an expectation that conflict would escalate to nuclear war, is less effective in Southwest Asia than in Europe.

But, in part because Southwest Asia is less an East-West arena, the political and military unknowns the Soviets would face in an invasion are also greater than in Europe. The relative likelihood of internal or Soviet-inspired political upheavals within the major countries, or of conflicts between those countries, as against a direct Soviet military attack, is much greater than in Europe (even though a Soviet military move in Southwest Asia is itself also more likely than one in Europe). And the likely negative political impact in much of the region if the United States pushed for a major military presence on the ground could dangerously increase those already greater internal threats. A limited Soviet military action could polarize the region against the Soviets, or it could frighten the nations of the region into accommodation. In sum, these factors make a U.S.-Soviet force ratio in Southwest Asia as high as the NATO–Warsaw Pact force ratio in Europe both less necessary and less feasible.

If the United States could arrange to station even one or two divisions in the region, along with one or two wings of fighter and attack aircraft, this would serve as a major deterrent to a quick Soviet military grab for the Persian Gulf. The ground forces could be interposed against a land attack across the 600 miles between the Soviet border and the Gulf, and the air wings could be used to prevent an assault by airborne troops. Such a deployment might become feasible sometime during the 1980s, but at present the political disadvantages of such a step in the region—if it could even be arranged at all—probably outweigh its military value. Until that changes, the industrialized democracies must rely on rapid deployment of U.S. forces—and Western European forces, to the degree available—into facilities previously prepared in the region, on rotation of ground and air forces in exercises of modest length, and on naval forces stationed offshore, many hundreds of miles from the important areas of the region. With or without permanent deployments in the region, most of the forces to slow a major Soviet attack—two or three divisions and four or five air wings—would have to come from reinforcements. Those would have to be moved by airlift or fast sealift from the United States or from Western Europe on the basis of intelligence and other indications warning of such a Soviet buildup.

In any of these scenarios, the response of the nations and peoples of the region to a Soviet invasion—in the form of political activity, conventional military action, or guerrilla operations and harassment—would have a major effect—perhaps the decisive effect—on the outcome. The Iranian forces, for example, especially the Revolutionary Guards, have shown in the war with Iraq that they can defend their country very effectively. The Soviet Union is not Iraq, but Afghan insurgents have demonstrated that Soviet forces can be impeded by indigenous capabilities, given determination and a knowledgeable use of difficult terrain. If the Soviets were to invade Iran in a drive toward the Gulf, the Iranian response would greatly influence U.S. political decisions on how to react as well as U.S. ability to succeed in repelling a Soviet attack.

Military: Prevention of Soviet Political Domination

Designing a strategy to deter or counter Soviet efforts to gain political domination of Southwest Asia by infiltration or other nonmilitary means is still more complex. Inevitably, the Soviets will pursue such efforts. They will use internal communist parties, the animosities and aspirations of such ethnic minorities as the Kurds and Azerbaijanis in Iran, conflicts between the states of the region (Israel and the Arab states, Iraq and Iran, Syria and Jordan), opposition to westernization, proxies (South Yemen, Cuba), arms transfers, and other tools in whatever mixture suits the situation and their view of the world and of history.

The United States cannot prevent such attempts; it can only seek to reduce their effectiveness and to respond. The role of U.S. military capabilities in meeting this challenge is limited but significant. A U.S. military presence, an ability to introduce military forces into the region, arms transfers, and joint military planning and exercises with countries in the region can all be influential in dampening regional conflicts, helping the important states of the region to achieve internal stability, and encouraging political resistance to Soviet influence. A U.S. military capability seen as usable in the region will also affect Soviet perceptions of the costs and gains of political penetration.

At the same time, and in contrast with the situations in Western Europe and East Asia, any significant U.S. military presence could have extremely adverse political effects, especially if it is mistimed or if it is perceived to be directed at the countries of the region or at control of rather than access to their resources. Many in the region object to westernization and the role of the United States as Israel's guarantor. They remember the history of European domination of their region. Consequently, even if the resources were available for U.S. military deployments or other military actions clearly sufficient to prevent Soviet political domination or military conquest, they would probably have to be scaled down and stretched out to avoid counterproductive political effects that would outweigh the direct and indirect benefits. The United States instead must exploit more fully the political value of Islamic resistance to communism and nationalist opposition to Soviet hegemony; depend on its diplomatic skills to increase its influence in the area, especially in its role as the only nation that can put nonmilitary pressure on Israel and also influence the key Arab states; and provide the economic, technological, and managerial assistance with which only the industrialized democracies can promote development in the region. The Soviets have demonstrated in the region and elsewhere that they either lack or are unable to apply these tools of development.

Some factors in the regional situation are a real aid in resisting Soviet political and military penetration. But some of the same factors make it more difficult to contain other political threats and instabilities. The central feature of the region is its Islamic faith and culture. In general these produce a strong resistance to communism as well as to westernization and/or modernization, but the Islamic revolution in Iran produced political chaos. The sense of individual nationhood is growing in many of the countries of the region, and this nationalism is often expressed in anti-Soviet terms; but many nationalist governments are also stridently anti-American. The region as a whole is rich, and properly used, its oil riches could stabilize it; but the richest countries are the least populous and the least able to defend their own independence. This situation contributes to regional instability. Finally, Israel, as a democratic nation and the strongest military power in the region, contributes elements of strength to the Western position; but its conflicts with its Arab neighbors are at the same time a major element of regional instability.

The United States will have many difficulties in building a security framework in the region. Some commentators have questioned whether the political infrastructure necessary for a security framework can be put together in a region with so many internal conflicts. In contrast, the security framework in Western Europe and in the Pacific after World War II was built upon nations with a strong heritage of literacy and technical training, with existing governmental institutions, and with industrialized economies. But the rivalries that had existed between Germany and France, or between Korea and Japan, were as long-standing and virulent as any in Southwest Asia. In the late 1940s, Great Britain turned away from Western Europe, and the communist parties in France and Italy gained 30 percent of the vote. The Western European framework did not seem so easy to build then. The task is more difficult in Southwest Asia, but that does not make it hopeless. It is hard to envisage the United States sponsoring a regional alliance like NATO there or signing as explicit a security treaty with most of the nations of Southwest Asia as it has with Japan, at least in the near future; but the United States has no choice but to try to create a security framework—loose and shifting though it may be—with the nations of the region.

Economic and Military Assistance

In designing a security framework for Southwest Asia, the United States will have to orchestrate the provision of economic development assistance to those more populous and militarily important nations of the region that do not have the economic resources that come from oil production. These nations include Egypt, Turkey, and Pakistan. The countries of Western Europe, Japan, and the oil-rich states can all contribute to this assistance. The United States should combine its economic and developmental assistance with judicious arms sales.

U.S. arms sales to both Israel and the moderate Arab states will be a major tool in building this security framework and in reaching a resolution of the Arab-Israeli dispute. But the history of arms sales to Saudi Arabia illustrates that such sales can be a double-edged sword. The question is how to tailor arms sales packages for both Saudi Arabia (and the other Arab states friendly to the United States) and Israel to meet any reasonable set of U.S. policies toward each. The problem—and it is a serious one—arises when those policies conflict, whether because of Israeli and Saudi attitudes or because the United States has failed to reconcile its own objectives sufficiently.

In the end, U.S. arms sales policy must be determined, where there are conflicts, by what the United States considers as its own security interests, broadly construed to include all the military, diplomatic, economic, and moral factors. U.S. and Israeli security interests are inextricably intertwined. So are U.S. and Saudi interests. The United States cannot decide security policies unilaterally for either nation, but it should take the lead in fashioning an overall security framework in the region.

Increasing strains in U.S.-Israeli relations have marked the years since the Israeli-Egyptian peace treaty of 1979, as the U.S. Government's perception of its interests in the region has conflicted more markedly with the Israeli Government's perception of its interests. Either may judge its own interests wrongly, but the conflict in perception is a sure recipe for strain. The Begin government's perception of Israeli interests has appeared to include the functional equivalent of annexation of the West Bank as the only reliable insurance against the emergence between Israel and Jordan of an armed, radical Palestinian state dedicated to Israel's destruction. To this end Israel has expanded Jewish settlement on the West Bank and deposed elected Arab officials. But the conflicts arising from the unsatisfied aspirations of the Palestinian Arabs for a homeland of their own cannot be solved by such Israeli actions; nor can they be solved by Israeli proposals to designate Jordan as the Palestinian Arab state, thus overthrowing a regime that could play a constructive role in the evolution of Israel's relations with its neighbors. The U.S. perception is that movement toward a solution of the problem of Palestinian rights and self-rule is needed to end the nearly four decades of wars between Israel and its neighbors, to avoid some probable further dangers to stability in the Persian Gulf region (including more oil cutoffs) as well as among Israel's immediate neighbors, and to deprive the Soviets of an important tool in their attempt to dominate Southwest Asia.

The Camp David agreements left the outcome of negotiations on these issues open for five years, while committing the parties first to negotiate autonomy for the West Bank and Gaza and withdrawal of Israel's military forces there to smaller areas as required for Israel's security. That appears to me still to be the most promising basis for peace—though events of the 1980s suggest that optimism is not at all in order. Implementing the Camp David agreements for Gaza could have been a useful initial step, but time has now probably made it impossible.

The Reagan proposals of 1982 indicated that the United States could not support either Israeli annexation or an independent Palestinian state but would support an autonomous Palestinian entity in federation with Jordan. Territorial boundaries, Israeli security provisions in the West Bank, and the future of Jerusalem would have to be worked out. This general approach is consistent with the Camp David agreements and the views I expressed above. The task is to work out an arrangement in which territory occupied by Israel in the 1967 war would be traded for peace, defensible boundaries, and guaranteed Israeli security, insofar as that is possible in the real world. This is the only formula that has any chance of long-term stability. It will require the participation of Jordan, probably Saudi Arabia, and other Arab states, as well as Egypt and representatives of the Palestinian Arabs. The United States must continue to play a leading role. The Western Europeans, through their peacekeeping forces and their political influence in the Arab world, can also play a significant role. It could be a supportive one, but European views of the region and of Western interests in it have frequently differed from U.S. views. The role the Soviets will play remains uncertain. During the war in Lebanon in the summer of 1982, they were hardly visible. But they have interests and clients in the region, so they cannot be ignored.

An alternative path is an attempt by the superpowers to compel their clients to accept an imposed solution. That approach is even more likely to fail than the course charted by President Carter in

1978 and 1979 and by President Reagan in 1982. Or the states and factions of the region could be left to fight it out among themselves. But the area Israel and its neighbors occupy is itself of great strategic significance. Events there also have a major effect on the Persian Gulf. The interests of the industrialized world and of both superpowers are involved. Thus, even in the unlikely event that a hands-off policy would lead to anything but chaos and disaster, it could not be followed. The United States should continue to take the initiative in moving the participants toward resolution of the disputes, including the issue of Palestinian home rule. Only the United States can provide the assurances to Israel that are necessary—but perhaps even then not sufficient—to gain Israeli acquiescence in any such development.

AN APPROACH TO U.S. POLICY

U.S. security policy in Southwest Asia must take into account this complex set of interacting threats, tensions, conflicts, power centers, and histories. Synthesizing such a policy has proved, not surprisingly, to be a major undertaking. The expressions of that policy by the Carter administration and by the Reagan administration show as many resemblances as differences, but even with a policy consensus within the United States, carrying out that policy will be an enormous task. If it is to be managed at all, the United States must produce an international diplomatic and political framework, both among the nations of the region and among U.S. allies, and take primary responsibility for creating a strengthened military capability. However necessary they are, it is not clear how possible many of these actions will prove to be.

The United States must implement a short-term and medium-term energy program—and an encompassing economic program. Overall, the United States should reduce its total oil imports to 10 percent or less of consumption (even though that would not be economically efficient) and thereby insulate itself somewhat from the direct effects of the price increases and shortages that would result from a cutoff of Persian Gulf oil. Continuing major efforts in conservation and a new effort in synthetic fuels both seem to have dropped from the national agenda during the Reagan administration. Both are vital. Otherwise, the dependence on Persian Gulf oil that hangs heavily over the 1980s will persist through the 1990s and beyond.

But even with a successful domestic energy program, the United States would still have reasons for maintaining a capability for the projection of military forces into the Persian Gulf region—the still important matters of the protection of access to oil for its allies and the general containment of Soviet expansion. The United States must, therefore, increase its military activities in Southwest Asia. It has taken the first step by setting up a new joint military command called the Rapid Deployment Force to provide military planning in peacetime and to exercise operational control in wartime. The United States has deployed maritime prepositioning ships at Diego Garcia in the Indian Ocean. These ships contain the equipment and a month's supplies for a reinforced Marine brigade and several Air Force fighter and attack squadrons. They could combine with ground forces and aircraft—which could be flown into the region within a week or ten days—to make a total force of about 15,000 to 20,000. The United States is maintaining one or two carrier battle groups and other naval forces on station in the Arabian Sea, thereby dominating the naval situation there. U.S. airborne warning and control aircraft operate in Saudi Arabia. These would be able to monitor and control operations of U.S. F-15 aircraft that could be flown into the region within a matter of days, thus providing air superiority in the Persian Gulf region. In three successive years, the United States has carried out modest joint exercises in the region with Egypt and with other nations. Design, construction, and expansion of military facilities has begun around the region—in Egypt, in Kenya, in Somalia, and in Oman. For the longer term, the United States has begun major expansions of its airlift and sealift capabilities.

All of these activities must be substantially increased. The United States should seek to preposition military equipment and supplies for air and ground forces in the region. To the extent that it is politically feasible, the local facilities should be built up beyond what the indigenous military forces require. U.S. air and naval forces should be rotated periodically into the region for exercises so that some are there at all times. More frequent and more substantial joint ground exercises should be undertaken with the friendly countries of the region. But even after such measures are taken, the deterrence of Soviet military adventurism will depend largely on Soviet concern that such action would lead to a direct U.S.-Soviet confrontation, which would in turn lead to a military conflict of unknowable intensity and location.

What numbers and what kinds of military force should the United States plan to be able to deploy in Southwest Asia? A reasonable short-term goal (say by 1985) would be the ability within three weeks to deploy a total of two or three divisions, including stationed forces and reinforcements. U.S. longer-term goals for the late 1980s should be the ability to provide forces of double that size. Corresponding tactical air power goals would be three or four wings of fighter aircraft

in the short term and more than twice that force in the long term—
to arrive within a week or ten days and to be sustained indefinitely.
In other words, in a conflict in Southwest Asia the United States
may well ultimately need to be able to deploy a number of ground
force divisions (though a smaller number of air wings) comparable
to the number programmed in *reinforcements* for Europe. But Southwest
Asia is more than twice as far away, so the task is more than twice
as great, even in purely logistical terms. The political problems would
be still greater.

The United States should seek to strengthen the political infrastructure of the region by extending economic development aid to
the poor and less stable countries and by making progress on the
settlement of the Arab-Israeli disputes, which do affect the stability
of the region and the attitudes of all its Islamic countries, rich and
poor, moderate and radical. Another reason for strengthening the
political structure is that threatened countries must be willing—and
must be *seen* to be willing—to fight in their own defense, as the
people of Afghanistan have. The political framework must project
the appearance—and reflect the fact—that the United States is not
trying to dominate the area itself, but only to counter the threat of
Soviet domination.

The United States should be sensitive to the potential adverse
political effects of an increase in its presence in the region. There is
a strong current of opposition to both superpowers. Too visible a
U.S. presence will increase the risk of internal unrest in many nations
of the region. This has led some governments to ask that the United
States not be present at all but somehow be able to appear immediately
with massive military forces at the first indication of an active or
imminent Soviet threat. Unfortunately, this is not possible. To be
able to move rapidly into the region at the first sign of such action,
the United States needs to preposition equipment and supplies and
to maintain a modest handling capability to receive U.S. forces. Little
of this need be in the form of a U.S. military presence on the ground.
Contract personnel and indigenous support could be made available
instead. As evidence of U.S. commitment and as a deterrent to the
Soviets, even a small U.S. presence on the ground would be useful.
But at present the adverse political effects in the countries of the
region probably outweigh those benefits. Even a small permanent
presence, for example, could create major political problems in and
around the nation in which it was located. Small peacekeeping or
symbolic forces, such as the U.S. force sent to Lebanon in 1982,
need not raise such concerns. They have little military value for use
in the region as a whole, but some political value—and some political

risk. Over time it should be possible to ease fears that such a U.S. force would be directed against those nations or that the United States would use the presence of such forces to gain a predominant political influence in the region by intimidation.

Adverse political change could come about in Saudi Arabia and the United Arab Emirates as a result of several factors, including the interaction of the indigenous populations with large numbers of foreigners from many countries in the work force; and conflict between upholders of traditional Islamic culture and proponents of western-ization. Conflicts could possibly occur within the Saudi royal family, especially between its different generations, or in the modernized Saudi Army and Air Force, which are oriented to defend against outside attack, and the National Guard, which is oriented to preserve internal security. A Western intervention after a change in a Persian Gulf state could well polarize internal attitudes and forces against the intervening power. A quick Western intervention before such a coup succeeded, in response to a request from what was seen as a legitimate authority resisting such a change, might be the only way to save the situation.

One sensitive issue is whether the United States should plan to protect the oil fields against internal or regional threats. Any explicit commitment of this sort is more likely to upset and anger the oil suppliers than to reassure them. The determinant of a potential U.S. response should be whether, in the event of such a threat, a legitimate regime asks for assistance and whether it and its people are themselves prepared to fight to that end. Such situations could arise, so it is appropriate for the United States to prepare plans and maintain the corresponding capabilities. The required capabilities are much less than, and somewhat different from, the capabilities required to counter the threat of a massive Soviet invasion.

But two cautionary notes are in order. First, such Western forces—even the larger ones needed to counter the Soviets—are unlikely to be able to keep the oil flowing in the quite different circumstances of a legitimate regime's wishing to turn it off. Second, the differing but related attitudes of the Persian Gulf states toward being defended from Soviet forces and being intimidated by Western forces make an explicitly declared policy on defense against local threats unwise.

Given the value of Israel as a democratic, moderately industrialized, and militarily strong ally in the region and the need to promote an Arab-Israeli settlement and move toward a resolution of the issue of Palestinian rights, what are the prospects? The Arab-Israeli conflict has already led to five wars and many other clashes. It is unlikely that a sudden peaceful settlement will be reached. Probably the best the United States can hope for—and encourage—is a series of complex ameliorations, trying to avoid catastrophe for a few years at a time. The progress between Egypt and Israel is an example of such a step, unfortunately not yet matched in other directions. U.S. policy should be to oppose actions and attitudes that impede further progress. These include Israeli moves toward de facto annexations, such as expansion of Israeli settlements on the West Bank or the continued presence of Israeli forces in Lebanon in a de facto partition of that country with Syria. They also include Palestine Liberation Organization (PLO) terrorism and the refusal of the PLO and Arab governments to recognize Israel's right to exist peacefully within secure borders. In the end, the United States may have to be prepared to station some forces in the region as part of a general guarantee of boundaries.

In 1980, President Carter made a U.S. commitment to deny control of the region's resources to the Soviet Union. President Reagan in 1981 extended this commitment to include internal threats, but in a way that may have frightened U.S. friends in the region more than it reassured them. To carry out this commitment, and to retain the support of the American people for this commitment, some Western European participation in the security framework will be required. After all, the Western Europeans and the Japanese depend on Persian Gulf oil much more than does the United States. France has significant forces in the Indian Ocean, and Great Britain is considering commitment of modest forces. These are steps in the right direction. Others among the U.S. allies will also need to participate. Such participation will in turn introduce more complexity, because it will make increased consultation necessary on political as well as military matters connected with the region. Various allies may have or may think they have different interests, or they may have different estimates of the situation. But all U.S. allies must cooperate in providing enroute staging and airlift and sealift capacity to increase the capability for military response in the region. And because much of the U.S. reinforcement capability that would have gone to Europe will, in the case of simultaneous threats to Western Europe and Southwest Asia, have to go to Southwest Asia instead, U.S. allies in Europe and in the Far East will have to increase their own military efforts to substitute for those reinforcements.

It will be necessary to balance these overlapping, often conflicting factors to create the political and economic structures and military capabilities that together will constitute a security framework for Southwest Asia, including the Persian Gulf region. To do so, in order to deter Soviet military adventurism, contain Soviet political penetration, and help the people who live in the region to stabilize their political and economic situation, is probably the most difficult current challenge to geostrategic and military planning for the United States, and to its international political skill.

9

U.S. Security Interests in Latin America, Sub-Saharan Africa, and Other Third World Areas

U.S. foreign and security policy must also take into account Third World countries outside East and Southwest Asia. As sources of strategic materials, markets for U.S. goods, and strategically important locations, they have become an integral part of the open international economic order the United States seeks to promote, though their political and strategic roles in an international security framework are often more ambiguous. In some cases, their domination by an adversary power could be expected to damage or at least threaten the economic security of the United States. The nature of U.S. relations with individual nations will be strongly conditioned by their geographical position, trade, natural resources, and political traditions. Two areas of particular interest to the United States are Latin America and sub-Saharan Africa.

Both these regions are in themselves complex mixtures. Latin America includes some very poor countries as well as some that are industrializing, for example, Brazil, Mexico, and Venezuela. Argentina and Chile have substantial agricultural and mineral resources, and educated populations; nevertheless they have failed to achieve economic prosperity or political stability. Sub-Saharan Africa contains an enormous diversity of nations whose profiles in many cases reveal

tribal, religious, and political conflicts. Nigeria's oil wealth, the devastating effects of the drought in the Sahel, and the difference between
the mixed economic and somewhat open political systems of the
Ivory Coast and Kenya on the one hand and the Marxist regimes of
the former Portuguese colonies of Angola, Mozambique, and Guinea-
Bissau on the other are all examples of this diversity. Superimposed
on this situation is the racial division in South Africa between the
dominant white minority and the other segments of the population
whose human and political rights are denied.

But there are some similarities both within each of these regions
and between them. In the first place, recognizable democratic institutions are few and far between. Only a handful of the fifty nations
in the two regions permit a free press or regularly hold free elections
between parties of which more than one has a chance to win. Second,
both areas are relatively far from the Soviet Union, making a direct
military threat or Soviet political intervention less likely than in
regions closer to the Soviet Union. U.S. military capability to project
force to these regions is in most cases superior. Both U.S. and Soviet
influence are more likely to be indirect. The Soviet threat will be
effected principally through arms sales, internal subversion, and proxy
attacks by another country in the region.

In many ways, the fate of the countries in these regions lacks the
centrality to U.S. security or to Soviet ambitions that Europe, East
Asia, and Southwest Asia all have. Some analysts have tried to
attribute to southern Africa the same resource importance to the
industrialized democracies as Southwest Asia, citing the very large
fraction of the world's supply of certain nonfuel strategic minerals—
for example, chromium, cobalt, diamonds, gold, and the platinum
group—found there. These resources are indeed important, but the
relatively small scale of annual world trade in them and the relative
ease of substituting for them or exploiting lower-grade ores or more
expensive sources of the same minerals strongly refute the parallel
with oil. International trade in oil amounts to more than $300 billion
a year, while trade in these other minerals constitutes only a few
billion dollars a year. Thus stockpiling and substitution would be
correspondingly easier than for oil.

The location of Latin America in the Western Hemisphere makes
it an area of traditional U.S. security interest, dating back to the
Monroe Doctrine. Even though Buenos Aires is farther from Miami
than Paris is from New York, Central America and the Caribbean
are so close to the United States that the potential presence there
of a major hostile influence, particularly that of the Soviet Union, is
inevitably a matter of major concern. And the effect of what goes

on in Mexico, Central America, and the Caribbean on economic and immigration matters, especially in the southern part of the United States, has been demonstrated repeatedly during the last decade.

Both regions are developing. Both have a history of political instability, race and class injustice, and colonialism—which has persisted to recent times in Africa and to this day has left the perception in Latin America of economic dependence on Europe and the United States. All of these factors make revolutionary rhetoric and action likely in both places. Specifically, in many developing countries of sub-Saharan Africa and Latin America, Marxist-Leninist ideas promise a road to revolution and industrialization. That promise, and even more the demonstrated ability of the Leninist state to keep the individual members of its ruling classes in power over a period of decades, appeal greatly to opposition forces who aspire to power, and to some regimes in power. The political and economic characteristics of these countries are very different from those of Western Europe and much of East Asia. They also differ from those of Southwest Asia, where Islamic tradition exercises a strong influence and wealth derived from petroleum has a profound effect on political and economic development.

Each country, each subregion, and each region must be treated according to its own particular problems. Nevertheless, there are some general principles that should guide U.S. policy. In the first place, political and diplomatic skill are central in dealing with these matters—much more important than the details of U.S. capability for unilateral military action, especially as U.S. military capability to intervene in these regions is and can remain greater than that of the Soviet Union. Such military capability should serve as a sufficient deterrent to direct Soviet military intervention. Consequently, the contest becomes more one of politics, ideology, and economics, in which the goal of the United States is to encourage stability, economic development, and as far as is possible, an evolution of the political systems toward greater democracy and toward peace between the countries of each region.

As previously mentioned, Marxist-Leninist claims are powerful tools for acquiring and consolidating power in these regions of the developing world. Of perhaps even greater importance, however, in conditioning the attitudes of the ruling political classes in the developing countries of Africa and Latin America—whether Marxist or capitalist—is the knowledge that their economic needs can be met only by the industrialized democracies, which possess the material resources, the technology, and the management skills they need if they are to modernize and prosper. The Soviet Union has provided major industrial aid—steel mills, hydroelectric projects—to some developing countries. But the nature of the Soviets' own economic system severely limits the amount of financial and technological assistance they can provide. Soviet management systems in Egypt, in Cuba, in Mozambique, and in North Korea have been a continuing disaster. The Soviets have been considerably more successful in transferring arms to developing countries and in encouraging them to attack their neighbors, but that is of only marginal value to regimes facing severe internal social and economic problems. The failure of the Soviets to provide credible and effective nonmilitary assistance in these regions suggests that the peaceful economic penetration of Africa and Latin America by the Soviet Union is not a major concern.

Certainly political skill is of central importance in taking advantage of the fact that the economic needs of these countries can be met only by the industrialized democracies. The essential goal then becomes to encourage economic and political development while preventing or at least containing military adventures sponsored by the Soviets, who use sales or gifts of their military equipment to disruptive elements, or actions by their regional surrogates, to that end.

A frequent goal of U.S. policy in many countries of these regions has been to try to find within the spectrum of political factions a democratic center (whether social democrats, Christian democrats, or capitalist democrats) that the United States would be comfortable supporting. In this the United States has usually been unsuccessful. The level of political and economic development in these countries and the nature of their political traditions have not been such as to nurture such a democratic center, enable it to achieve power, or keep power if it did achieve it. It has proven impossible to maintain such regimes with U.S. support alone, or even with U.S. intervention, just as it has proven impossible to maintain repressive regimes in power over an extended period through U.S. support or intervention. The possibility of gradual development toward more democratic forms of government remains, and it should be encouraged by the United States, but without illusions that it can come quickly, if at all, during the rest of this century.

Thus U.S. interests will probably best be served by struggling along in support of the least bad alternatives to be found among the political leaders of Third World countries, helping these countries economically, and putting some pressure on their governments to democratize gradually, in the cautious belief that failure to progress along those lines will alienate whole populations. But U.S. policymakers should not assume that those in opposition who say that they are against the older forms of repression would, on achieving power, themselves be less repressive. In many cases they have proven to be more so. Some U.S. opinion makers have assumed that political leaders or aspirants in developing countries who dislike U.S. influence are by that evidence lovers of freedom. That has also proven to be false more often than not. Yet there have been and will be right-wing regimes so oppressive that the proper U.S. stance is to let them go under, despite their professed pro-U.S. and anti-Soviet stance, and take the chance of trying to achieve a bearable relationship with a successor regime rather than accept so distasteful an association on the poor chance that the right-wing regime can stay in power with U.S. help. In other regions, in the cases of China and Yugoslavia, seeking good relations with communist successor regimes was not initially U.S. policy. But mutually helpful, though prickly, relations have been achieved as those regimes came to see the Soviets as a greater threat to their independence than the United States, and the United States came to realize that their geopolitical orientation was more important to the United States than their professed ideology.

Each case must be looked at separately and in detail. Adherence to Soviet views in international affairs, denial of human rights within a country (whether by a left-wing or a right-wing government), and economic policies likely to abort development should all be considered as negatives in forming U.S. attitudes toward a particular government. The difficult question is what relative weight to give these criteria. U.S. political relations with a developing country ought to be influenced most heavily by that country's behavior—peaceful, subversive, or aggressive—toward other countries, and especially toward the United States and its friends. Its behavior toward its own citizens should also be a factor. But the U.S. Government cannot know enough about the proper course of internal political evolution, especially in very different cultures, to try to shape that evolution. Thus, doctrinal Marxism on the left or lack of a two-party representative democracy on the right should be considered less central in determining U.S. attitudes than human rights and international alignments.

In southern Africa, almost all of the regimes are repressive. The Republic of South Africa is run by and for a large white minority, oppressing the largely black and Coloured majority. The racial injustice there makes that country even more liable to a tragic future than the other countries in the region and less liable to influence by U.S. actions. The United States should recognize that in most of those other countries, a black majority is politically repressed by a black minority, which at the same time usually treats the white and Asian minorities badly and often professes a Marxist orientation.

The United States is unlikely to be able to contribute as much to the solution of the problems in southern Africa as can some of its allies (as, for example, Great Britain did in Zimbabwe). In attempting to exercise any influence the United States should appreciate and weigh the diversity, complexity, and difficulty of the region, the likelihood that outsiders will be singed if not burned, the relatively limited U.S. economic interest, and the possibility of preserving that interest better by dealing primarily in economic terms. The United States should thus show a relatively low economic and political profile in the region. It should make clear its willingness to work even with regimes in the area that label themselves Marxist, provided that they do not become—or are prepared to move away from being—willing instruments of Soviet power. The United States should also make clear the unacceptability of South African racism by disallowing any military relations with that country and limiting, though not eliminating, economic ones. Finally, the United States should work with its Western European allies to find temporary solutions that will facilitate the ultimate independence of Namibia and use its limited economic relations to press South Africa (without optimism as to the results) toward a gradual opening up of its political system.

What tools does the United States have in influencing the behavior of these developing nations? Economic assistance is clearly one. Arms sales policies are another. The interest of developing countries in the life-style, culture, and even ideology of the United States—often a mixture of fascination and revulsion—is a third. It is truly a disgrace that U.S. official foreign aid is only a fraction of a percent of U.S. GNP. U.S. private investment is also an important tool for development that must be continued and even increased. But feeding the starving and helping the poorest people in the poorest countries improve their agricultural production and their capabilities in light and home industry are important needs that cannot be met fully by private investment. It is unlikely that such assistance will ever be popular among the U.S. electorate. But an important test of the statesmanship and the true dedication to peace and to national security of any U.S. president and any member of Congress is whether they support increases in such aid and try to educate the electorate about its value, even if such support is unlikely to help them politically.

The United States has correctly shown some hesitation in selling advanced arms, suitable for use in conflict between neighbors, to nations in regions where such sales would be more likely to encourage than to deter such conflicts. Such a policy is in principle correct, even though it has sometimes failed. In the mid-1960s, for example, the United States declined to sell jet fighter and attack aircraft in

South America in the correct belief that none of those countries needed them to defend themselves against their neighbors. Unfortunately, the consequence is that though there are few supersonic U.S. jet fighters in the inventories of these South American countries, there are many Soviet, French, and British jet fighters. When it becomes clear that others are selling such advanced arms, the United States can appropriately ease its prohibitions.

The United States should be prepared—if other criteria are met— to sell advanced arms where there is an outside threat, particularly one supplied or encouraged by the Soviets or their surrogates, be they Cubans in Latin America, Vietnamese in Southeast Asia, or Cubans, Libyans, or Eastern Europeans in Africa. If a government meets some reasonable criteria of legitimacy and acceptability, the United States should not stand by and see it overthrown because its internal opponents were able to receive arms from the Soviet Union, directly or indirectly, while the government itself was unable to receive them from the United States. That would run counter to both U.S. security interests and the interests of the inhabitants themselves. The Somoza government of Nicaragua, for example, did not meet the criteria of legitimacy and acceptability. The Duarte government of El Salvador did appear to meet them. That is less true of the subsequent regime dominated by d'Aubuisson, despite its victory in an election of restricted choices, in light of its actions to rescind land reform laws and the uncertainty of its intentions with respect to right-wing terror.

Such arms sales and economic help are unlikely by themselves to preserve acceptable governments that are under pressure unless those governments achieve or preserve legitimacy by sufficient economic success and political reform. That makes it appropriate for the United States to impose some modest requirements for such an economic and political program as a condition for the continuation of arms sales. Admittedly, the U.S. judgment about what program is likely to improve the chances of stability and political improvement is less well informed, as well as less biased, than that of the indigenous government. That makes it difficult to discontinue arms sales if the government fails to meet these conditions. Sometimes the United States has overdone its fine-tuning of controls—in El Salvador in 1980 the United States held up the dispatch of one helicopter and three military advisers—in order to demand some particular (occasionally unspecified) action from a recipient.

But the general approach is appropriate. In its relations with other countries, the United States should consider violations of human rights—especially torture, government terror, and racial or religious persecution, as well as lack of opportunity for political expression. It should also take into account the geostrategic importance of the particular country; the regional political and military situation in the region; the extent of its own leverage on, or dependence on, the nation; the other government's attitude toward U.S. and Soviet international policies; and the probable nature and evolution of a successor regime.

The attitude of another government toward the Soviet Union should not be the sole factor in determining U.S. responses to human rights violations. The anti-Sovietism of the right-wing Somoza regime damaged the United States more than it did the Soviet Union. The United States was never tempted to support the anti-Sovietism of the left-wing Hoxha regime in Albania, because anti-Hoxha Yugoslavia was more important to the United States, because Albania remained equally anti-American, and because Albania is especially repressive even in comparison with other Marxist-Leninist regimes. To take another case, the PRC's ability to tie down considerable Soviet military might, and the benefits this brings to U.S. foreign and military policy, call for a degree of U.S.-PRC cooperation despite internal repression in the PRC, which the United States cannot realistically expect to change by a carrot-and-stick approach to economic cooperation or military sales and aid.

In many cases, U.S. allies can exercise influence on one or another of the countries of the developing world more appropriately than can the United States—in the form of economic aid, arms transfers, or political influence. Past political ties—even when they were those of colonialism—or current economic or cultural influence, or simply the need to share tasks can all be offered in one case or another as arguments for such a course. It ought to be followed, even though it has the inevitable drawback of greater complication, and in the full knowledge that U.S. views and those of its allies will often differ on a particular situation. French equanimity about, or even support of, Marxist-Leninist revolutionaries in Central America is unlikely to be matched by a similar equanimity about such movements in their own former colonies, with which they continue to maintain close economic and political ties. Thus in Central America, France is not a suitable intermediary for U.S. interests, but in western or central Africa it is.

Other friendly Western Hemisphere governments have as great an interest in Central America as the United States does, and the United States should be prepared to modify its views and actions somewhat in order to gain their support and participation in political, economic, and military moves. Even some hedging of Western bets through support of leftist insurgents by a U.S. ally has been suggested as valuable. That is too clever by half. But it would be a great mistake for the United States to fail to encourage the skills and abilities of its allies and friends where they are appropriate in these geographical areas. It would be a worse one if U.S.-allied differences in these geographical areas resulted in allied disunity in the even more critical geographical areas of Europe, East Asia, and Southwest Asia or in such functional areas as international economic policy.

10

Cross-Cutting Military Issues

In defining a national security policy for the 1980s and the 1990s, the United States must address a number of military issues that cut across individual regions. War at sea poses special problems and must be planned for. Conflicts—or crises that threaten to become conflicts—that take place on many fronts at once also require special consideration.

NAVAL FORCES AND NAVAL WAR

The advent of the nuclear age and its evolution over the past four decades have produced a curious combination of effects on the purpose and function of naval forces. Nuclear submarines armed with ballistic missiles are the most secure strategic retaliatory force. The existence of massive stockpiles of nuclear weapons has overarched naval force, as it has other conventional forces, and become the ultimate arbiter of any war. At the same time, paradoxically, the existence of many nuclear weapons on both sides, and especially of parity in strategic nuclear capability, serves to deter nuclear war. This means that conventional war of some length might possibly occur, even between nuclear powers. In the nuclear age, conventional wars among states other than the superpowers, between a nuclear power and a nonnuclear power, or between the superpowers through the use of proxies are all possible—indeed, they have happened. Escalation of a conventional war between the major nuclear powers into a nuclear war might be avoided if two conditions are met: The command-and-control systems hold up, and the alternatives for either nuclear power are not reduced to unacceptable defeat or the use of nuclear weapons. In any conventional war, naval forces will play a part—and it can be an important part. But surface ships are not only vulnerable to nuclear attack; they are also increasingly vulnerable to conventional attack. The British fleet's losses in the Falkland Islands conflict were a reminder of how the well-known dangers to surface vessels from land-based air attack have been compounded by the introduction of precision-guided air-to-surface weapons.

During the 1960s, a good deal of emphasis was placed on the possibility of a war between the United States and the Soviet Union that was confined to the sea. Scenarios were devised, and potential naval responses were planned that could punish the Soviet Union for certain nonnuclear attacks (such as one against Berlin, too isolated to defend conventionally, or against some neutral territory that was not absolutely critical to Western security or survival but that warranted some kind of U.S. military response).

The idea of a U.S.-Soviet war confined to the sea is intellectually appealing, especially because the United States has advantages over the Soviet Union in naval forces. But relying on such a response raises a number of practical issues. First, even if the United States were able to wage such a war successfully and sweep Soviet naval forces and shipping from the seas without initiating a nuclear escalation, the Soviet economy depends only modestly on commerce from outside the Soviet empire. Such a defeat would be more of a punishment to Soviet self-esteem and prestige abroad than to the Soviet economy or Soviet ability to apply military force on the Eurasian landmass. It is precisely *because* access to the seas is not vital to Soviet national interest that such a war might not escalate. Second, Soviet land-based air power could pose a major threat to U.S. naval forces at substantial distances from the Soviet Union (for example, in the whole of the Mediterranean). To neutralize that Soviet capability, many war-at-sea scenarios call for U.S. conventional attacks on bases for long-range aircraft inside the Soviet Union. Such scenarios are dubious insofar as they assume that further escalation would not then occur. Surely the Soviets would at least retaliate on U.S. naval bases. Refueled Backfire bombers can reach Clark Field and Subic Bay in the Philippines and even Hawaii from bases on Soviet territory. Soviet retaliation by nuclear attacks on U.S. ships at sea would also be a significant possibility. A U.S. nuclear response against the Soviet fleet would not be of equal military utility, although it could serve the political purpose of demonstrating determination. The United States could be left with the difficult choice of moving up the escalation ladder with a U.S. nuclear attack on naval and air bases in the Soviet Union.

War at sea has also been suggested more recently as a possible "horizontal escalation," by which the United States could deter, or perhaps compensate for, a successful Soviet attack on the oil-producing regions of Southwest Asia. But the relative damage to the two sides is completely out of balance. The loss of Southwest Asia would be catastrophically damaging to the economic, political, and military condition of the industrialized democracies. Sweeping the Soviets from the seas would do no comparable damage to them.

Direct attack on Soviet naval centers has also been suggested as a way of forcing the diversion of Soviet power from the scene of its original aggression. The difficulty of such an approach is that those are precisely the centers of Soviet land-based naval air power that can probably dominate the adjacent sea out to a considerable distance. The Kola Peninsula would be a particularly tough area to attack, and even Petropavlovsk would by no means be easy. The Soviet Union would be hurt considerably if such attacks were even partially successful, but that would not begin to compensate the industrialized democracies for the loss of Southwest Asia.

The course of any naval conflict would depend strongly on both the political and military conditions that led to it or that were associated with the broader war of which it might be a part. One important factor would be whether at the time the actual combat began the Soviet fleets were inside or outside the straits through which they must pass into the global ocean from their home bases. Another would be who struck the first naval blow. The straits are a major problem for the Soviet fleet in either event. If it is inside, it risks being bottled up. If it is outside and the allies have control of the straits, the Soviets would have a serious resupply problem. This suggests that any naval war would be accompanied by a major Soviet attempt to control the Turkish straits, the Japanese straits, the Baltic straits, and Iceland (the center of the Greenland–Iceland–United Kingdom gap) through amphibious and airborne assault and air and naval attack. Gibraltar is probably too far away for an assault, but the Soviets might attack it by air. Though expanded in recent decades, Soviet naval infantry is about one-tenth the size of the United States Marine Corps. The importance to naval operations of islands, seacoasts, and straits suggests that U.S. amphibious capabilities will continue to be important. The United States must maintain and modernize its substantial marine amphibious assault capability, but there seems little advantage in increasing it, given other priorities for military resources.

All of these scenarios show considerable interaction between combat on land and combat at sea. Land-based air power is a major threat to ships within its range. Control of various straits will determine naval movements. Thus it appears unlikely that any war at sea between the United States (with or without its allies) and the Soviet Union could be confined to the seas for an extended period. Scenarios that so confine it have an air of unrealism about them.

Naval power can play several important political and military roles, even outside actual conflicts. First, naval forces can maintain a peacetime presence to remind friends, adversaries, and nonaligned or undecided nations of U.S. military capabilities without being a permanent irritant. Second, naval forces can be dispatched to the scene of a crisis within weeks—sometimes within days—to suggest U.S. ability to use force and to hint that it might be used. In the Iran crisis, first one and then two carrier battle groups were stationed in the Arabian Sea for more than a year. Though this, like other moves, proved to be of limited effectiveness in securing the release of the U.S. hostages held in the Embassy, it did serve to deter various other actions that might have taken place—Iranian moves against other Persian Gulf states, or Soviet adventures. Third, wars in remote areas over an extended period must be supplied by sea, even if an initial presence can be established by the use of air transport. Where air landing is not feasible, amphibious assault is required, as employed by Great Britain in the Falkland Islands. Fourth, the United States plans in a major conventional war in Europe, Asia, or Southwest Asia to resupply by sea.

In a conventional war in Europe or in Korea, naval resupply would become important after about thirty days. A central question in U.S. war planning is whether to devote major resources during those thirty days to attacking Soviet surface ships, and possibly naval bases, to sweep the seas. To do so would require diversion of naval and air forces, as well as of airlift and sealift capability, from missions more directly associated with the land battle. A second question is whether to set in advance a geographical order of priority for such naval operations, or to try to deal simultaneously with the North Atlantic (perhaps even north of the Greenland–Iceland–United Kingdom gap), the Mediterranean, the Indian Ocean and Southwest Asia, and Far Eastern waters. Ideally, the United States would want to sweep the seas all at once and push the Soviets back to their coasts, but this is clearly out of reach with reasonably available resources.

A central factor in deciding U.S. priorities in an actual combat situation would be the effect of Soviet diplomatic maneuvers and military threats in influencing the political behavior of the coastal countries. A substantial diversion of U.S. carrier-based air forces to the Indian Ocean is likely to be necessary, especially if the United States has neither a peacetime nor a crisis-inspired land-based air presence in that region. The United States should therefore plan to give priority for naval forces at the start of a global conventional conflict to the Indian Ocean and next to the Far East, on the theory that land-based air power can be inserted more easily elsewhere in peacetime and that the shorter distances in the Atlantic and the Mediterranean make the use of land-based air power more feasible in those regions. But the balance between the North Atlantic and western Pacific as destinations for U.S. naval reinforcements is likely to be determined more by political than by military factors. If a war were to break out in Europe first, naval reinforcements would go first to the North Atlantic and the Mediterranean.

In the balance of naval forces, the United States and its allies have advantages in total tonnage and in number of major combat ships, in civil and military transport, in bases, and in antisubmarine warfare capability. The Soviets, however, have greatly improved their naval forces over the past twenty years. Beginning with a navy that was only a coastal defense force capable of supporting the flanks of their land forces, they have established a capability for global presence and for force projection, albeit a modest one compared to that of the United States. They have added bases and carried out extended operations at sea. They now have many more submarines than do the United States and its allies, and they have paid substantially more attention to land-based long-range naval air power. Until recently, they had the lead in developing anti–surface ship cruise missiles and direct satellite surveillance of naval forces. The outcome of any potential naval war would probably turn on the relative surveillance capabilities of the two sides; on electronic countermeasures, cruise missile deployments, base structures, and training and operational experience; and on who strikes the first blow at the other's navy. The United States and its allies are clearly ahead in capabilities, but their tasks are much greater than those of the Soviets. The United States must, therefore, continue to expand its naval capability. By how much and of what kind are related questions, because the mix would appropriately be different at different levels of overall naval force strength.

A major question has been the relative merits of a smaller number of large combat ships (and of more capable aircraft) and a larger number of small combat ships (and of less capable aircraft). Too often this question has been dodged with the answer that more ships *and* larger ones are needed, but funds are never unlimited, so this answer is not useful. A combination of more capable large ships and less capable small ones, called a high-low mix, has also been suggested. This is the correct answer in the abstract, but its effectiveness has been considerably undermined by cost escalation for smaller ships and for aircraft. Still, at likely funding levels, a mix is probably the best answer.

Sea-based air power belongs on relatively large carriers, though "large" can vary for this purpose between 55,000 and 80,000 tons. The reason for this variation is that so many aircraft are needed for self-defense of a carrier force that its offensive capability increases steeply when the total number of aircraft on the carrier (and therefore the weight of the carrier) increases only modestly. Moreover, the operational effectiveness of a large ship is greater because of its greater stability in rough seas and its flexibility in handling the launch, recovery, storage, and maintenance of aircraft. Vertical take-off and landing (VTOL) aircraft have long been promised as the way to make small aircraft carriers more effective, but their performance in the air is inherently inferior at a given level of technological development to that of conventional take-off and landing aircraft. (The performance of British Harrier VTOL aircraft operating from small carriers around the Falkland Islands was respectable but limited to short ranges.) In its older carriers the United States has platforms that can be used effectively for deploying VTOL aircraft if the performance penalty is considered acceptable.

Within the range of large carriers, those at the lower end of the range offer an advantage because of the lower cost per ship. It is then possible to build more carriers for a given total cost. That in turn allows better geographical coverage; no matter how capable a ship is, it cannot be in two places at one time. It also spreads the inevitable ship losses over a larger base, making a few extra losses less likely to cause a catastrophe.

Existing and planned surface ships—from frigates on up to cruisers—and submarines should be fitted with from a dozen to several dozen conventionally armed medium-range and long-range cruise missiles to pose a threat to Soviet naval forces and their land bases. Such a fleet would force the Soviets to deal with a large number of U.S. ships, each of which was capable of inflicting a powerful blow. This is one effective response to the increased vulnerability of surface ships that results from improved surveillance and potential Soviet use of cruise missiles. The United States should also add more land-based naval aircraft and use Air Force aircraft to carry out surveillance and to attack naval targets with medium-range and long-range cruise missiles.

Can aircraft carriers survive a large-scale conventional war at sea? The answer depends on the effectiveness of enemy surveillance measures in locating and identifying them, the countermeasures to such measures, the development of cruise missile capabilities on both sides, and the defenses against those cruise missiles. I believe that aircraft carriers, even though they are protected by more concentric rings of defense than other surface ships, will be quite vulnerable to air-launched cruise missiles. But if they are kept at a considerable distance from land and used with other ships that are equipped with cruise missiles, aircraft carriers could probably survive long enough to produce a favorable outcome in a sea war fought more than 1,500 nautical miles from Soviet land bases.

The decision by the Navy and the Reagan administration in 1981 to take old battleships out of mothballs and use them for naval gunfire in support of amphibious operations, for command facilities, to maintain a visible presence, and later to fit them with substantial numbers of cruise missiles and convert them into long-distance attack ships is not the most effective way to proceed. The rejected alternative of bringing additional Essex-class aircraft carriers out of mothballs would have provided additional strike-aircraft power, at a cost comparable to that of the battleships, assuming that aircraft would be provided from those to be retired from the active force. To send a battleship into an area of high risk requires that it be defended. Such defense can be provided adequately only if the task force includes a carrier, but if a carrier is in the vicinity it can use its own attack aircraft to deliver a conventional attack. A battleship could be replaced in regions where the threat from air attack is low by a mix of such smaller ships as frigates and destroyers, which can also launch cruise missiles and are less concentrated and appealing as targets. Granted, in peacetime a battleship is a more impressive presence. Moreover, the argument that battleships can be taken out of mothballs in two years while smaller ships would take five years to build has some weight. But the decision should not have turned, as it apparently did, simply on the Congressional popularity of the battleship.

The use of many small ships as cruise missile launchers will ease the dilemma of deciding whether naval forces should be designed, developed, and deployed primarily for sea control or for the projection of force in a land attack. Smaller ships (destroyers, even frigates) can provide sea control in areas of ocean far from land-based enemy air power, leaving the carriers the responsibility for sea control closer (but not too close) to the enemy land bases and for force projection.

The United States and its allies have natural geographical, technological, and historical advantages in conflicts at sea. In training, skills, and operational experience, they generally have a significant advantage. But the United States also has a more difficult task than does the Soviet Union—preserving rather than disturbing sea lines of communication. And the Soviets have increased their relative naval capabilities in many dimensions—only in sea-based manned aircraft and antisubmarine warfare do they continue to lag considerably. The United States must emphasize and work from its advantages, concentrate its efforts, and define its priorities, especially in detailed plans for the sequence of functional and geographical operations to be used in different naval warfare scenarios. U.S. and allied fleets have the skills to carry out such plans and operations. More attention must be devoted to the development, procurement, and operational use of some kinds of equipment and materiel—electronic countermeasures and counter-countermeasures, for example. U.S. antisubmarine warfare (ASW) capability far exceeds that of the Soviets, but the United States has paid inadequate attention to coordinating sea-based and land-based aircraft, surface ships, and submarines as an ASW team and to mining and minesweeping capabilities. In the land-based Backfire bomber with antiship cruise missiles, the Soviets have a severe threat to allied surface ships. The United States and its allies could mount a substantial defense in the form of land-based interceptor and AWACS aircraft in Iceland, Japan, and elsewhere, but they have yet to do so.

Finally, the United States must modernize its naval forces, though a balanced force would not require an increase of more than 5 percent in either the present naval and marine personnel levels or in the number of vessels now active. Ship production schedules and lifetimes are so long, compared to those of most other equipment, that modernization will take time. Meanwhile, a great deal can be done much more quickly by upgrading or replacing existing equipment aboard present ships. A strike fleet of twelve or at most thirteen carrier battle groups, supplemented with cruise missiles on the other surface vessels, is a force of appropriate size given the need for the flexibility of being able to attack from sea bases, the vulnerability of surface ships, and the probable availability of resources.

MULTIFRONT CONFLICTS

In providing an appropriate overall military force posture, the United States must take into account the possibility of simultaneous military conflicts in more than one region. Four major theaters could be the arenas of a global conflict—Europe, Northeast Asia, Southwest Asia, and the high seas. In several other land areas the United States might have to commit smaller forces. A conflict in Europe would almost certainly also involve a conflict at sea. A conflict between the United States and the Soviet Union in one of the land areas might or might not involve conflict in the other land areas, depending on the way events unfolded and the way each saw the potential advantages and disadvantages to itself of expanding the conflict.

At first glance, the Soviets appear to have some substantial advantages in a multifront war. They have much larger ground forces than the United States—about five times as many divisions, counting regulars and reserves (though the Soviet divisions are smaller)—and comparable advantages in tanks and artillery. They almost certainly have larger stockpiles of ammunition and war reserve materiel. Moreover, they can move their forces in Europe and Asia on interior lines of communication, with no troop ships to be sunk. To some degree they can redeploy troops in peacetime or crisis less openly than the United States, which has to move them over oceans or by air in a highly visible way. U.S. intelligence would detect major Soviet movements, but that is not the same as having the world press watch.

These are correct and relevant comparisons, and they pose formidable challenges to the United States. But it should be remembered that in none of the three land regions mentioned would (or could, or should) the United States fight alone on the ground against the Soviets. In Europe, the bulk of the ground forces would be provided by U.S. allies. In East Asia an even smaller percentage of ground forces would be U.S. forces. In Southwest Asia the United States would probably have to provide a larger percentage of the total regular ground forces. But again there would be no way of mounting a successful defense, and little realistic prospect that U.S. forces would go in, without major indigenous resistance to a Soviet attack, as in Afghanistan, or without some Western European military forces participating as well.

U.S. and allied airlift and sealift capabilities greatly exceed those of the Soviets. They are two or three times as great now, and the United States can and should increase that advantage during the 1980s. The periphery of the Soviet Union is much closer to each of the three critical land areas than is the United States, so Soviet forces can get close to Iran, or West Germany, or Japan in large numbers before a war or a crisis begins; U.S. forces, without peacetime stationing overseas, cannot. But the Soviets will not find it easy to reinforce their advance forces or to transfer forces from combat in one area to another. They would need to move their forces, equipment, and supplies over thousands of miles, relying largely on railroads because there is no Soviet road network of sufficient capacity connecting these distant parts of the Soviet Union with each other. That would impose substantial logistical limitations, especially on transfers between the Soviet Far East and the other borders. In Europe, supply would be the easiest and most straightforward, especially because the Soviets have been war-gaming Warsaw Pact operations in Western Europe for decades. But some of the terrain outside the Soviet borders where fighting would be expected to occur—in Southwest Asia, for example—is rugged and difficult and contains many choke points. In the Far East, water or vast and difficult terrain separates Soviet forces from their main military objectives. This should add to Soviet concerns about fighting a war with China and one in Europe simultaneously. Expanding a European conflict to involve the USSR along its border with the People's Republic of China (PRC) has a corresponding appeal to the United States. The PRC is much less likely to see such an expansion as being in its interest.

Finally, the U.S. ability to move its tactical air power and conventional heavy bombing capabilities around the world is excellent and could play a significant role in the early stages of a conventional war. Resupply and wartime reinforcement from the United States, especially of ground forces, would depend substantially on keeping sea lines of communication open to carry equipment and supplies over and above what had been prepositioned. Here the principal Soviet threat would be from land-based naval air power and submarines. U.S. antisubmarine warfare capability is such that within a few weeks—roughly the time at which resupply becomes important—it should be possible to eliminate the threat from Soviet submarine forces in the open oceans if the Soviets choose to send them there to attack the sea lines of communication. Defense of the sea lines of communication against the long-range capabilities of the Soviet Backfire bomber is more difficult, but U.S. carrier capability should, if combined with properly placed land-based interceptor aircraft, make the problem manageable.

Even given these balancing factors, the Soviet ability to pose military threats to any or all of the key land regions is formidable. Too many possible scenarios exist for the initiation and conduct of major conventional conflict to examine them here. If a conventional war occurs either in Europe or in Southwest Asia, the Soviet Union would want to avoid simultaneous conflict with China or Japan. The Soviets might well consider it to their advantage to have tied down U.S. forces some months earlier or simultaneously in an attack by North Korea against South Korea. But they would not want to commit their own forces in the Far East, both because such a commitment would be an additional drain and because it would raise the chances of Chinese or Japanese participation against them.

The Soviets *would* probably find it useful in preparing for an incursion into either Europe or Southwest Asia to raise the level of tensions in the other of these two areas in order to divide the forces and complicate the planning of the United States and its allies. An actual diversionary attack in the theater the Soviets regarded as secondary would be quite possible. Moreover, the Soviets could be expected to initiate or to threaten conflict through surrogates in Central America and the Caribbean, with the Cubans attacking shipping in the Straits of Florida or the Yucatan Channel, through which many of the U.S. resupply lines to Europe and to Southwest Asia run. The United States would then have to divert substantial forces to suppress or to deal with the threat of such attacks.

As noted earlier, it has been suggested that under these circumstances the United States might find it advantageous to launch a diversionary attack of its own at some remote periphery of the Soviet Union. Petropavlovsk is one conceivable possibility, as it is isolated and not as well defended as Vladivostok or the even more heavily defended northwestern coast (Arkhangelsk and the Kola Peninsula). In any event, the number and concentration of U.S. carrier battle groups required for such a diversionary attack make its wisdom somewhat questionable. If such an attack were called for it would be better to launch a major force of conventionally armed cruise missiles, at ranges of up to 1,000 miles, from surface ships and submarines. Such a capability could be built over the next five or six years, and the large number of launch platforms involved makes it less vulnerable than carrier forces. Even if such a diversionary attack is not carried out, the capability for such an action, like the Soviet capability for diversionary attacks and multifront attacks, complicates planning on the other side.

Perhaps the clearest conclusion from this consideration of two-front and three-front wars is that the United States and its allies must plan for a variety of contingencies while retaining a mix of forces stationed both in the United States and overseas. The overseas forces should be large in Europe, small in East Asia, and larger than those at present in Southwest Asia—provided that arrangements can be made for stationing them there without unacceptable political penalties. In almost all cases U.S. forces will be only a modest percentage of the total allied capability; nevertheless, they serve important military and political purposes. U.S. forces in the United States should constitute a central reserve of ready forces that can be moved very rapidly into a threatened region, or between theaters of combat, in a time of crisis. This rapid mobility is already available to a significant (though not sufficient) degree for U.S. air and sea forces. It must be greatly improved for U.S. ground forces. For this purpose greatly increased airlift and sealift capability will be needed. For the ground forces to be mobile after they arrive in a combat zone, heavy equipment, including helicopters and armored vehicles, must be lifted with them. Thus mobility of forces, once they arrive, is not associated with lack of heavy equipment; if anything, the opposite is true.

Finally, in a multitheater crisis or conflict U.S. forces prepared to go to any of two or more regions will have to be split or (more likely) principally directed to one of them. Resource constraints are almost certain to prevent the most obvious response to this possibility, namely, adding to the force structure a half-dozen divisions and a corresponding number of air wings and the needed lift capability. Consequently, U.S. allies and friends—in Western Europe, in East Asia, and to the extent possible in Southwest Asia—will need to provide the majority, and in most cases the great majority, of the ground forces in their own defense. Without that contribution, U.S. participation—and indeed a successful defense of their regions—is both politically and militarily impossible.

11

Arms Limitation and Reduction

The arms competition between the superpowers is fueled by political conflicts around the world, by hopes of gain from military superiority and fear of loss from inferiority, and by the uncertainties of each superpower about the present and future military capabilities, as well as the potential military and political intentions, of the other. Solving or ameliorating the political conflicts would slow the arms competition and might even halt it, but in the absence of such progress, geographical or functional arms control agreements are one of the few methods of placing an actual ceiling on arms. Without such agreements, arms competition will continue (within economic constraints) to produce higher levels of military capability on both sides without necessarily increasing the security of either. The purpose of this chapter is to describe some recent arms control efforts, evaluate what they have accomplished, and consider what they may be able to do in the future.

The world in general would be better off, and U.S. national security would be greater, if nuclear weapons had proved impossible to devise—even though their existence has helped to prevent war between the superpowers and to keep Europe at peace for almost four decades. Complete nuclear disarmament is a desirable goal, but it does not seem to be possible during this century or even at any foreseeable time in the next. The ability to design and produce nuclear weapons cannot be uninvented. Even if all nuclear stockpiles, reactors, and uranium and plutonium separation plants were destroyed, nuclear weapons could be produced again within a few years by any of an uncomfortably large number of nations. Only a repressive world empire, or an end to the use of force in international and even internal conflicts, would remove the motive for producing nuclear weapons.

Unilateral nuclear disarmament is sometimes suggested as less dangerous than the present course of events. But there is no chance that unilateral nuclear disarmament by the United States would be followed by disarmament in kind by the Soviet Union. A world in which the Soviets had nuclear weapons and the United States did not would be rather more dangerous, as well as—to put it mildly— less free than the present one. Thus unilateral disarmament appears undesirable as well as unrealistic.

Limits on the development and production of nuclear weapons and their delivery systems are possible, as are reductions, even deep ones. Effective steps against further proliferation of nuclear weapons are also feasible. Agreements on arms limitations and reductions can in principle serve any of several different objectives:

• They can improve security and stability, even though there will always be the possibility of covert violations or of a breakout (an abrupt withdrawal from the treaty agreement after making preparations to exceed the limits) by one side.

• They can lead to a more accurate understanding of the size and character of the adversary forces, through such provisions as those that ban interference with national technical means of verification.

• They can increase the ability of each side to calculate and predict the future military capabilities of the other and thus reduce the likelihood of overreaction.

• They can reduce the level of damage in a war—though only extremely deep reductions could mitigate the catastrophic destructiveness of nuclear weapons.

• They can improve deterrence of both nuclear and conventional war—in the first case by increasing the ability of retaliatory forces to survive an attack and in the second by favoring defensive weapons and dispositions of forces, thus tilting the balance against the initiator of an attack.

• They can reduce the likelihood of surprise attack, accidental war, and escalation through misjudgment, by providing for relocation of forces to make surprise less feasible, by including inspection and other confidence-building measures, and by arranging for exchanges of information both in normal times and in times of crisis.

Measured against these glittering possibilities, the achievements of arms negotiations to date have been modest indeed, as are their immediate prospects. The ABM Treaty has helped stabilize deterrence by ensuring the continued mutual vulnerability of the urban and industrial centers of the superpowers. The Nuclear Test Ban Treaty ended nuclear testing in the atmosphere by the superpowers—a move that affected the environment more than it did the arms race. SALT I limited the numbers of some kinds of strategic weapons, but that only channeled the efforts of the superpowers increasingly into qualitative improvements. SALT II imposed important qualitative limits and some reductions, but the failure of the U.S. Senate to approve that treaty has left it in the unstable limbo of voluntary observance. The Mutual and Balanced Force Reduction (MBFR) negotiations have had useful political results within NATO and have favorably influenced decisions for some unilateral reductions on each side. But they have not produced any agreements between the NATO and Warsaw Pact nations. The hot line agreement provides modest emergency communications capability. In all, not much to show for thirty-five years of negotiations and twenty years of treaties. And yet the arms control efforts of the past have not been a trap. They were worth all the effort, and the prospects justify even greater efforts in the future— not as a substitute for defense programs, but as a companion to them. Both are required to improve national security through an adequate and stable military balance.

REQUIREMENTS AND RESULTS

The complementary relationship of arms control and arms development programs in ensuring national security is paralleled by their relationship in encouraging agreements. Each side's perceptions of what the other would deploy in the absence of agreed limits affect bargaining positions and outcomes. Severe overall imbalances are not politically tolerable to either superpower in agreements (or outside them). Weapons programs can play a role as bargaining chips, but so far the United States has had little success in using them as such. Often a new strategic system develops a constituency inside the government, and the arms control agreement must protect rather than trade away the bargaining chip. Cruise missiles are an example. In other cases, the program loses public support, especially when budgets are constrained or other doubts about whether the programs can be carried out make them appear expendable. The MX may be an example of such a case. Without close coordination of arms control negotiations with these domestic political concerns, such programs are more likely to be given away than bargained away.

Verification of arms limitation agreements must be adequate to ensure that any evasion of the limits cannot significantly affect the balance in the armaments being limited. Unilateral intelligence (national technical means) provides the irreducible basis for such verification. This works well in determining the numbers of strategic arms deployed and the characteristics of strategic nuclear or conventional weapons. It works less well in determining production rates or the size of tactical deployments of conventional arms. For example, verifying strategic missile production is probably possible, but it would entail intrusive inspection requirements or at least such elaborate cooperative verification measures as displaying the output of production plants in open holding sheds visible to reconnaissance satellites.

Arms limitation negotiations are sometimes viewed as valuable independent of the nature of the agreements reached, or even of whether agreements are reached at all. The hope is that such negotiations will produce a momentum of their own that will carry them through political difficulties between the two countries and even provide a means for improving political relations generally. Some claim that the United States and the Soviet Union are not the most dangerous threats to each other, but that the arms competition is the real threat to both. To the extent that this is true, arms control negotiations—even if they reach no agreements—focus the attention of the adversaries on the dangers of the competition and thus improve political relations.

This last approach is rather naive. It is true that modern arms make war enormously more dangerous and destructive to all participants than it has ever been and that the nature and the quantity of armaments can only amplify everyone's suspicions and concerns. But were it not for the political differences between the superpowers in goals, ideology, and institutions, the arms competition would lose its principal driving force, and the superpowers would find few occasions for military conflict. Great Britain and France have nuclear arsenals that could annihilate each other, but neither feels any concern. The regional powers that may now move to produce nuclear weapons are motivated by fears of or ambitions toward their neighbors. In the absence of these various clashes of political interest on the regional and superpower levels, some technologists would still feel the urge to carry out new arms developments, but the necessary government support would be lacking.

Arms control negotiation cannot substitute for the settlement of political differences, but such negotiations can in some circumstances serve a useful purpose even if they are not carried through to an agreement. They may be able to lead each side to a clearer understanding of the purposes and military doctrines of the other; this can reduce uncertainty and instability and may even lead to helpful parallel unilateral actions—restraints in weapons developments or deployments, for example.

When are negotiations likely to be fruitful? The two governments must also share some degree of motivation to ease certain aspects of their political competition, even if, as in the case of strategic arms control and reduction, they already share a common goal—avoiding a nuclear war that would destroy both. It is not desirable to tie nuclear arms control negotiations to the state of political relations between the United States and the Soviet Union, but a degree of such linkage is a fact of political life. It is difficult to say in advance exactly how the state of political relations will affect the attainability of arms agreements. If the negotiations are far enough along, they may be able to survive some political differences. The SALT I negotiations were concluded despite Soviet concerns about the U.S. mining of Haiphong harbor and U.S.-Soviet differences over the India-Pakistan war. (In the United States, on the other hand, even favorable arms limitation agreements can be derailed by popular and congressional concern about Soviet behavior in other areas, as happened to SALT II when the Soviets invaded Afghanistan.)

Agreements also depend on a sense on both sides of approximate equality in the arms to be limited, before and after the negotiations. Neither side can agree to terms that will be widely seen as unequal; and if either side is far ahead when negotiations begin, it is unlikely to give up that lead by agreement.

NEGOTIATIONS TODAY AND IN THE YEARS AHEAD

Strategic Nuclear Forces

The most extensive and detailed negotiations on arms limitation have dealt with strategic nuclear forces. These negotiations will continue to hold the greatest promise, because the two superpowers, whatever their separate unilateral goals, have a common motivation to reduce the danger of nuclear war. Moreover, these negotiations have a long history, dating back to 1969 (preliminary discussions date back to 1967). This longevity provides a foundation for further discussions and potential agreements. In Article VI of the Nuclear Nonproliferation

Treaty (NPT), the superpowers have also subscribed to a commitment to reduce their nuclear arsenals.

It is probable that, by midsummer of 1979, more than two-thirds of the Senate had been convinced that ratification of SALT II would be a favorable development for U.S. security. But suspicions of the Soviets had grown, and the next year's election campaign loomed. Senate consideration was then stalled by the mishandled "discovery" of the Soviet combat brigade that had been in Cuba for seventeen years in various forms. But that incident would not have prevented ratification once the Administration publicly agreed to commit itself (as it had already agreed internally) to a further overall military buildup, principally in conventional forces. Then in December the Soviets invaded Afghanistan; that did prevent ratification.

Various—and conflicting—lessons can be drawn. Negotiations that drag out for more than two or three years are likely to run afoul of Soviet misbehavior in other fields or of electoral politics in the United States. On the other hand, U.S. concessions to speed the process would be likely to result in an agreement that will be seen as inequitable and will fail to gain support of the U.S. security establishment (including military leaders) and thus of the Senate.

The United States should now lock in, and attempt to build on, the limitations and provisions of SALT II regarding the total number of bombers, ICBM launchers, and SLBM launchers; the total number of MIRV-equipped ICBM and SLBM launchers; the total number of bombers capable of launching long-range cruise missiles; the maximum number of MIRVs on an ICBM; the development of new missiles; and verification. It is also worth pursuing deeper reductions and further test limitations. Other kinds of limitations—on total payload weight, for example, or on the production of missiles—have also been suggested, though production limits would be difficult to monitor, and payload limits could lead to interminable arguments about the equivalence of bomber payload and missile payload and about the effect of range on each of the two.

Probably the outstanding example of successful arms control negotiation was the agreement on the Antiballistic Missile (ABM) Treaty, signed in May 1972. The United States and the Soviet Union agreed not to deploy nationwide antiballistic missile defenses, limiting the number of sites allowed to one and sharply limiting the allowed numbers of ABM interceptors and radar installations allowed. In this way, they greatly decreased the chance that a clever briefer might persuade political authorities to undertake a first strike against opposing strategic forces by arguing that deployed air defense and ABM systems could limit to acceptable levels the damage the opposing forces that survived the attack could inflict on the attacking power. Unlimited competition in antiballistic missile deployment would have made outcomes less predictable and could have led to dangerous misconceptions. Since the signing of the ABM Treaty, questions have been raised about whether the Soviet early warning and air defense systems have been given some capabilities in preparation for a future breakout from the ABM Treaty. In the United States, the ability to use ABMs to defend land-based ICBMs' retaliatory capability has been suggested as a possible reason to modify or abandon the ABM Treaty. But no convincing evidence or rationale has been advanced in support of either the charges against the Soviets or the wisdom of such action by the United States.

An alternative approach to nuclear arms limitation is the nuclear freeze, involving a bilateral U.S.-Soviet agreement not to build any more nuclear weapons or delivery systems. The proposal for a nuclear freeze is prompted by understandable concerns and has laudable aims. It serves a useful political purpose by focusing attention on the urgency of nuclear arms control. But a freeze is more a slogan than a program. Attractive as a nuclear freeze may seem in principle, it is not clear whether it would result in an acceptable balance or whether it would aid or damage the ability of U.S. nuclear forces to survive an attack. It is no substitute for detailed negotiation. In the absence of an agreement, the movement for a freeze may erode public support for U.S. nuclear weapons programs.

Determination of what is to be frozen would be lengthy and difficult. If, for example, air defense and antisubmarine warfare (generally nonnuclear) continue to be developed and deployed but ballistic missile submarines, bombers, and cruise missiles are frozen, the stability of deterrence would be undermined. Some parts of a freeze could be verified, some could not. Working out such issues could take as long as reaching agreement on a treaty to reduce nuclear arms, or even longer. And what would be the effect? Tens or even hundreds of millions of deaths would result from a strategic war involving the *present* nuclear forces on which the freeze proposals are based. Thus, a better course than a general freeze is the aggressive prosecution of strategic arms talks, aimed at major reductions of some forces where that is possible, freezes of some forces where that is possible, and changes in the characteristics or numbers of other forces to increase stability and ensure equality.

Concern about the possibility of nuclear war in Europe has prompted renewed interest in nuclear no-first-use pledges. Some have even suggested that adoption of a no-first-use doctrine would encourage Western European and U.S. efforts to increase NATO's conventional capabilities in the face of the economic and political difficulties such efforts now face. In my view, it is at least as likely that U.S. adoption of such a policy would increase pressure for withdrawal, first of U.S. nuclear weapons and then of U.S. troops, from Europe.

The United States should not seriously consider adopting a no-first-use policy until the balance of conventional forces between NATO and the Warsaw Pact becomes such that the Soviets could have very little confidence of success in an invasion or a territorial grab. A no-first-use policy, then, could have clear political advantages in gaining public support for Western nuclear doctrine and programs. On the other hand, it would reduce—to the extent that the Soviets believed it genuine—the added deterrent effect provided by Soviet concern that a conventional attack could escalate to nuclear war. On balance, even if an adequate conventional force posture is reached, the risk of losing this deterrent effect argues for maintaining the possibility of first use in U.S. declaratory policy.

Nuclear Weapons Tests

Another set of nuclear arms control negotiations would limit or ban nuclear explosions or weapons tests. These negotiations date back to 1958; they culminated in a partial success with the atmospheric test ban in 1963. Subsequently, in 1974, the United States and the Soviet Union signed the Threshold Test Ban Treaty limiting the size of underground nuclear explosions to 150 kilotons. The Senate has not acted on that treaty, in part because the United States began negotiations with the Soviet Union and Great Britain in 1977 aimed at a comprehensive test ban (CTB). These negotiations have fallen into indefinite recess since the Soviet invasion of Afghanistan and the U.S. failure to ratify SALT II.

Proponents of a CTB offer both political and military arguments for it. Politically, they argue that a CTB is an important part of a nonproliferation strategy. Some nations indicate that without an end to superpower testing, they will not adhere to the Nuclear Nonproliferation Treaty. But in fact few if any of the present nonnuclear nations would decide to adhere to the treaty on the basis of a CTB entered into by the superpowers. A CTB may be a necessary precondition to such compliance, but it is unlikely to be a sufficient one. It deprives such nations of an excuse for going nuclear but not of their principal reasons for doing so. On the military side, proponents argue that a CTB would lead to the elimination of one dimension of the arms race, nuclear weapons testing. It could also decrease the possibility of nuclear war, because existing stockpiles would become less reliable, thus making governments less certain that they would work. The problem is, however, that such military effects may not operate equally for both sides. Below some yield, probably in the range of 1 to 5 kilotons, verification becomes difficult or even impossible. This in turn raises the complicated questions of whether the Soviets could maintain confidence in their stockpile with tests at that yield and how much and how quickly confidence in the U.S. stockpile would erode without tests. Those questions are not easily answerable without (or even with) access to information on U.S. and Soviet nuclear weapons designs.

Opponents of a CTB tend to focus on the problems of verifying a zero-yield test ban, that is, one forbidding nuclear explosions that are clearly not detectable by the other side. But they also argue that major additional advances in the characteristics of nuclear armament can be made through testing. This claim is rather questionable, at least in terms of relative advantage to the United States if both sides make such advances. It is realistic to expect that greater safety against accidental detonation or use by terrorists could be attained through further testing. Most important, opponents of a CTB conclude that continued stockpile testing is needed to maintain the reliability of the nuclear weapons in the U.S. stockpile in the face of a Soviet stockpile whose reliability they believe would be higher because of its design and because the Soviets could test below some verification threshold.

In light of these continued uncertainties, a reasonable approach would be for the United States to ratify the 150-kiloton Threshold Treaty and for the signatories to lower the threshold to the minimum level that can now be verified with the goal of lowering it to zero as verification improves. The United States and the Soviet Union should also incorporate into a successor treaty the important verification provisions agreed to in the course of the 1977–1980 negotiations for challenge on-site inspections, no peaceful nuclear explosions, and the introduction of seismic monitoring stations on each other's territory.

Europe

Another set of arms control negotiations, under way in Vienna since 1973, involves Mutual and Balanced Force Reductions (MBFR) in Europe. Several of the Warsaw Pact and NATO countries have been seeking an agreement on the levels of conventional forces in Europe. In the beginning, the United States insisted on the MBFR negotiations to balance the Helsinki Conference on Security and Cooperation in Europe (CSCE) that the Soviets pushed to legitimize post–World War II European boundaries. The Soviets achieved their objective in the

Helsinki negotiations, but they also had to agree to economic provisions and to human rights principles that have subsequently embarrassed them. For U.S. defense planners in the early 1970s, a second reason to begin MBFR negotiations was to avoid congressional approval of the Mansfield Amendment, which would have removed substantial numbers of U.S. troops from Europe. It was sensibly and successfully argued that any such reductions should come as a result of negotiations that would also lead to removal of Soviet troops from positions in Eastern Europe that threaten NATO. These MBFR negotiations so far have had a primarily political purpose—perhaps even a propaganda purpose—for each side. They have not produced an agreement.

The two sides in the MBFR negotiations have agreed on the objectives of a common collective ceiling for conventional forces and a first-phase reduction in U.S. and Soviet forces. But the negotiations have stalled on the issues of whether to establish separate ceilings on individual Western forces (which the Soviets desire as a way of gaining the right to influence and limit West German force levels separately); the measures to monitor the reductions and ceilings; and the actual number of Warsaw Pact troops now in the geographical region under negotiation. The Soviets claim that the forces on the two sides are now equal, while the NATO allies insist—and there is reason to believe that the Soviets know—that Warsaw Pact forces are about 150,000 to 160,000 stronger than the Warsaw Pact admits.

Though no agreement has been reached in these negotiations, they have been useful in several ways. The NATO governments have come to a common understanding of the nature of the actual conventional force balance and have demonstrated their ability to define and maintain a common negotiating position. In 1979, the two sides undertook unilateral reductions in forces and weapons that had originally been part of the negotiations: for the United States 1,000 nuclear warheads and for the Soviet Union, 20,000 troops and 1,000 tanks. Before my years as Secretary of Defense I believed that negotiations that did not reach agreements had no value, or even negative value. This is sometimes true, but I now believe there are cases in which negotiations change attitudes for the better and stimulate beneficial unilateral actions. Such negotiations are of value even if they do not lead to any formal agreement. MBFR is an example.

The problem in the MBFR negotiations is that NATO's stated objective of getting the Soviets to give up a perceived edge in numbers of troops is unrealistic, especially in the light of Soviet concerns (unfounded or not) about Western technological superiority. At the end of the 1970s it seemed that the NATO allies' agreement to improve their conventional force capabilities by following the NATO

Long-term Defense Program might push the Soviets to negotiate more seriously in MBFR. Since then the United States has increased its military forces and equipment in Europe, but Western European economic and political problems and the political difficulties between the United States and its allies may have convinced the Soviets that their apprehensions about a NATO buildup were unfounded. In any event, it is probably now time to turn these negotiations away from major reductions in the number of personnel under arms and the amount of equipment in the region and toward what are called confidence-building measures (CBMs). These are arrangements for keeping track of the size and position of the other side's forces and for making surprise attack more difficult.

Inhibiting surprise attack is clearly a most desirable goal for NATO. One way would be to station observers with the forces of the other side or to provide for inspections. Another is to place limits on peacetime military activities, for example, on the number of forces out of garrison. The second would be more useful in preventing surprise. The Soviets would be hard put to object publicly, though it is quite possible that they see their ability to execute a surprise attack on NATO as contributing to their security. But there is disagreement about the possibility of designing measures that make a surprise attack on NATO less feasible without inhibiting NATO's own ability to respond quickly to a warning of a surprise attack if it comes. Properly defined, CBMs probably could promote stability in a crisis. But there are potential pitfalls.

One festering issue in the MBFR negotiations is the geographical area that should be covered. The negotiations now exclude military forces in the Soviet Union, Hungary, France, and Italy. There are strong political reasons to have any limitations cover the territory of the Soviet Union if they cover West Germany. Militarily, it would be useful to include Soviet reinforcements in the forces to be limited. At the Madrid Conference on CSCE in 1980 the French presented a proposal for a conference on disarmament in Europe (CDE). One of its attractions is that it would include the western part of the Soviet Union, as well as all European countries, in the areas for confidence-building measures. Events in Poland have, however, stalled efforts to convene such a conference.

Space

One area in which a special arms limitation agreement already exists is in space. The United States and Soviet Union have agreed not to emplace weapons of mass destruction there. Specifically, this ban covers nuclear weapons, although presumably it also includes death-rays aimed at populations on earth. This is a safe enough prohibition considering the unlikelihood and impracticality of developing and deploying such a science-fiction system. Both sides now use satellites in space for civilian purposes and for military support purposes (communications, surveillance, navigation, and early warning, for example). By and large the United States relies on them more, because its lines of communication and supply are global rather than interior and because of the global disposition of U.S. forces. (There are, however, some exceptions: The Soviets rely more on satellites for ocean surveillance.) It is thus to the advantage of the United States to inhibit warfare in space. There are two ways to inhibit such warfare: arms limitation agreements and the deterrence that comes from building or at least developing systems to retaliate against hostile Soviet actions. Because of the higher U.S. stakes, the first approach is more desirable, but some development of a deterrent force is probably also wise, both as an incentive for the Soviets to negotiate and as a fallback if negotiations fail.

In negotiations to limit or ban ASAT (antisatellite) systems, one problem is that even a modest ASAT capability can be significant. That is to say, one side's ability to launch a few dozen, or even a few, antisatellite weapons could have a devastating effect on the other side's intelligence and communications capabilities. That makes verification a greater problem. A few dozen undetected ICBMs would not change the strategic balance between the United States and the Soviet Union in any meaningful way, but successful use of a dozen ASAT weapons could change the balance of space support capabilities enormously. Verification is correspondingly more difficult, especially because the Soviets use the same facilities and launchers for some of their antisatellite systems that they use for some of their space launch systems, and distinctions would be difficult to make.

Despite these difficulties, it is worth trying to inhibit actions against satellites in situations short of war. (In war, any such agreement would clearly go by the board.) One way of doing this would be an agreed declaration that an attack on a satellite will be seen as a belligerent act. That might have the effect of slowing down an unproductive and potentially dangerous trend toward "space wars."

Biological and Chemical Warfare

The United States and Soviet Union have agreed not to use or produce biological weapons. Most knowledgeable observers believed—before the events described below—that biological weapons were so unpredictable and of such uncertain usability that there would be no motive to break such an agreement, despite the great difficulty of verifying compliance with it. The same difficulty of verification has, on the other hand, served to prevent an agreement banning chemical agents, although both the United States and the Soviet Union have pledged not to use chemical weapons first.

Over the past few years the Soviet Union has improved its chemical warfare capabilities, demonstrably in defensive measures and equipment and probably in offensive deployments as well. Concern has thus arisen in the United States, because an attacker gains a tactical advantage from substantial superiority in chemical warfare capability, even if that superiority is only in protective equipment. If the two sides are more nearly equal, the slowing of movement resulting from the need to carry out operations in protective clothing and sealed vehicles might well help the defender, who more often operates from fixed positions.

To give the arms control negotiations a chance, the United States postponed the modernization of its offensive chemical weapons capability in the 1970s. But the negotiations have not progressed, so the United States should now act to improve substantially its ability to protect its military forces from chemical attack and to enable them to operate under such an attack. But defensive measures against chemical warfare are not sufficient. If the Soviet Union alone were to use chemical weapons—against air bases, for example—NATO forces would have to labor under the crippling handicap of protective clothing and equipment, and the attacker would not. Some observers suggest that the United States should plan to retaliate against the use of chemical warfare with nuclear weapons. The theory that such a threat may serve as a deterrent is questionable. Few of those who advance this proposition would be likely to advocate retaliation with nuclear weapons after an actual use of chemicals in warfare.

Existing U.S. stocks of chemical warfare agents are effective but aging, and questions about their safety in peacetime have limited their deployability. The new binary agents would solve that problem because they are not lethal until combined. But their production at this time could well create more problems domestically and with the NATO allies than this advantage is worth.

ARMS CONTROL PROSPECTS

The future of arms control negotiations and agreements is very much in doubt. Three concerns merit specific attention here.

The Soviet Union has been unwilling to discuss seriously with the United States questions about Soviet compliance with some existing arms control agreements. The first involves an outbreak of anthrax in the Sverdlovsk region in the spring of 1979, which would appear to have resulted from an accident at a plant producing biological warfare agents. The second is the detection in Southeast Asia of the mycotoxin trichocethene, a poison produced by a moldlike product of fermentation, which is then dispersed as, and acts on the body as, a chemical. Samples obtained on the scene, together with a good deal of anecdotal and clinical evidence, suggest that Soviet client states or proxies have used such agents in Southeast Asia. There is also evidence that Soviet troops in Afghanistan have used various toxic agents. The evidence in all these cases is strong, but there may be reasonable explanations. But Soviet unwillingness even to discuss or share information about these events casts a shadow on the arms control process.

A corresponding difficulty arises from Soviet refusal to provide technical information about their nuclear weapons test program and about their observance of the 150-kiloton yield threshold, even though the Nuclear Threshold Test Ban Treaty calls for an exchange of information. The treaty is unratified, but both sides have indicated that they will do nothing to undercut it. Opponents of arms control agreements with the Soviet Union can allege violations and point out that the Soviets do not now give the required technical data. But in the much more important case of SALT compliance, the Soviets have been adequately forthcoming with the required information.

A second major concern is the possibility that the Reagan administration is not willing to proceed with serious arms control negotiations in the absence of a prior favorable alteration of the military balance, an alteration that it claims could easily take four or five years. This concern has been fueled by its ambiguous attitude on abiding by the provisions of SALT II. In this regard, the action of the Reagan administration in November 1981 in resuming negotiations to limit intermediate-range nuclear forces is a favorable sign, however much it may have been motivated by a need to placate the NATO allies. President Reagan's proposal for a "zero option," forgoing Pershing II and ground-launched cruise missile deployments in return for a Soviet dismantling of all SS-20s, SS-4s, and SS-5s, may well create negotiating problems, but it was nonetheless a reasonable and fair proposal.

The Reagan administration's continued attachment of new political conditions to the resumption of negotiations on strategic nuclear forces was less encouraging, but in June 1982 those too were resumed. The Administration's initial proposals in those START (Strategic Arms Reduction Talks) negotiations called for reductions in the total number of strategic ballistic missile (ICBM and SLBM) warheads by about a third, to 5,000 on each side, with no more than half of these on ICBMs. It would also allow 850 ICBMs and SLBMs on each side. These limits would force major reductions in the Soviet ICBM force and the U.S. SLBM force. The Soviet force of 2,500 ICBM warheads would, however, still have a large residual capability, even after destroying the U.S. ICBM force in its present basing mode of fixed hardened silos—and the United States would have to reduce that ICBM force in size to meet the proposed limitations on missile numbers.

Those proposals were not inequitable, but they were incomplete. They dealt principally (though not adequately) with U.S. concerns about imbalance and instability. Issues involving bombers and cruise missiles, and the numbers of warheads they carry, will also have to be dealt with. Predictably, the Soviets have raised those issues in the START negotiations as matters of concern for their "equal security." It is not clear whether the two sides can find a formulation that meets their respective security, political, and negotiating needs in the early 1980s. It would be most desirable to incorporate the limitations and modest cuts of SALT II and to go beyond them to major reductions and new limitations aimed at stability and equality. But to do so, the political motivation and political will must be present on both sides.

A third problem is that many people suspect arms control negotiations have in the past been used as a reason to increase levels of armament rather than to limit or reduce them. Both SALT I and SALT II were accompanied by new strategic programs because neither the United States nor the Soviet Union was prepared to forgo all modernization in these agreements—not because the agreements provided a rationale for a continuing arms buildup. Moreover, in the absence of arms control agreements, the United States would have found an imbalance in favor of the Soviet Union unacceptable and would have responded with an even larger arms buildup. The weight of the evidence is that arms control agreements have in fact limited arms. But the contrary argument was used by both opponents and the undecided in the SALT II debates to prevent its approval by the Senate. That argument will continue to be used.

Few agreements have come from arms control negotiations. But there have been some real accomplishments in limiting strategic nuclear weapons: the ABM Treaty, SALT I, and SALT II. The atmospheric test ban, the Moscow-Washington hot line, and the various other provisions that have been made to reduce the chances of an accidental war have been useful. Notably, none of these agreements has eliminated the need for U.S. force improvements nor—except the ABM Treaty—greatly altered those that had been planned.

Some of the negotiations and agreements have been of value in easing political tensions between the United States and the Soviet Union, though this relaxation has proven to be only temporary. Limitations on forces and armaments have been difficult in geographical areas where the United States and the Soviet Union have major political conflicts or where the military balance appears to favor the Soviet Union, as in Europe. This should be no surprise. In such places, arms negotiations can be an adjunct to but not a substitute for achieving a balance of military capabilities or resolving political differences.

Finally, it is worth saying that arms control negotiations by no means must be, nor have they been, a trap leading to unilateral U.S. disarmament or to a failure to redress dangerous military imbalances. The U.S. negotiators, like the Soviet negotiators, have always been closely controlled from the top levels of government. The United States has not agreed to forgo a military program that it would otherwise have carried out, even though it has made concessions that critics may argue to have been unnecessary. By and large, the United States has gained at least as much in negotiations as it has given up in return. No agreement between the superpowers can be reached, and certainly none can be maintained, unless each side thinks that reaching and observing the agreement is more advantageous to it than rejecting it.

At the same time, arms control agreements cannot substitute for U.S. or allied military programs to ensure an acceptable military balance. The United States and its allies cannot negotiate their way into a military balance more favorable than the one they are prepared to achieve unilaterally if the arms negotiations fail.

12

Organizing and Reorganizing for National Security

U.S. national security rests on, among other elements, military strength, economic programs, and diplomatic efforts. The political, managerial, and financial resources available for these efforts will always be limited. In principle, one way to improve U.S. national security for any given level of resources is to reorganize the way the government formulates and carries out national security policy. Many such efforts have been made, through legislation and through executive branch reorganization. Moreover, Congress has altered its own procedures. Some of these changes have been improvements but some have not.

In defining and executing national security policy the government acts within three major sets of organizational relationships: the executive branch with the legislative branch; the President and White House staff with the executive departments and agencies; and the offices within each of the various executive departments.

CONGRESS AND THE EXECUTIVE BRANCH

Congressional procedures in the past fifteen years have changed most notably in staffing patterns and in committee functions. Congressional staff personnel are about four times as numerous as they were in the mid-1960s. The expansion was in part an understandable reaction to the previous situation, in which executive branch officials had maintained a monopoly on detailed information and expertise. The legislators in Congress found it difficult to compete with the executive, and the subdivision of their attention among a growing variety of issues lost them the advantages of their lengthier tenure. Congressional committees accordingly now examine individual national security programs in much greater detail, whether they deal with weapons or foreign policy. The result has been an increase in Congressional oversight and thus in the degree of executive branch accountability. It is doubtful that this has improved the efficiency or effectiveness of either branch of the government.

Senior policymakers in the executive branch—in the Department of State, the Department of Defense, and other agencies—now spend much more time testifying before Congressional committees and answering detailed questions prepared by Congressional staffers but asked by individual legislators. Members of the Senate and the House have no more time to attend to the details of these matters than they had before. They are elected to office to serve a variety of political interests, not to act as executives; so it is no surprise that their staffs are not organized to produce a smooth evolution of consistent foreign or defense policy positions, even for the individual legislator. The legislators themselves are responsible to their constituencies for their actions, but one legislator is almost never the final individual decider of an issue. As one vote among 535, he or she is unlikely to be held accountable for the consequences of the legislation itself. Moreover, the authority of party leaders and committee chairmen within Congress has weakened greatly over the last two decades, so each Senator and Representative must be negotiated with separately. The Congressional staffer is much less accountable than the executive branch policymaker or even a low-level bureaucrat and need not know much about some military subject or program to be *the* expert among Congressional staffs.

Congress not only examines but also legislates foreign and defense policy and programs at a much more detailed level. For example, Congress now reserves the right to veto military sales to foreign countries. Reasonably enough, the responsibility for initiating that veto process has been assigned to the Senate Foreign Relations Committee and the House Foreign Affairs Committee. In fact, no major military assistance sale has been rejected, but negotiations between the United States and foreign governments on these matters now have an invisible third party (or rather, 535 of them) present. Again accountability is improved, and unjustified and careless executive branch actions are inhibited; unfortunately, necessary foreign assistance and military equipment transfers have also been made more difficult.

Congress passed the Budget Impoundment and Control Act of

1974 to force President Nixon to make expenditures for domestic programs that had been voted by Congress. The act also forced Congress itself to make an overall decision, in a "budget resolution," on tax revenues, entitlement programs contained in authorizing legislation, the appropriations of individual departments, and the resulting effects on the economy. Supervision of just these concerns is what the Office of Management and Budget is supposed to do in the executive branch. As usual, things did not work out as simply as Congress intended. The budget resolution process gradually gained strength through the late 1970s as the congressional budget committees and the resolutions they pushed through Congress came to have more and more effect on individual authorizations and appropriations. The budget reconciliation process also began to affect revenue and entitlement legislation. Often the government was forced to operate for long periods of time on continuing resolutions. In its consideration of those resolutions Congress as a whole assumed the functions that it had previously delegated to the authorizing and appropriating committees. Those committees, bested in the struggle to control overall budget totals for domestic programs and defense, turned to closer micromanagement of individual departmental budgets, in part in an attempt to compensate for authority lost to other Congressional power centers.

In 1981 President Reagan successfully used the budget reconciliation process to force a single up or down vote on his proposed budget and tax legislation, threatening to veto any substantially different programs, an action that would have brought the government's functioning to a standstill. This showed that the process can be used to give a powerful and popular President the last word. This procedure is unlikely to work more than once for a given administration or session of Congress, but it does highlight the need for the legislative branch to find some way to make modifications in executive programs—domestic and economic as well as national security programs—without falling into one of two traps. The first trap is getting into so much detail that a coherent program is impossible. The second is making policy changes the individual parts of which (defense, taxes, entitlements) Congress approves but the consequences of which (deficits) it is unwilling to take responsibility for. Of course, Presidents must avoid the same traps, but their responsibility is clearly fixed.

Two additional examples of Congressional limitations on executive authority in foreign policy and national security matters are the laws covering covert action and the War Powers Act. Both have restricted or inhibited executive branch actions on occasion, but in fact they represent the limits that U.S. public opinion now sets on the nature and length of any U.S. combat involvement or covert activities in foreign countries. A determined President, confident of public support for his foreign and military policies, will not be unduly hampered by the present laws and practices.

A reorganization of Congress delineating committee responsibilities more clearly, reducing overlaps, increasing the authority and responsibility of the leadership, and reducing the size of staffs would produce more coherent national policies and legislation. But that seems even less likely than the comparable changes that Congress frequently urges on the executive branch.

WITHIN THE EXECUTIVE BRANCH

National security policy has diplomatic, military, intelligence, economic, and domestic political components. It must therefore be formulated by several executive agencies, individually and through interagency coordinating procedures. When there are differing views among the agency heads, and for sufficiently important matters even when they agree, the President must make the decision. With the agency heads, the President's national security staff develops criteria for what issues must be taken to the President and frames those issues for decision. Both in the interagency consultations and in the interactions of agency heads with the President and the White House staff, personalities will inevitably play an important role. This factor makes it difficult to lay down hard and fast procedures.

The Assistant to the President for National Security Affairs (also known as the National Security Adviser) heads the staff of the National Security Council (NSC) and must do more than just ensure that differing agency views are debated and where necessary brought to the President for decision. He should also offer his own advice, given from the standpoint of one who represents the President's (and, one hopes, the nation's) interest and who has an overarching viewpoint rather than the particular functional perspective created by the departmental bureaucratic pressures that inevitably influence the Secretary of State, the Secretary of Defense, the Director of Central Intelligence, and other agency heads.

But the effectiveness of the National Security Adviser in offering advice, as well as in coordinating interagency activities and in ensuring that Presidential decisions are in fact implemented, is determined by whether he acts to facilitate decision making or is seen as an independent player. In this regard appearances, press conferences, and "backgrounders" are usually unnecessary and can even be counterproductive. They should occur rarely and then only with explicit and specific Presidential approval, usually when the President wants something said but for some reason cannot or should not say it himself and does not want the Secretary of State or the Secretary of Defense to issue the statement.

The President must also make decisions that weigh the foreign aspects of national security (military and diplomatic) in the balance with economic and domestic political considerations (including those that also affect national security) and adjudicate between the differing views and perspectives of his domestic political advisers and his advisers on foreign and defense policy.

It may be possible to make organizational improvements to aid the President in this task. Making economic advice a recognized component in national security policymaking would be an important step. But that will not be easy. The governmental structure does not provide a single preeminent economic adviser for the President, as it does a foreign policy, a defense, and an intelligence adviser. The Secretary of the Treasury, the Chairman of the Council of Economic Advisers (CEA), and the Director of the Office of Management and Budget (OMB) all have a clear claim, and the Chairman of the Federal Reserve Board has a major effect. Moreover all of the domestic agencies—the Departments of Agriculture, Labor, Commerce, Health and Human Services, and so on—not only represent domestic constituencies but are likely to have views on the economy as a whole. Each President should select a single agency head to be the principal adviser on economic affairs as they relate to foreign policy and national security policy. Presumably the principal adviser will usually be the Secretary of the Treasury, although it might be the Director of OMB or the Chairman of the CEA. The economic expertise of the NSC staff should also be strengthened.

The White House staff will have to deal with the effects of national security on domestic politics and of domestic politics on national security. It would help if the President were to designate a single person to be the preeminent adviser on the interaction of domestic policy and national security policy. Assuming that the National Security Adviser reports directly to the President, that top adviser on domestic interactions ought to be the President's chief of staff—the senior adviser for everything else.

THE DEPARTMENT OF DEFENSE

Secretary of Defense

A Secretary of Defense has a variety of responsibilities. Some of these are mutually reinforcing and some are conflicting. His first task is to advise the President on and to manage for him the military aspects of national security policy. The Secretary of Defense must inevitably be part of a national security team. He plays the leading role in defining military policy, as the Secretary of State does in defining foreign policy. But foreign and military policy are closely connected, so the Secretary of Defense and, under his direction, the Joint Chiefs of Staff (JCS) influence foreign policy, and the Secretary of State influences military strategy and programs.

The Secretary of Defense, for example, appropriately advises the President about the probable effects on the U.S.-Soviet military balance if the United States and its allies tighten or loosen restrictions on transfers of technology to the Soviets. The Secretary of State would, however, usually take the lead in formulating and negotiating such a policy. The Secretary of Defense can comment on a recommendation that the United States distance itself from, say, some East Asian nation whose internal policies are distasteful, in light of the effect such a policy would have on U.S. security in the Far East. Correspondingly, the Secretary of State can make recommendations on the deployment of weapons systems, e.g., enhanced radiation weapons, to allied countries in the light of the effects of the proposed deployments on U.S. relations with those allies. He can also assess the effect than changes in U.S. fleet-deployment levels in the Far East will have on Japanese attitudes or on how proposed deployment modes for U.S. land-based ICBMs are likely to affect European attitudes toward accepting U.S. land-based nuclear weapons. But in such cases, the primary responsibility for formulating and implementing these defense policies rests with the Secretary of Defense. Depending on the President's interests and on the state of world and domestic affairs, the President's Assistant for National Security Affairs, other White House staff members and advisers, and the Director of Central Intelligence will also play major roles in both kinds of national security decisions.

A second responsibility of the Secretary of Defense is to act as the President's deputy in the military chain of command. For example, the Secretary of Defense approves, or returns for modification, requests from the Joint Chiefs of Staff for authority to move military units— even a single aircraft or ship. He also approves plans drawn up by the Joint Strategic Target Planning Staff in Omaha for the use of U.S. strategic forces in case of a nuclear war.

A third major function of the Secretary of Defense is to manage the Department of Defense—an enterprise that spends more than $200 billion a year—with all the major domestic political effects and pressures that engenders. The Secretary determines, subject to Presidential approval and to very considerable congressional review (1) policies for procuring and awarding contracts for military systems; (2) the number and location of military bases; and (3) regulations for the recruitment, training, and compensation of personnel. Industry, families of service personnel, and Congress all have special interests at stake in these decisions.

Thus, in connection with his duties, the Secretary of Defense often finds himself communicating with the public, the press, Congress, and also foreign governments and publics—sometimes persuading, sometimes bargaining.

Finally, the Secretary of Defense must be familiar with the ideas and views of numerous interested parties and constituencies—domestic and foreign, political and bureaucratic. He must build a consensus about defense policy across the widest possible range of those perspectives. A corresponding task exists for most senior government officials, but the Secretary of Defense has one of the most difficult, given the differences in perspective of the various Military Services, the differences between military and civilian officials, and the variety of interests—domestic, foreign, economic, and budgetary—involved in defense issues. The difficulties of building such a consensus are greatly compounded by the bureaucratic process and by individual personalities. Nevertheless, a substantial degree of consensus on policy can be established within the Department of Defense, given reasonably effective leadership.

The Office of the Secretary of Defense (OSD)

Every Secretary of Defense must make a choice—or rather, his personality makes it for him—about the degree to which he and his immediate assistants will run the day-to-day operations of the Department. Both a hands-on and a hands-off management style are workable, and the practice tends to shift from one to the other every five years or so.

Probably the greatest single innovation in managerial style and organization since the Military Departments were subordinated in 1949 to the Secretary of Defense took place in the early 1960s when Secretary of Defense Robert McNamara and Assistant Secretary (Comptroller) Charles Hitch instituted a formal planning, programming, and budgeting system (PPBS).

PPBS is a system that, in a highly idealized description, operates as follows. First, the Secretary of Defense and the JCS decide on a military strategy. Then PPBS determines the optimum force structure to carry out the chosen military strategy or plan. It devises a five-year program to produce and maintain those forces in the most cost-effective way, revising the program annually and rolling it forward one more year. Then it budgets annual increments of the program. PPBS compares alternative forces by objective rather than by military service and uses overall program costs, including maintenance and personnel, rather than initial acquisition costs alone. An office of systems analysis (now called Program Analysis and Evaluation) carries out the corresponding studies.

This was the first example of such a system in the U.S. government, although it had been prefigured to some degree in the Department of Defense (DOD) itself during the tenure of Secretary Thomas Gates (1959–1961). PPBS remains in use. It has spread throughout the government, even while its prophets, the Systems Analysis Office in the Office of the Secretary of Defense, have sometimes seemed to be without honor in their own country and have seen their own numbers and influence wax and wane.

Since 1959, the Director of Defense Research and Engineering (now the Under Secretary of Defense for Research and Engineering) has exercised strong staff supervision over the development and acquisition of major systems. But much more attention needs to be paid to the mechanics of acquiring weapons systems and materiel, both in the Office of the Secretary of Defense and in the Military Services. The problems of high costs, delays, and unsuitable products are largely traceable to the lack of personal responsibility and accountability on the part of anyone for any particular weapons program as a whole. Instead, overly detailed military specifications are drawn up for standard items, piles of documentation accumulate that no one looks at but that protect procurement officers when Congress starts investigating, and lengthy and repeated reviews settle nothing. All of these contribute to the problem rather than to the solution. The best evidence for this thesis is the relative success of programs carried out at a high level of secrecy, e.g., the U-2, the SR-71, various satellite programs, and the "stealth" aircraft programs. In these cases, very few individuals in the Military Services, in the Office of the Secretary of Defense, in the Office of Management and Budget, or in Congress—and none in the public or in the press—knew about the programs until they were well along, sometimes even until after they were deployed. Documentation in such cases is minimal, decisions are made and approved by a small number of people, program managers have long tenure, and personnel and overhead are minimized—in part for security reasons.

Such expedited procedures are almost by definition not possible for the entire defense development and production program. For one thing, such an approach demands outstandingly capable, and correspondingly rare, people. But the much better record of highly classified programs suggests that modifying the overall development and procurement system along those lines would be a great improvement. Whether such a modification is feasible is uncertain, for the American public, press, and Congress have come to demand accountability in great detail and extremely quickly.

The position of Under Secretary of Defense for Policy, created in 1977, has staff responsibility for the interaction of foreign policy and defense policy, for planning, and for helping the Secretary of Defense evaluate the advice of the Joint Chiefs of Staff on military strategy and operations. The Secretary of Defense also needs a small operational staff to review the adequacy of military contingency plans. The best way would be to share such a staff with the Chairman of the JCS.

The Military Services

Any organization as large as the Department of Defense must be divided into major operating units, with appropriate authority delegated to them. Historically, having an Army, Navy, Air Force, and Marines has made considerable sense. Each service has definable functions, and the land, sea, and air environments differ sufficiently to call for differing skills, experience, and sometimes even equipment. The morale and esprit in the military have largely come from service identifications. Recruiting, training, and personnel functions up to a certain level are clearly best carried out in such a structure. Attempts to substitute for service identification some general professional military identification, or a functional identification that would go with the activities of particular unified or specified commands, are unlikely to work as well.

Nevertheless, the division into four military services has led to some large and wasteful overlaps. The most obvious is the maintenance of four separate tactical air forces. Others include separate medical services, separate development and procurement of communications equipment, competing public relations organizations, and duplication of expensive military bases and facilities.

Service divisions have increasingly contributed to operational difficulties. In Vietnam, for example, the air war was directed in part by the theater commander in Vietnam, in part by the Commander in Chief of Pacific Forces in Hawaii. U.S. Army and Air Force units in Europe have difficulty communicating because their systems were developed separately and are not interoperable. Because the Navy and the Air Force use different refueling equipment, tanker aircraft of one cannot refuel fighters of the other without an equipment change. Until recently, even that option was not available. Each service has its own model of transport helicopters, and crews are generally not cross-trained.

Conflicts also exist over service roles and missions. The Army, the Navy, and the Air Force all see a role for themselves in space systems and operations; these ambitions compete. Both the Navy and the Air Force operate parts of the strategic deterrent forces. The Army and the Marines have differing views on which service should take the lead in providing the ground forces for the Rapid Deployment Force. The services themselves cannot eliminate the waste, correct the operational difficulties, or resolve the conflicts over roles and missions. Efforts by civilians in the Office of the Secretary of Defense to resolve them, through procurement decisions or new ideas about strategy and tactics, are better than nothing. But they are not nearly so appropriate as military efforts to that end, in the JCS, for example, and their Joint Staff. Unfortunately, those bodies as now constituted are unable to resolve such issues.

Two major organizational issues in the Department of Defense require attention. These are the role of the Military Departments and the responsibilities of the Joint Chiefs of Staff.

Military Department (or Service) Secretariats are intended to ensure civilian supremacy and to insulate the Service Chiefs from political pressures from Congress and the public. Sometimes the Secretariats are able to carry out these tasks; the key is the relationship the Service Secretary (the man in the middle) has with the Service Chief and with the Secretary of Defense. In some cases the Service Secretary has actually increased the service pressures on the Secretary of Defense and his immediate staff in the OSD. In recent years Assistant Secretaries of the Military departments have often been appointed from the ranks of Congressional staffers in an attempt to cement departmental relations with Congress. Unfortunately, this practice has increased the likelihood of Service Secretariats' trying to bypass the Secretary of Defense in dealing with Congress. The insulation fails, and short circuits result, as the former Congressional staffers revert to their earlier loyalties.

To reduce the number of levels in an overly layered managerial structure, it would be desirable to eliminate the Service Assistant Secretaries and to combine the staffs of the Service Secretary and the Service Chief into a single staff serving both. The Service Secretariat would then include only the Secretary, the Under Secretary, and a total staff of four or five professionals. A more streamlined option would eliminate the Service Secretaries altogether, vesting most of their functions in the Service Chiefs and the rest in the Office of the Secretary of Defense. This could make sense if the Service Chiefs were severed completely from their JCS responsibilities. Then the chain-of-command and combat functions (planning and operations) could be separated from the support functions of personnel, training, development, and procurement. If a less sweeping revision of the present JCS structure is adopted, the retention of a modest Service Secretariat is appropriate.

The Joint Chiefs of Staff

The Service Chiefs who now, together with the Chairman, constitute the JCS, have a built-in and insuperable conflict of interest. They have individual responsibility for running their services and confront strong internal pressures to fight for their service interests. They are also expected to provide joint military advice to the President and the Secretary of Defense on political-military issues and operational military planning. But the Chairman of the JCS has no power of decision and commands no forces. In fact, he does not even command the Joint Staff.

Service Chiefs must spend so much time running their services that on interservice issues, and especially political-military issues, their reliance on subordinates is great. Those subordinates, who depend for their promotions on the approval of their immediate service superiors, are unlikely to advise the Army Chief of Staff to assign a high priority to defending air bases with Army surface-to-air missiles or to go along with a plan to have British units serve that function for U.S. Air Force bases in Britain. Nor is the Air Force Chief of Staff likely to support Navy suggestions for sealift increases unless the Chief of Naval Operations supports the Air Force's airlift program.

Preparations for military operations, including command arrangements, logistics, and plans, must go through an elaborate interservice procedure. This sytem has its advantages: The interrelationships in a combined operation are examined beforehand, and different perspectives are advanced. But the result is often the lowest-common-denominator resolution of differences in service positions, adding together requests rather than making hard choices either between services or between operational theaters. It is easier, for example, to assume that enough airlift and sealift will somehow be available for multiple contingencies than to face up in advance to the difficult choice as to which front will get priority. And when the Joint Chiefs do face the fact that the requirements will exceed the available lift capacity, their peacetime compromises are likely to be the wrong ones for wartime exigencies.

A variety of views, backgrounds, and experiences must be brought to bear on military advice. Experience across the boundaries of land, naval, and air forces is rare. The President and the Secretary of Defense therefore need a senior interservice advisory body. The JCS, if it is to give coherent advice and to take an effective position reflecting professional military views, should not be a collective body. By far the best solution would be to have a Chief of Military Staff (with a deputy from the naval forces if he is an Army or Air Force officer, or vice versa) and a Joint General Staff drawn from all the services but responsible *to him alone.* He should have the principal authority for promotions on that staff. Some movement back and forth between the general staff and the service staffs would be possible, but obviously there would be a difference in career paths— some officers choosing or being chosen to remain largely within their services, others following a career path of joint service except for occupying, on occasion, some very senior positions in the service in which they were commissioned.

Such an approach would be an attempt to introduce a clearer and less parochial military view on issues of military strategy and capabilities, and the relationship between the two. It would provide a means to clarify roles and missions and to improve the procedure for establishing the requirements for operational capabilities. A General Staff would be able to review, compare, and suggest changes in the plans of commanders with different geographical or functional responsibilities and to decide among their competing demands for limited combat resources. Decisions would be less likely to be influenced by (or go unmade because of) questions of whether individual unified and specified commanders are from one service or another, whether the functions are oriented toward one service or another, or how the decisions would affect service roles, missions, opportunities, futures, and personalities. The President, the Secretary of Defense, and Congress would be able to get much clearer and more accountable military advice than they get now—if they want it. U.S. military planning and strategy would become more responsive to the changed needs of military operations and to complex political-military situations.

The Service Chiefs would continue to have responsibility for structuring, equipping, and training their services. They would make budget recommendations on behalf of their services through their Service Secretaries. But they would no longer make recommendations in a separate chain under JCS auspices. The Chief of Military Staff would make an overall budget recommendation, including a ranking of priorities from among the programs of the different services. He would also review budget decisions and their implications for joint operations.

What is proposed here is to separate those charged with training and procurement (the Service Chiefs) from those charged with strategy and operations. The Chief of Military Staff and the Joint General Staff would provide not a second channel for service inputs but a separate perspective on these matters. It is notable that such a structure and military posts (whatever their names) already exist in so disparate a collection of nations as Great Britain, Canada, West Germany, France, and the Soviet Union.

Are there drawbacks to this Chief of Military Staff–Joint General Staff approach? Surely. It does tend to create an elite group, and strains between that group and the operational forces would be inevitable. Operational commanders at the high level, however, already have multiservice responsibilities and should prefer getting their guidance from a General Staff alone to receiving additional informal but influential pressures from service headquarters. This proposal will not necessarily resolve the problems of, or bring a clear and unique military insight to, choices among weapons systems or procurement levels. And there is a risk in not having at the top levels of the General Staff some of the immediate service experience involved in training, weapons development and procurement, and service doctrine that the Service Chiefs now provide in the JCS.

General David Jones, the recently retired Chairman of the Joint Chiefs, has proposed a more modest modification of the present JCS system. This would give the Chairman—who would be provided with a deputy—more authority. The Chairman would replace the JCS as a group in their role as principal military adviser to the President, the Secretary of Defense, and Congress. The Service Chiefs would continue as members of the JCS. In that role they would advise the Chairman, and each would be given a small interservice staff for that purpose. The present participation of the service staffs in JCS matters, where they effectively have a veto at each of four steps, would disappear. The Joint Staff would be responsible to the Chairman alone. He would have influence in the promotions of officers assigned to the Joint Staff, and they in turn would be allowed to serve longer in those assignments. This proposal is a reasonable way to begin. But it would not fundamentally alter the dual responsibilities of the Service Chiefs.

One concern about any JCS reform is frequently expressed, but in my judgment it has no substance. This is that it will produce something analogous to the German General Staff and threaten democratic principles. The problem with the German General Staff in World War I—which was an army staff rather than a joint staff—was not that one service dominated the others; it was, at least in that war, that it dominated the civilian authority. In World War II the German General Staff probably had too little capability to plan or direct combined operations—for example, the Luftwaffe, through Göring, remained a political force on its own. A Chairman of the Joint Chiefs, or a Chief of Military Staff, is no more likely to dominate civilians than is a committee.

A more legitimate question is whether divergent views would be suppressed. Though that possibility will always exist—as it does now—a Secretary of Defense or a President can see to it that alternative choices are presented and can reach down into the services, or to the Unified and Specified Commands, to get dissenting views. Enforced conformity of view is much less likely in a Joint General Staff than within a specific military service. Strong traditions and a sense of cohesion and community make the headquarters staff of a military service more monolithic than any other organizational unit of the U.S. military. Plenty of argument goes on, but it is kept inside.

A reform of the JCS would have several additional benefits. First, it would almost certainly greatly improve the quality of the Joint Staff. That is not to say that the present Joint Staff is of poor quality. It is composed of fine officers. The real stars among the lieutenant colonels, colonels, commanders, and Navy captains, however, are guarded jealously by the individual services. Thus, though the Joint Staff gets its full share of good officers, it probably gets less than its share of the very best. This, almost as much as the existence of service vetoes during the formulation of JCS positions on policy or operations, affects the quality of all Joint Staff work, most importantly their operational planning and their review of the plans of the unified and specified commanders.

Second, military officers in such a Joint General Staff could take over many of the current roles of the OSD staff. Civilian analysts in the Department of Defense have been making military recommendations for more than twenty-five years, and they will undoubtedly continue to do so, no matter what organizational changes are made. But the degree to which their recommendations are accepted over those of military staffs will depend on how well-conceived and responsive the recommendations of the military staffs are, both to the situation and to the needs of civilian decision makers. In principle, the best recommendations would come from a joint military staff or from teams of military officers and civilians, with the military officers usually in charge of those teams. Under present arrangements the JCS organization and the Joint Staff cannot meet the above tests for quality of recommendations. Secretaries of Defense have, therefore, turned to civilian staffs in the Office of International Security Affairs and in the Office of Program Analysis and Evaluation to get policy and planning advice whose content comprises at least as much of military as of political or technical matters or of international relations.

Usually, but not always, Secretaries of Defense have also turned to the Chairman of the Joint Chiefs of Staff as a personal adviser. This has inevitably caused the Chairman problems with his colleagues on the JCS and forced him to rely on a staff of four or five—a special assistant and a Chairman's special staff group. He uses the Joint Staff as well, to whatever degree is feasible with a Joint Staff that reports to the Joint Chiefs of Staff as a group. All joint staff actions are also monitored and influenced at every step by the staffs of the Military Services.

A third reason for such a change would be to improve the interactions of the Joint Chiefs or of any successor organization with the unified and specified commanders. Almost all modern military operations are joint operations and have been since World War II. Today reconnaissance and target acquisition and designation are largely done from the air or even from space. The ranges of manned and unmanned attack vehicles—ballistic or aerodynamic, launched from land or from the sea—are much larger than they were before. Land and sea battles are now strongly influenced, if not dominated, by control of the air; and air and sea forces require land bases. For all these reasons, the operational commands charged with planning and executing combat operations require a much closer integration of the different services than was necessary in the past, even in World War II. Some of these Unified and Specified Commands are functional and involve only a single service (the specified commands—the Strategic Air Command and the Military Airlift Command); others are geographically defined and tend to be dominated either by naval forces (the Atlantic and Pacific commands) or by ground and ground-based air forces (the European command).

In every case, the unified commanders in the field should have greater control over their component service commands, which now respond more to service headquarters staffs in the Pentagon. The unified and specified commanders (CINCs) should also play more of a role in defining military requirements and budgets and in the initial planning for military contingencies. The Chief of Military Staff, using the Joint General Staff, should then review and balance the plans of the CINCs, reconciling them within limited resources, ensuring their compatibility with overall operational plans for various single-theater or multitheater contingencies, and evaluating them in light of international political considerations. Then, ideally, the CINCs' plans would be redrawn to be compatible with all those constraints, or the constraints would be adjusted where possible.

If these radical JCS and military service reorganizations make sense, why have not previous DOD administrations (specifically my own) put them forward? The answer is simple: Ripeness is all. Such changes are best proposed by either a departing or a recently departed administration, which cannot be accused of self-aggrandizement. They also require the informed support of the incumbent administration. All the organizational changes I have discussed are feasible, given an administration that is strong enough and a modicum of acceptance in the Congress. But until now they have not had a high enough political priority when that political strength was present. The 1980s are a good time to move at least some distance in these directions.

13

Managing the
Department of Defense

The Congress established the Department of Defense in 1947, incorporating and reorganizing the elements of the old War Department and Navy Department. The experience of World War II and the immediate postwar years provided much of the impetus. One goal of the reorganization was to integrate the military policy of the United States more closely with its foreign policy, a task that could be more effectively addressed by a single, central, civilian management of the various armed forces and their activities. A second goal was certainly to address the perceived need for efficiency of operation. This was to be done by avoiding waste and duplication and applying sensible business practices in procurement and in other areas where they could reasonably be expected to save the taxpayer money. The original Congressional hearings on the legislation establishing the Department of Defense (DOD), the legislation itself, and the testimony on and text of the amendments that have since gradually restructured the department all make frequent reference to such principles.

In the years since 1947, there have been many calls for better, more efficient, and more effective management of the Department of Defense. Some come from the General Accounting Office (GAO), which offers many suggestions every year—some practical and some not, some useful and some not, some adopted and some not. In 1981 the retiring Comptroller General, Elmer Staats, indicated that he had delivered to the new Secretary of Defense a list of fifteen suggestions. The savings from their adoption would, he said, reach an "absolute minimum" of $4 billion a year by 1985. A further list, which would take longer to implement, could be expected to increase the annual savings to $10 billion. Some of the proposals were new, most were not, but none of the good ones was at all easy to implement or they would have been adopted before.

Suggestions also come from political candidates. As a Presidential candidate in 1976, for example, Governor Carter advocated a $5 billion to $7 billion reduction in the defense budget through the elimination of waste. In office, President Carter explained that such savings, if achieved, would mean a budget lower than it would otherwise have been, rather than a budget lower than the previous year's budget. Innumerable Congressmen, retired military officers, academics, and journalists call for savings, for rationalization, and for reorganization.

It should be no surprise that every Secretary of Defense also takes office declaring that he will cut back, eliminate waste, reorganize, and manage better. And each succeeds—to a certain extent. Some are more successful at that particular duty of the office than others. But each—and I include myself—has left office at least as frustrated by what he had failed to get done as he was pleased by what he had accomplished along these lines. There are still four tactical air forces, and there are still too many military bases and installations for the present or any reasonably anticipated size of U.S. armed forces. There is still a mismatch between the procurement of initial systems and equipment, and the procurement of spare parts. There are still fifty-cent fasteners that cost fifty dollars. Why?

Many (though by no means all) of the disappointed hopes and expectations of Secretaries of Defense can be traced to some common confusions and misconceptions. In many cases, Secretaries of Defense have in mind—and express in word and deed—different and even conflicting objectives. Pursuing some can make others difficult or impossible, or can undo them once they have been done. Furthermore, the comparison to business, useful in some contexts and in some areas of defense management, breaks down in others.

The management procedures followed in spending the $110 billion for research and development (R&D) and for procurement included in the fiscal 1982 defense budget certainly bear many resemblances to those in the private sector. But the overall size and expenditures of the Department of Defense continue to dwarf most individual business enterprises. Even Exxon, number one in the *Fortune* 500, has annual sales that are only about half the annual expenditures of the DOD. In personnel, the differences with the private sector are more obvious: The DOD has more than 2 million uniformed personnel and about 1 million civilian employees and in fiscal 1982 supported about 3 million workers in defense industries. By contrast, Exxon has about 139,000 employees, and AT&T, the single largest private employer, has just over 1 million.

The Department of Defense also has an enormously diverse set of products, but only one line of business. Consider the following list of objectives and activities of the DOD:

• The Armed Forces must deter armed conflict and, if necessary, fight. They must be organized. This organization includes the formulation of doctrine, the creation of strategy and supporting war plans, the recruitment and training of personnel, and the deployment and maintenance of forces. Each of these activities requires a very different kind of management, although they certainly influence one another.

• The DOD must procure, repair, maintain, and often develop materiel ranging from aircraft carriers to light bulbs.

• DOD policies, programs, and operations must support the foreign policy of the United States—a truism, but not one that applies to business activities in the private sector.

• The DOD must deal with a vast and diverse set of constituencies—including the public, Congress, the media, organizations of retired military people, and the various nongovernmental associations interested in national security. The acceptability of defense budgets, programs, and activities all depend on the attitudes of some or all of these constituencies. Their views must therefore be taken into account. A great deal of consultation, explanation, and persuasion is required.

Most important, the Department of Defense differs from business because it is part of the government. There is no single number that provides a bottom-line measure of how well the DOD or any other government agency is being managed. And there is a whole set of conflicting and often legitimate forces whose pull is neither toward improved efficiency nor toward increased combat capability.

Beyond this difference, there is also a balance to be struck between cost and combat effectiveness. For any particular level of combat effectiveness, there should be a way to do the job at the lowest cost possible. Doing so makes resources available, either for additional military capability that can be translated into greater confidence of being able to support or extend U.S. foreign policy goals, for nonmilitary foreign aid that can serve the same purpose, or for support of domestic goals, including a balanced budget. But there are differences in judgment, even among well-informed, experienced, and dedicated people, about the relative effectiveness of different military forces.

The criteria that define effectiveness vary with external circumstances and with the internal assumptions on which the comparison is based. Some of this variation is susceptible to economic analysis or systems analysis, but some is not. There are also differences between what is efficient in peacetime and what is effective in wartime. In principle, the United States wants to structure its military forces for optimum wartime use, but it is less likely to pay the high premium for such a configuration if the likelihood of war appears remote. Readiness for combat is expensive. So long as crises that require such readiness do not arise, it may come to be thought of as unnecessary insurance.

It is therefore not possible to manage the Department of Defense exactly like a business and to try to get to a bottom line that indicates profit or any other single measurable criterion. Even the management criteria used in private nonprofit organizations or in other parts of the government cannot be applied to all the various operations of the DOD.

Each of these differences from private business management is worth more detailed consideration. The problems of a government agency are familiar. Clearly there is and always will be great political pressure from local officials, members of Congress, and the White House staff on decisions, for example, to realign military bases in a way that would reduce the number of jobs at any location. There can be equal or even greater pressure on awards of defense contracts. Such pressure undermines efficient management by any economic standard.

It was easy to show in 1979 that it made sense to reduce from nine to five the number of defense contract and supply centers in the Defense Logistics Agency. And it was not too hard to determine, by economic analysis, which four should go. But only one was eliminated. The political forces in the regions concerned did not agree with the analysis and came up with alternative calculations. These were not correct, but they were difficult to prove incorrect to their authors.

In the business sector, the arguments would be heard and a decision would be made and implemented. Moreover, the final decision could be made privately, with the appropriate executive considering and judging the various arguments and calculations submitted by the parties within the organization, interested and disinterested. But in the Department of Defense there is no privacy in decision making except in the Secretary's own office, and by no means always there. Given an arena to perform in and a captive audience, officials of the military services, Congressmen, and countless other parties engage in a debilitating amount of posturing.

The story on military bases is much the same, but it has several dimensions. There is little doubt that by the time a choice must be made between eliminating a military base in the Northeast or Midwest and one in the South or the West, analysis will show that it is cheaper to keep the one in the Sunbelt. There is some merit to the opposing contention that a more uniform distribution of bases is needed both to retain a geographically diversified infrastructure and to ensure broad political support, but I have never found that argument decisive.

My own examination, though, has indicated that there is a story behind the story. A major reason the Sunbelt bases look more cost effective by the time the choice is presented to the Secretary of Defense is the way in which many smaller decisions, sometimes biased in nature and always biasing in effect, were made well down in the organization for decades beforehand. Generally these decisions were made by senior military officers, who were thinking not only of the most cost-effective way to manage the base structure and operate the forces. They were also weighing which organization of facilities would provide a larger number of senior managerial spots. They were thinking as well about where they and their friends would prefer to serve—in the snow or in the sun. When it came time to retire, they wanted to retire near a military hospital and a commissary—and those will be where the bases are. Under such circumstances, there is little inclination to improve or expand a base in the Upper Peninsula of Michigan when you can expand one in Florida or Texas or California instead. Another well-known cause of the existing geographical base structure is the functioning of the Congressional seniority system, which put southern Democrats from safe districts in committee chairs in the days when chairmen ruled and bases were built. Those states and districts benefited accordingly.

These earlier decisions were not improper, nor have they necessarily led to the wrong result. Sunbelt bases have better flying and training weather, and in the past facilities were less expensive to build there. To some degree these remain factors in today's decisions. The personal factors do demonstrate, however, that when the time comes for a critical decision, what may seem to be a decision based entirely on cost effectiveness will often depend on other elements, influential or even decisive, that developed for quite different reasons.

It is instructive to examine some other examples of the forces that affect management in its drive for efficiency. Shouldn't procurement be centralized? Yes, it should. But the real question is, for which items? It seems appropriate to centralize procurement of standard items, and the Defense Logistics Agency was set up to do just that. Light bulbs and raincoats can be most efficiently procured that way. But what about aircraft engine parts? They have a critical effect on combat readiness, and a good argument can be made that they should be procured by the particular command that will be carrying out the maintenance and repair.

What about centralized training? The example of undergraduate helicopter-pilot training is a good one. There is no fundamental reason that initial training in helicopters cannot be the same for the Navy as for the Army. Indeed, the Army has done the first-level training of many Marine helicopter pilots. But even during the brief period when the Navy agreed to such a change, members of Congress from Florida, where separate Navy undergraduate helicopter training is carried out, reached a different military conclusion and were able to sustain that position in Congress.

The arguments about cost and efficiency will be further complicated by different judgments as to the relative combat effectiveness of the less expensive way of doing things. Some of these differences can be analyzed and quantified, but others cannot. The same is true, of course, of many aspects of business. Not even the best opinion poll will predict consumer preferences with high accuracy. And a revolution in Iran affects the price of gasoline and sales of automobiles as much as it affects the feasibility of a given U.S. military strategy in Southwest Asia. But combat capabilities and military posture bring a sense of urgency and importance to the debate that can easily outweigh the analytical arguments for efficiency, or even for effectiveness measured by some particular criterion. If this urgency does not overwhelm the decision making of the executive branch, it can still do so in Congress, especially when it is reinforced by the political interests of members whose states or districts will be affected.

Moreover, though the separate services develop and procure equipment and recruit and train personnel, they do not make decisions about force deployment or about the use of forces in combat. Those decisions are made in the field by the unified and specified commanders, based on instructions transmitted by the Secretary of Defense through the Joint Chiefs of Staff. This means that when the services give advice on alternative ways of accomplishing a given combat mission, they do so primarily as suppliers rather than as users. That is, they are interested in selling more, not spending less.

Examples abound. The question of the effectiveness of land-based or sea-based tactical air power in conventional warfare goes beyond the issue of which deployment mode is able to deliver a certain amount of ordnance on target for a given cost. The answer to that is rather clear: Over a campaign of several months or more, land-based airpower will be more cost effective, *if* both are equally available. But will land bases or bases to support naval forces be available? How soon after a crisis arises will they be available? How much materiel can be prepositioned at land bases for land-based air forces? What about the relative vulnerability to attack of land bases and the ships of a carrier task force? Answers to all of these questions depend on the particular contingency envisioned. All such answers are also subject to geopolitical judgments about the way they interact with U.S. foreign policy. And all are quite removed from the simpler issue of whether land-based or sea-based air forces, when in place, will be more accurate, more responsive, more efficient, and more economical. Many of those simpler questions can be answered by quantitative analysis—though different analysts are likely to come to different conclusions. The diplomatic and geopolitical questions are much more difficult to analyze and cannot easily be stated numerically.

Another illustration: The so-called "light" ground forces require much less airlift capability for their deployment than do armored forces. But once they get to a combat zone they will have less mobility and less punch, because they will lack the armored vehicles and helicopters needed for local mobility. Thus decisions on the mix of armored forces, helicopter-borne air-mobile forces, and infantry will depend largely on such issues as the nature of the forces they are expected to fight and whether they will be defending a limited though valuable area or moving forward from wherever they disembark into surrounding areas against enemy resistance. These issues, as much as the questions of accuracy of ordnance delivery, target detection and identification, and sortie rates that are the usual stuff of systems analysis, are likely to be the critical ones.

The list of examples could be extended almost indefinitely. The management of the Department of Defense must also choose between a B-1 and a bomber based on new technology, and between a land-based MX missile and a sea-based alternative. It must select the right mix of aircraft carriers, attack submarines, and surface ships equipped with cruise missiles. These choices depend on much analysis and even more on judgment. When a choice is made with which a particular commentator disagrees, that commentator will often characterize it as "waste." And so it can be, in one sense. Suppose a decision turns out to produce less combat capability for a given expenditure than some bypassed alternative. Or suppose a particular weapons system's deployability or usability is incorrectly evaluated because of misjudgments of international factors. In either case, the decision produces less capability than the same funding could have done if invested elsewhere. And judgments about the best choice will vary widely, not only before the system is procured but even after it is procured and deployed or even after it is used. It is not improper to call such mistakes "waste." But that is not the same kind of waste as the unnecessary extra military bases in the United States, which add nothing to U.S. capability.

This is the nature of some of the problems. What are the solutions? The first step is to acknowledge that the conflicts and contradictions of managing defense cannot be fully resolved. They can only be traded off against each other, well or not so well. It will be argued that such insoluble conflicts obviously exist in any large organization: External political forces act on every government agency; every corporation faces difficult choices, with many of the factors largely matters of judgment and only partly quantifiable. All this is true. But the intensity of the pressures and the importance of the stakes are so much larger in the Department of Defense as to produce a qualitative difference. Individual corporate mistakes can have catastrophic financial effects for many people; wasteful or misguided domestic policies can damage the country; but mistakes in defense and foreign policy can kill us all. That alters the nature of management in these areas. In that sense, the DOD cannot be fully managed— or at least, much of it cannot be managed like a business.

Organizing parts of it in a businesslike way is desirable; it improves efficiency and saves money. The defense establishment is more efficient now than it was in, say, the 1950s. But the management of the Department of Defense still needs major improvement.

The Office of the Secretary of Defense must exercise close policy control over military strategy, force structure, arms control, research and development of weapons, force deployments, and interactions with the military establishments of other countries. Only in that way can there be reasonable assurance of a coherent defense policy and assurance that defense policy supports foreign policy. Moreover, the Secretary of Defense must have the responsibility for dealing with the various defense constituencies. These practices have generally been followed for the past twenty years, and they are being followed now. But there are some signs that they may be weakening, as they have from time to time in the past. Then the individual services follow separate global strategies, procure hardware and forces that fail to match, and conduct public relations and Congressional lobbying activities that compete even more than usual. The need for the Secretary of Defense to exercise these particular powers, though, is so clear that in the long run they will always come back to him and his staff.

The Military Departments should probably have more authority than they have had recently in contracting and procurement and in training and experimenting with different kinds of combat organization. Then the Service Secretaries and Service Chiefs must be held accountable for the results. This is one area in which I am not particularly satisfied with my own performance. The problem is that it is difficult to hold subordinates (especially middle-rank civilians) accountable for their performance in government. It is then often fairer—and easier in the short run—to pull the authority back to the top level.

It is neither feasible nor desirable to abolish the Military Services, which create and foster the kind of morale and loyalty on which military organizations so much depend. Moreover, the Military Departments offer one of the few forms in which necessary decentralization of business-type responsibilities can be effected in the Department of Defense.

The need for improvement and some ways to achieve it have been described; fairness demands an overall assessment. Mine is that despite its difficulties, the Department of Defense is nevertheless the most efficient and the best managed—even in business terms—of all the major departments and agencies of the U.S. government. (Unfortunately, that is damning it with faint praise.) It operates more effectively than the others and is (along with the Department of State, perhaps) the most ably staffed—by military and senior civilian officials alike. Presidents, White House staffs, governors, and mayors turn to DOD when they need something done even outside the military sphere. This is not only because the Department has such substantial financial and hardware resources; it is also because DOD is organized to get things done.

But the major lesson to be drawn from any study of management in the Department of Defense is the basic limitation that any attempt to manage DOD in an ideal fashion will confront. The need to be able to fight a war will always limit the peacetime efficiency of the defense establishment. So will domestic political factors. The problem remains—and will always remain—one of balancing the need for combat readiness and capability with the need for efficiency by exerting strong leadership within the democratic political process. The pull of highly demanding requirements for flexible combat capability—employable in a variety of unpredictable circumstances against opposing forces whose capabilities cannot be confidently foreseen—is a crucial element of our national security. Neither the democratic political process nor the requirements of combat capability can or should be totally overridden in the name of cost-effectiveness. To manage the nation's defense efficiently at the lowest possible cost, along the lines of private-sector business management and organization, is a useful standard. But meeting it exactly entails prices the United States cannot afford to pay. One is the abandonment of democratic control. Another is the loss of a war. Defense cannot be managed like a business, but it can be *led* in a way that preserves U.S. national security interests while operating effectively in a world of limits and amid the pull of conflicting interests.

14

Technology, Military Equipment, and National Security

Just about everything that has to do with national security, in both foreign and defense policy, has been a matter of substantial controversy since the mid-1960s. But since about 1979 what was formerly a minor theme in the usual dissonant symphony of views has become perhaps the most popular of all. It has to do with the place of advanced technology, and of the military equipment that incorporates it, in the U.S. defense posture. Discussions of this matter have become as adversarial as discussions of U.S.-Soviet relations or of the proper U.S. policy towards the Middle East.

THE SIMPLE MYTHS AND THE COMPLEX FACTS

There are three main complaints about the development and procurement of military weapons and equipment:

• U.S. military equipment has become too complex over the past couple of decades. It incorporates too high a level of technology and aims for too high a level of performance. Because of this, the equipment is too expensive and is unreliable and unsuitable.

• The effort put into the technology of modern weapons is one reason, perhaps the major reason, for the decline of the United States' relative position in modern civilian technology and productivity, because it detracts from efforts that would otherwise go into civilian functions.

• There is an iron triangle of Congressional committee members and their staffs, military and civilian officials in the Department of Defense, and contractors that works to produce this overambitious, unreliable, colossally expensive, and dangerous armament.

These concerns are expressed by a variety of commentators. Their numbers include people who have participated in weapons development programs, experienced members of Congress, and middle-level or (more rarely) senior military officers. They also include journalists and other commentators, whose less thorough familiarity with the intricacies of defense procurement does not necessarily make their allegations less worthy of serious attention.

These arguments are set forth here in their most extreme and therefore least defensible form. In fact, there is at least a little truth and sometimes a substantial truth in more moderate expressions of each. But the facts do not support the allegations. The conclusions that are in turn drawn from these allegations, and the remedies proposed, are often wildly out of line. The situation can be more realistically summarized as follows.

The United States has no real choice but to adopt advanced technology for its weapons systems, given the relative advantages it can provide over potential adversaries, and the fact that the American public and its political leaders are willing to maintain only a certain level of defense spending. Moreover, if correctly handled, U.S. reliance on advanced technology is likely to produce a more effective military capability.

There is less spinoff from defense-oriented research and development to the civilian sector today than there was in the 1950s. That is, the civilian sector profits less from military research and development (R&D). In fact, U.S. military research and development now rides, to a considerable extent, on the back of civilian technology, especially in the areas of advanced electronics and integrated circuits. But military R&D still contributes to civilian technology substantially. And the deficiencies of U.S. industry in productivity and in competition with other countries, notably Japan, are very much less a consequence of the diversion of technical talent to military R&D than they are of a variety of cultural factors, of business organization and labor union practices, and of government regulatory, employment, tax, and antitrust policies. The relationships between military and civilian R&D differ in the Soviet Union, Western Europe, and Japan. None of these is a better model for the United States.

Institutional, operational, and industrial forces create pressure to use insufficiently mature technology in military weapons systems and, more often, to use mature technology to achieve peak performance while slighting the features of low cost, reliability, and maintainability. These forces typically cause contractors to overpromise performance and military user agencies to push for the higher performance that the contractor offered in the brochure that won the contract, to the detriment of those other factors. Together the contractor and the operator often push the developing agency and the program manager into an impossible situation. When the program manager is squeezed, so are the virtues of reliability and affordability. It takes a strong program manager, backed by the most senior military and civilian officials in DOD, to withstand those pressures. Some have—and these are not always the ones who are given credit for being great program managers. The Congressional role in this matter is equivocal. Sometimes knowledgeable legislators (or their staffers) without a constituent interest or personal ax to grind will side with sensible management. More often, contractor pressure expressed through Congress, or the lure of power without responsibility combined with a Congressional staffer's whim, will exacerbate the problem.

THE LESSONS OF HISTORY

Historians can speak of the advantage of the then inferior but less expensive (and therefore more numerous) iron swords over bronze ones to the Dorian invaders of Mycenaean Greece, of the iron-beaked prow to the Roman navies, of "Greek fire" in prolonging the life of the Byzantine empire, or of the rate of fire of the longbow to the English at Agincourt. There is some question of how relevant any of these examples is to the choices the United States faces today or to the appropriate criteria in deciding which technologies to choose and how to employ them for military purposes. The lessons of World War I and World War II are more applicable.[1]

During World War I, the United States was behind both its allies and the Germans in technology, in aircraft, in tanks, in artillery, and probably even in naval design. During World War II, the United States was again behind at the start in quality and sophistication of most military equipment. Never during that conflict did the United

---

[1]The Korean War showed that superior technology and materiel resources can compensate for inferior numbers of personnel. The Vietnam War showed that technology, along with an enormously superior GNP, larger forces, and more materiel will not win a war in the absence of an adequate political infrastructure in the nation being defended, a determination comparable to that of the forces on the other side, or a willingness to use those advantages.

States outdistance the Germans in quality of basic military hardware—tanks, artillery, or aircraft. The antisubmarine warfare problem remained unsolved, although the combination of technology and tactics that went into U.S. aircraft carriers came to dominate the naval war in the Pacific. Moreover, in jet aircraft and guided aerodynamic (V-I) and ballistic (V-II) missiles the Germans remained ahead to the end of the war. It was primarily the quantity, not the quality, of equipment that gave the United States its advantage.

But there were some notable exceptions. These proved critical, at least in limiting the duration of the war, both by preventing the Axis powers from making even greater gains at the beginning and by terminating the war in the Pacific. The critical developments included radar, the proximity fuse, the atomic bomb, and cryptanalysis. The British did the initial work on radar, but during the last three years of the war the United States carried out most of its application. Neither the Germans nor the Japanese were able to match it in quality or quantity. U.S. researchers were also responsible for developing the proximity fuse and nuclear weapons. Great Britain and the United States cooperated in using cryptanalysis for major military gain.

THE SITUATION TODAY

The present situation differs in two important ways from that of World War II. First, the number of troops and the amount of equipment available by 1943 clearly favored the United States and the Allies. Second, as in World War I, the United States had a period of years between the time that U.S. participation was clearly envisioned, or at which it entered the war, and the time the crucial battles were fought.

If one considers the likely combat scenarios in which the United States today might find itself engaged, neither of these conditions would be fulfilled. In the first place, the United States and its allies would not have an advantage in numbers of personnel or quantity of materiel. Even cursory examinations of the current economic, political, and social situation make it clear that the United States would enter any such confrontation with the Soviets with a much smaller active-duty and reserve military force. The active-duty forces of the Soviet Union are about double the size of those of the United States. U.S. and European allied forces do not fully balance those of the Warsaw Pact on the central front, and if Soviet reserves are counted, the Soviet numerical advantage is substantial. In East Asia, the United States would be at a disadvantage relative to the Soviets, even after U.S. reinforcements arrived. The overall ratios would depend on the belligerent status of other major nations or of various proxies. In Southwest Asia, the United States would find it difficult to bring forces to bear comparable in size to those of the relatively nearby Soviets.

An even more important difference in a prospective conflict is that the United States could not expect to have a year or two to prepare before the critical battles were fought. The United States must be prepared to fight from a standing start against what would undoubtedly be Soviet blitzkrieg tactics, whether in Europe, in East Asia, or in Southwest Asia. Had that been the case in World War II, the Germans and the Japanese would have won. But the United States then had the good fortune to be allowed three years to build up its capabilities.

Technological quality, quantity of materiel, and size of forces are all important factors in the military balance. But there are many examples of military victory by numerically inferior forces with proper doctrine and tactics. Neither technology, quantity of materiel, nor numbers of troops can be counted on to substitute for morale, political and military strategy, and superior generalship. The incorporation of advanced technology into U.S. weapons systems must not, and need not, preclude its integration into such a political and military strategy for execution by innovative military strategists and commanders.

Can greater quantities of military hardware substitute for technological superiority in U.S. strategy, as it did in World War II? The amounts of materiel the United States now deploys are appropriate to the size of its peacetime forces. Those forces will not be much increased. If the United States were willing to raise and rely on very large reserve forces, it might be willing to pay the immense price of stockpiling the corresponding quantities of equipment for their use—tanks, planes, ships, and so on. But even that would make sense only if the United States could be sure of bringing those military forces to combat readiness and of transporting them to the theater of combat before the critical battles were fought. It now takes two years from initial order to produce a tank, three to produce an aircraft, and at least five to produce a ship. Most personnel can be trained in a short time, so it would make sense to buy and stockpile the equipment beforehand if the U.S. anticipated (as I do not) that a global or even a European war could last for years. It does make sense, within economic constraints, to shorten those procurement lead times so that the United States could increase its forces during a period of much higher tensions lasting two or three years.

If the United States looks for comparative advantages against a potential Soviet adversary with superior numbers of forces, one of the most obvious is the relatively lower cost of incorporating high technology into U.S. military equipment. The same is true for U.S. allies. In contrast, a low technology–high manpower mix is more advantageous to the Soviets, who are behind on technology but have greater numbers. What follows is a discussion of a few areas in which U.S. high technology can and must be applied to counter Soviet numerical advantages.

Tanks

The Soviets have 40,000 tanks in their inventory, as compared to about 10,000 first-line U.S. tanks. On the NATO central front, which is a more relevant measure of what might be encountered in a combat situation, the ratio is about 2.5 to 1 in favor of the Warsaw Pact. If the United States were to try to redress this difference by manufacturing and deploying a comparable number of tanks, the initial equipment cost (not the total systems cost) for 30,000 tanks would probably be about $50 billion (1982 dollars). Over ten years, such an inventory buildup might be economically feasible. But it would also be necessary to provide crews for those tanks. Given pipeline and training figures, that would probably require 150,000 to 200,000 additional troops in the tank crews alone, and given the U.S. support ratios (or even the much more austere Soviet support ratios), it would probably require an increase in the U.S. Army of 300,000 or 400,000. There is no prospect that this will happen in peacetime, even if the United States returns to conscription.

The United States and its allies must therefore counter this advantage with some combination of innovative tactics and technology. One way to do this would be to have much better tanks. But in technologies for ground forces the Soviets are able by and large to match the United States. In fact, they produce new variations of armored vehicles at about twice the frequency of NATO, so that most of the time the best of their deployed technology tends to be ahead of NATO's. The Soviet T-72 is at least a match for our most modern versions of the M-60 tank. The U.S. M-1 tank is better than the T-72, but the Soviets will follow that up within a few years with a successor probably more advanced than the M-1. In some areas of tank technology, such as materials for armor protection, stability as a platform for target acquisition and firing, and crew comfort, the United States is ahead. In others, such as tank guns and low tank height to make the tank more difficult to see and to hit, the Soviets have advantages. In view of the claims that Soviet systems are less complex, it is interesting to note the presence of an automatic gunloader on the T-72. One more mechanical system to go wrong—but for

lack of it the M-1 needs one more crew member (four, as opposed
to three on the T-72) to lift and insert the 50-pound shells. The M-1
turret must also be bigger, and it must frequently revolve for loading
and again to retarget.

The appropriate comparison, especially in a situation in which
NATO would be defending against a Soviet attack, is that between
Soviet tanks and NATO antitank capability. This is where the technology of the industrialized democracies, and specifically of the United
States, can play a critical role. The United States took the lead in
antitank guided missiles in the mid-1960s. Since then, the Soviets
have made gains. But the United States has now introduced laser-
guided artillery shells and bombs, and infrared imaging systems to
guide air-to-ground ordnance. It is developing ground-launched and
air-launched missiles that will contain submissiles guided by millimeter
waves to acquire tanks as targets and penetrate the thinner armor
on their tops from above. Such technological innovations, based on
U.S. capabilities in sensor technology and in data processing, can be
expected to make a major contribution to the allied ability to stop
Soviet tank attacks.

Air-to-Air Missiles

A second example of the uses of technology in offsetting numerical
deficiencies is in air-to-air combat capabilities. U.S. tactical air forces
now hold a distinct advantage because of the longer range of U.S.
air-to-air missiles, coupled with longer-range radars, more advanced
data processing systems, and the ability of shorter-range, heat-seeking,
infrared-guided missiles (such as the AIM-9L version of the Side-
winder) to home in on opposing aircraft from the side or even from
the front, as well as from the rear. The ability to fire such a missile
and then have it home in on its own, without continued attention
by the firing aircraft, will inevitably be incorporated into the next
generation of air-to-air missiles, thanks again to U.S. advantages in
integrated circuits and data processing.

There are, as always, limits to how far such advantages can be
pushed. Extensive tests in simulated air combat indicate that even
the best air-to-air combat system cannot overcome a ten-to-one
numerical advantage when combat takes place in an adversary's air
space, with ground radar controlling the adversary's aircraft. And
much of the advantage of long-range air-to-air missiles is lost if the
air-to-air combat doctrine does not include firing at long range on
any aircraft that fails to give the correct IFF (identification friend or
foe) signal. U.S. military doctrine has in the past been at best ambiguous
on this point, and restrictions have been placed on the use of long-

range missiles in air combat tests. As a result, some analysts have drawn incorrect conclusions, overvaluing the advantages of superior numbers of fighter aircraft engaged (say, two-to-one or three-to-one ratios) as compared with the advantages of superior long-range air-to-air radars and missiles.

The United States must pay more attention to the competition in electronic countermeasures and counter-countermeasures, in which the Soviets have by no means lagged behind. But overall, U.S. capability in air-to-air missiles is one area in which U.S. technology has paid off.

Precision-Guided Air-to-Surface Missiles

A third general area in which U.S. technological sophistication has become to a substantial degree a substitute for large numbers is precision-guided munitions. The ability to destroy military targets is greatly dependent on the accuracy of delivery of ordnance. In many cases only a tenth or even a hundredth as many sorties by tactical aircraft are needed to accomplish the same mission, provided that they carry such precision-guided munitions. The cost and complexity of the munitions is therefore repaid many times over, not only in the reduced numbers of rounds of ordnance that are needed, but also in the reduced loss of aircraft and pilots, which constitutes the most severe price paid to accomplish a given military mission.

The U.S. Technological Lead

The three examples given share the common features of advanced electronics, integrated circuitry, and computers and data processing. In that area the United States and its European and Japanese allies maintain a five-to-seven-year lead over the Soviet bloc. This is perhaps the most solid single technological advantage possessed by the industrialized democracies. They have a much smaller, though real, lead in aircraft engines and aerodynamics and a substantial lead in antisubmarine warfare capabilities, which again results largely from advantages in data processing and sensors. As for new applications of materials science, the Soviets are ahead in some and the industrialized democracies in others.

There are thus several critical areas in which U.S. technology leads that of the Soviets. To a considerable extent these leads now offset and will continue to offset some of the Soviet numerical advantages. There are limits, however, to the numerical disadvantages they can offset, and they are not a substitute for wise strategy, effective tactics, strong leadership, trained personnel, or any of the other elements of military strength, let alone for the nonmilitary aspects of national security policy. But to fail to take advantage of them would be to throw away a major equalizing factor, much of whose cost has already been paid in any event because, for other good reasons, the United States has a large civilian and a relatively small military sector in its industrial economy. Among the technological areas in which the United States can expect in the future to enjoy such an advantage are precision-guided munitions, cruise missiles, air-to-air missiles and their associated sensors, low-observability "stealth" technology, technical systems for intelligence to offset the Soviet advantage of tighter military security, and antisubmarine warfare capabilities. Without these advantages, the comparative military position of the United States and the other industrialized democracies would be much more precarious than it is.

There is some experimental evidence that supports this assessment of U.S. military technology. When U.S.-equipped forces have engaged Soviet-equipped forces in recent years, U.S. tanks and antitank equipment, advanced fighter aircraft, air-to-air missile systems, and U.S.-inspired air battle and antiaircraft suppression tactics have worked well. These results were not against the most modern Soviet equipment or against Soviet forces, and factors other than equipment have played an important part in the outcome. But even making allowances for those factors, U.S. military equipment and doctrine for its use acquitted themselves well in both the Iran-Iraq War and the Arab-Israeli conflicts of 1973 and 1982.

THE HORRIBLE EXAMPLES

Whenever a new weapons system reaches the testing stage, a predictable pattern emerges. Test failures occur and are highly publicized. No one explains that tests would not be necessary if it were not expected that some of them would result in failures, or that these failures illuminate the changes that need to be made in the system's design. Cost overruns are announced by officials or Congressmen or discovered by investigative journalists. One source from which the cost overruns are unearthed is the so-called Selected Acquisition Report program cost summary, mandated by Congress for military systems (though not for civilian entitlement programs or for Congressional office building construction). These include as overruns the effects of overall cost inflation in the economy, for which some think

Congressional actions bear part of the responsibility.[2] The General Accounting Office conducts investigations and finds that some characteristics of the system are not (or might not be) what was advertised or are (or might be) disliked by some of the people in the testing organization or the potential user organization. The new system is compared unfavorably to an existing system a few years older, now in the inventory. Exactly the same negative comments were being made about the existing but now praised program by the same critics a few years earlier: Compare the situation of the F-18 in the early 1980s with that of the F-16 five years before. It is all great sport, but it is not a very useful contribution to decision making or to national security policy.

The cycle of research, development, systems design, testing, and procurement is an extremely complex one. Judgments are difficult to make about when a technology is ripe for incorporation in a weapons system, what performance trade-offs should be made, and what degree of concurrency there should be in the development, testing, and procurement schedule. The need to balance such factors and to make such trade-offs naturally produces differences of judgment, even from those who have spent their professional lives considering such matters. The people of the United States are trusting both their money and their lives to these judgments. The decisions have often

---

[2]The costs of defense systems or of decisions made about them have come to be expressed publicly in terms of lifetime acquisition costs or overall system costs (including operation), because the analyses in the Department of Defense are sufficiently detailed to take a stab at such numbers. Defense critics sometimes object (correctly) when only acquisition, not personnel, spares, or maintenance costs, are included. For a social program, the annual costs are given, often for the first year (before full implementation). Presumably this is because, the program being likely to go on forever, there is no systems "lifetime" cost. The result is that some legislators and analysts will press for a choice between a new weapons system and a domestic social program. In principle, the comparison may be feasible. They announce that the weapons system, estimated at $40 billion current dollars, will probably cost $80 billion considering inflation and overruns. They may well be right. The social program will cost only $3 billion. Right again—and the comparative cost (and by implication, the priority) seems clear. But the cost of the weapons system is a twenty-year cost and includes the effects of inflation. The cost of the social program is an estimated first-year cost. In fact, the social program is likely to cost $5 billion in current dollars the first year, $10 billion the fifth year (because eligibility will be expanded and because benefits are indexed to inflation), and even more thereafter. At the end of twenty years, the weapons system will have cost $80 billion in current dollars, and a new one will be in process. The social program will have cost, over the same twenty years, say, $300 billion in current dollars and will be spending $40 billion a year. It can be expected to be continued, at an ever-increasing rate, thereafter. Comparisons are not easy.

left much to be desired, resulting in high costs, delayed schedules, and imperfect performance. But the American public should not place more trust in the conclusions drawn about these matters by journalists and television personalities.

Some defense critics conclude from the problems they find in new systems that what is needed is a return to the good old days of wooden ships and iron men, or of spit and baling wire. Such an attitude is dangerous nonsense. Large numbers of low-technology weapons cannot be counted on to outfight smaller numbers of modern weapons. Even if they could, the United States cannot, as explained above, expect to have enough troops to operate larger numbers of weapons. The United States would almost surely end up with about the same numbers of weapons as at present, but of much less capable systems. The United States does need the cruise missile, it does need the F-18 fighter aircraft, it does need the M-1 tank.

It is a sensible management practice on the part of the Secretary of Defense to have the production of each new system carried out at only a low rate until the development and operational testing .have adequately demonstrated performance and reliability, thus encouraging the contractor to meet those requirements before going into a high rate of production. In peacetime, a crash program substantially telescoping development and production is justified only when the availability of some single weapons system at a particular time is seen as representing the difference between peace and war or between victory and defeat. With the present multiplicity of weapons systems, such a situation almost never arises. But caution in approving high rates of production early in a program is quite different from concluding, as some critics have, that the modernization of U.S. systems has caused reduced military capability, or that more modern systems are necessarily more complex to operate or even to maintain. The jet engine goes longer between overhauls than the piston engine. The F-4, much older than the F-16, requires more hours of maintenance for each hour of flight time. And modern electronic technology has made radar and guided missiles more reliable than they were in the 1940s or 1960s.

A new generation of "smart bombs" allows the operator to designate the target and then have the munition itself hold to that designation while the operator turns his attention elsewhere. This requires less training for the operator, not more. A "joystick" approach, in which a bomb or antitank missile is flown into the target, requires much more training and experience on the part of the operator than does a system in which the operator keeps the crosshairs on the target. The electronic and control systems that in the latter case automatically steer the munition to the target will be more complex. In both of these systems the operator must watch the target until impact. The "fire and forget" approach will require still more design complexity, and will cost more, but it does not require operator attention after target designation, and it does not expose the launcher or operator to counterfire after target designation.

There is much to be said for separating the responsibility for operational test and evaluation of a new system from the developing agency when making the decisions on whether to proceed with procurement. But those who advocate separation of this responsibility from the military service that will use the system go too far. Moreover, development objectives and the needs of operational evaluation must often be met in the same test. Efficiency therefore dictates that the developer be involved in some operational testing. But there should be an operational organization to evaluate the performance of systems before they are bought in large numbers. It should consist not of personnel specially selected for their technical skills, but of ordinary troops. And it should report to the Service Chief outside development channels. The Navy's Operational Test and Evaluation Force does just this.

HOW SOME OTHERS DO IT

It is often alleged that the Soviets have solved all these problems of judgment, while the United States has not. There are cases in which the Soviets have emphasized simplicity with some success. Moreover, they tend to keep a much larger number of development programs going at one time in a given area. By and large they introduce about twice as many models of tanks, armored personnel vehicles, aircraft, and air defense systems, and they tend to blanket all the fields of technology more completely. They can do this because they are willing to devote to military expenditures more than double the percentage of GNP and to spend about 50 percent more on military research and development than the United States does and to pay their troops and workers much less. Massive Soviet military development and production place a substantial premium on the United States's making correct judgments both on which technologies to push and on which weapons to develop and produce. Because U.S. military R&D funding is smaller, the United States has chosen to concentrate on a few choices rather than playing the entire field. Inevitably this leads to a few big systems and leaves less room for errors. If U.S. judgments are generally correct, this approach is more efficient than the Soviet approach; if incorrect, less effective than theirs.

There is another alternative. The United States could adopt the Soviet approach and pursue almost everything of interest in technology, doubling the number of full-scale systems brought through development and production. That would require the United States to augment by about 50 percent its present military R&D expenditures—now more than $20 billion a year and growing at a rate of more than 6 percent a year in real dollars.

In my view, such a switch would probably be a mistake, even if it were politically and economically feasible. There is more to be gained by achieving a more efficient and rational allocation of development and production tasks with U.S. allies. Major steps in that direction have been taken since the mid-1970s. Allied defense-oriented R&D spending, at a current level of about 40 percent of that of the United States, helps offset the Soviet advantage, despite the existing inefficiencies. Furthermore, there is a large civilian R&D infrastructure in the United States and the other industrialized democracies, especially in microcircuitry and data processing and to a lesser extent in aerodynamics and even in materials, that is not duplicated in the Soviet Union.

One generally unrealized sign that the U.S. development approach is comparable in its effectiveness to that of the Soviets is that U.S. systems take about as long to develop and procure as do theirs, though the United States could probably shorten this if some changes were made in the industrial base and in our Congressional appropriations and executive procurement procedures. For the Soviets, the time from initiation of development to achievement of an operational capability is limited by the level of their managerial efficiency, which is better in their military than in their civilian sector, and sometimes by their technological shortcomings. Soviet decisions to proceed through the key stages of development and production for major systems are made at the top level of the party and government. Once that decision is made, resources are assured and programs are seldom modified—even when they should be.

Development times in the United States benefit from the advanced state of U.S. technology and the support of an efficient civilian sector, though competition from the civilian sector has lately lengthened the lead time for some components. Delays result from the number of levels of government that can delay execution after development is initiated and from the stop-and-go funding associated with multiple reviews.

THE REAL PROBLEMS

If the widely heralded criticisms are often off the mark, what are the real problems in choosing technologies to push and in applying them to the weapons systems needed by U.S. military forces to give them an edge against potential adversaries?

One problem is the tendency to try to achieve the best possible performance (speed, payload, range) in systems and to take full advantage of the newest technology only for that purpose. The operating commands have often insisted, for example, on the highest possible speed for a given aircraft design, without asking what value the last 100 knots provides and what is sacrificed, to achieve that capability, in other desirable performance characteristics or in reliability. In other cases, fleet air-defense missiles have been given ranges considerably beyond those at which the radar associated with them could provide reliable target information. This situation is reversed in the new Aegis fleet air-defense system: There the radar outperforms the missile. Almost always, these unnecessary increments of performance have been paid for in unreliability, demonstrated in either more frequent equipment failure or more frequent maintenance requirements. Accepting a performance 5 percent or 10 percent lower than the peak that could be obtained from new technology and using the design freedom thus achieved to operate engines at lower temperatures, structures at lower stresses, or circuits at higher redundancy pays rich dividends in reliability. Moreover, it is better to achieve higher reliability by using for that purpose part of the capabilities of advanced technology (for example, the redundancy made possible by microelectronics) than it is to seek reliability by using older technology or older equipment beyond its time. Failure to use modern technology to get the right combination of performance and reliability creates a high risk that the Soviet materiel will be superior. Given the inevitable Soviet advantage in numbers, that is an unacceptable risk.

A second real problem is the need to train U.S. military forces, both the combat forces who will operate the equipment and the support personnel who will maintain it. The increasing unit cost of weapons has reduced their use for practice and training. More realistic simulators provided by modern technology can ease this problem.

It is U.S. practice to do much of the equipment maintenance in the field, as opposed to the Soviet system of maintaining large stocks of equipment and replacing complete units from replacement depots. There has been a real erosion since World War II in the mechanical experience of military recruits and in their technical education. The decline in the mathematical and technical course work in the high schools and even in the universities over the last fifteen years, after the brief renaissance engendered by Sputnik, is alarming. One new craze may help: The generation raised playing computer games may find that experience as useful in operating some kinds of military equipment as the World War II generation found its experience repairing a simpler generation of automobiles in dealing with the materiel of World War II, the first really mechanized large-scale combat operation.

It will take a variety of skilled and educated personnel to conceive, design, manufacture at acceptable cost, operate, and maintain the advanced and complex weapons and support systems that will be needed. These personnel include research scientists, design and production engineers, technicians, and technically trained military people. The erosion of training of technician-level personnel in the civilian educational system, the poor mathematics and science curricula in U.S. elementary and secondary schools, the declining proportion of students in science and engineering at the undergraduate and graduate levels, and the lack of growth or even the shrinkage in federal support for research, teaching, and equipment in these fields during recent years are real and serious problems.

Distinctions must be made among complexity of function, complexity of design, difficulty of maintenance, and difficulty of operation. The first is inevitable; the United States has often overdone the second, which has led to the third; U.S. equipment usually avoids the fourth. Reliability and ease of maintenance must be emphasized from the time requirements are set and design begins, even at the expense of performance. Greater automaticity will inevitably involve greater complexity, which will reduce reliability and increase maintenance requirements. The former can be compensated for, to some degree, by providing redundancy of subsystems where that is made possible by the lower weight and smaller size associated with advanced technology. Very-high-speed integrated circuit technology and designs now being developed under DOD sponsorship are one example of a way to achieve this capability.

The extra maintenance that complex equipment may require is best split. One segment of a maintenance program could include the replacement of modular sections in the field. If the design is modular and the equipment is self-testing, equipment replacement would not require highly-trained personnel, but it would require that replacement modules be available at field maintenance facilities. The other segment should include rear-echelon repair of faulty modules and of subsystems or systems that cannot be either replaced or repaired in the field.

Another real and serious problem is the inflation of major defense systems costs at a rate higher than the general inflation rate in the economy. This phenomenon was experienced from 1978 to 1980. Its effect was to cut the quantities of major systems procured by 10 or 15 percent below what had been planned. This is a separate phenomenon from the increase in unit costs as a result of reductions in the rate of procurement. It can be traced instead to competition for resources with a then-healthy part of the economy. The civilian aerospace industry had a brief boom as a consequence of the need to replace an earlier generation of jet aircraft with a new generation that is quieter and consumes much less fuel per ton-mile. At the same time, the airlines projected an increase in passenger traffic, largely as a result of the airline deregulation scheduled to be phased in from 1978 to 1985. This increase has since proven illusory. Simultaneously, a growth in consumer electronics products using integrated circuits (video games, pocket calculators) increased the demand for the same kind of electronic components that are used in major weapons systems. This competition for air frame, engine, and electronic components drove up prices for those items more rapidly than the average prices in the civilian economy. There emerged correspondingly and simultaneously a shortage of engineers, which drove up their salaries. There was also a rapid increase in the price of certain strategic materials heavily used in defense systems.

All of these phenomena were exacerbated by the shrinkage in the defense subcontracting structure that had taken place over the previous fifteen years. The decline in levels of defense procurement, the uncertainties in the program as a result of the cycles of increased and decreased defense procurement, the relatively low profit, and the opening up of new civilian markets all pushed some subcontractors (especially the second-tier and third-tier subsubcontractors) entirely out of defense subcontracting and caused most of the others to reduce the percentage of their business given over to defense. These factors made it more difficult for the prime contractors on defense systems to get competitive bids from subcontractors for the components of their systems. This in turn raised prices. As a result, major defense systems rose in price at an annual rate 5 percent or even 10 percent higher than the budgetary figures assumed by the Office of Management and Budget in its government-wide projections for those years. Inflation in overall defense procurement, about half of which is in major systems, corresponded rather closely to the producer price index.

This phenomenon suggests a more general problem connected with the fact that the political process tends to produce unsteadiness in programs, with an off again–on again cycle. At the very least there is likely to be a four-year cycle, corresponding to Presidential elections. But there are also annual budget cycles. Defense spending is set forth as a five-year program, but even during the 1960s, when more stability in programs was politically possible, the funding for a given weapons system such as the F-111 could be seen after the fact as five one-year segments of five different five-year programs. Such unsteadiness in funding clearly makes for inefficiency and cost escalation; it is compounded by the instability of personnel assignments, especially for program managers. This complex of deficiencies is far more serious in its effects than the allegations of the new generation of defense critics that are listed at the beginning of this chapter.

SOLUTIONS

If these are the real problems, what are some of the real solutions? There are no panaceas, and few really new ideas. Fundamental solutions must be contingent on fundamental changes not only in the management structure of the Department of Defense but in the way that the Federal Government does business, including such basic issues as the relations between the executive and legislative branches. But there are some important palliatives that suggest themselves strongly.

One is stable management. Broad policies, whether in international relations, military strategy, or procurement practices, change slowly even when administrations change. Individual weapons systems are considerably more subject to the attitudes of subordinate officials who, at the political level, change even more rapidly than administrations. The predilections, right or wrong, of individual legislators and their staffers also have a significant effect on the stability of programs, usually a bad one because programs become an element in political bargaining. Multiyear contracting, urged on Congress by previous administrations and pushed to partial adoption in the Reagan administration, should help to ease this problem. But what hurts most of all are the changes in program managers that tend to occur every two or three years as part of the normal military rotations. Continuity of assignments and holding program managers accountable would have a big payoff. Major program managers should be kept at the head of a given systems program office for six or seven years, allowing them faster-than-normal rates of promotion if they manage their programs well. This would be a change from the usual situation, which is that an officer at the colonel or Navy captain level who is not moved around among assignments has reduced chances for promotion. In such programs as the Special Projects Office of the Navy (which ran the Polaris and Poseidon missile programs), the ballistic missile division of the Air Force, and more recently the joint service Cruise Missile Program Office, this pattern has been followed. These programs have been among the most successful, although in their later phases all encountered production cost overruns.

A second measure that would improve the application of technology and the effectiveness of modernized weapons systems would be to give the systems contractors performance specifications rather than technical specifications. Performance specifications indicate the performance to be achieved; technical specifications detail the way to achieve it. To the extent that technical specifications are used, they inhibit contractor creativity. The prime contractor needs to have some leeway for trade-offs among the various performance specifications, giving substantial weight to maintainability and reliability. The development of the F-16 was a successful example of such an approach.

A third prescription, to avoid making inflation rates higher in defense than in the rest of the economy, is to have defense procurement grow at a modest rate in real dollars. Real growth of 10 percent a year in military systems procurement is not likely to cause inflation in unit prices. Overall procurement expenditure growth of 20 percent to 30 percent in a year will increase unit prices significantly. In extreme cases, more of the increased funding can end up in higher unit costs than in larger output of units.

One desirable change would be to use the profit incentive more effectively and to give more weight to past performance and less to the quality of the brochures that prospective contractors prepare as part of their bids in choosing among contractors. A larger return on investment than what has become common in defense work may be required to bring more subcontractors to bid on defense programs and to encourage both subcontractors and prime contractors to invest more of their own resources. This is not a popular idea. Such defense critics as John Kenneth Galbraith have argued that the defense industry ought to be nationalized, because it takes no risks and is not responsive enough to direction from the Federal bureaucracy. Professor Galbraith lauds the flexibility allowed by federal shipyards and arsenals. Such an attitude could be held only by one who has never tried to close down or reduce the size of a federal shipyard or arsenal. In my experience, that is enormously more difficult to do than to cancel a contract or allow a contractor to go into bankruptcy. There was much criticism of the famous "golden handshake," a government guarantee of bank loans to the Lockheed Aircraft Corporation in connection with the C-5 aircraft contract. That arrangement levied a $200 million loss on Lockheed, from which the company has not fully recovered, though the government has never had to pay out any money on the guarantee. The settlement was harsh but just. It is difficult to imagine treating a government facility as sternly. Because the private sector is by and large more efficient than the government sector, that sector should be encouraged to use on defense programs the efficiencies of which it is fundamentally capable.

SUMMARY

There are real problems in employing modern technology in defense weapons systems—although they are not the ones set forth by the current crop of popular critics—and the solutions to those real problems are not easy. But the United States cannot afford to abandon the advantages that modern technology offers. It also needs to keep its lead in military technology by employing in the military sector advanced technologies available in the U.S. civilian economy but not in that of the Soviets. There are alternatives to this reliance on technology: doubling the number of U.S. personnel under arms to approach Soviet levels, increasing defense procurement budgets by 50 percent over what they would otherwise be to compete with the Soviets in quantities of equipment, and substituting purchase of production by allies for much of the current U.S. production of military equipment. None of these would be acceptable to the American people. The defense procurement budget will have to continue to grow. The United States will have to share more rationally the task of defense development and procurement with its allies. U.S. defense personnel requirements will prove a difficult problem in any case. But to exacerbate the difficulty of all these choices by abandoning the advantages of technology is an unnecessary, unintelligent, and self-defeating course.

The military balance between the United States and its allies and friends, on the one hand, and the Soviet Union and the states subordinated to them, on the other, is not nearly so unfavorable as the denigrators of U.S. military capability have been proclaiming for the last few years. But it is precarious enough. The United States must not fail to take advantage of the advantages that it has—economic, political, ideological, or any other. And among all of these, the U.S. technological advantage is one of the most important and valuable.

15

Manpower and Personnel

U.S. foreign and national security policy requires a military strategy, which in turn demands a military force structure, which must be funded, equipped, and staffed. More than half of the defense budget goes for pay and benefits for military personnel and for the costs of civilian employees of the Department of Defense.[1] What numbers, skills, and experience are required in U.S. active and reserve military forces? How are these people to be attracted and retained? Can an all-volunteer force meet these needs effectively? Even if it can, are its monetary costs and other disadvantages so great that conscription is a preferable solution?

CONSCRIPTION: A HISTORICAL OVERVIEW

Historically, conscription—like large military forces—has been a rare phenomenon in the United States. It was first used during the Civil War, but even then an able-bodied man could buy his way out of military service in the Union Army by paying about $400 to a substitute. Resistance to the draft ran high in many northern cities, in part because the war was by no means universally popular and in part because the sale of exemptions was seen as unfair. The next use of the draft was in World War I. Many perceived that war as none of the United States's business, and draft evasion and resistance

---

[1] In defense jargon, the term "manpower" usually refers to numbers (of men and women) and skills required to operate the force. "Personnel" refers to issues connected with how to obtain, manage, and retain those civilians and military service people.

were again widespread. Peacetime conscription was instituted for the first time in the United States in 1940, after World War II had begun but more than a year before the United States entered the war. The extension of the draft in 1941, only months before the attack on Pearl Harbor, passed the House of Representatives by a single vote. But once the United States entered the war, resistance and evasion to conscription, though not entirely absent, were substantially rarer than they had been in either the Civil War or World War I. The most logical explanation for such compliance is that World War II was almost universally seen in the United States as just, the threat as a mortal one to the nation. Whatever the faults of the Allied side (which included the Soviet Union), the Nazis and the Japanese militarists were seen as the essence of evil. There were some pacifists and conscientious objectors, but service was widely expected and accepted.

After World War II the Selective Service Act remained on the books. Universal military training was proposed, but it failed to carry in Congress. The number of conscripts dropped to insignificance as the U.S. Armed Forces demobilized to a very low level. Only when the Korean War began in 1950 did substantial draft call-ups resume. There was also a call-up of reserves. During and after the Korean War—in the course of which there was some disaffection and draft resistance—a high percentage of eligible males reaching draft age entered the service. This continued through the 1950s and into the early 1960s; although there were some deferments and exemptions, nearly half of the young men in the United States served for at least a year in the armed services, either after high school graduation or, if deferred, after college.

Some reserves were called up in connection with the Berlin crisis in 1961, but no general call-up of reserves resulted from the protracted combat in Vietnam. Draft calls continued, and they were universally and correctly seen as inequitable. Large numbers of young men from the educated classes, in which there was the most disagreement with the national policies and actions in Vietnam, found ways to avoid service in an unpopular war. After the withdrawal of U.S. troops from Vietnam, senior officials in the Nixon administration concluded that the proper lesson to be drawn from that experience was that a way should be found to end the draft, at least in peacetime. A blue-ribbon panel under former Secretary of Defense Thomas Gates reached the conclusion that an all-volunteer force was feasible. Making military compensation comparable to civilian pay for positions judged to be comparable was seen as a necessary condition to ending the draft. This was done, and the draft was replaced by an all-volunteer force in 1974, with debatable (and widely debated) subsequent effects on the nature and quality of the forces, especially the Army. As one of the responses to the Soviet invasion of Afghanistan in December 1979, the Carter administration in 1980 reinstituted registration for the draft, while specifically disclaiming any intention to reinstitute the draft itself in peacetime. No new legislation, except for modest funding, was needed to restart registration. During the 1980 campaign, candidate Reagan took a position against draft registration, but President Reagan continued it in 1981 and 1982.

CURRENT PERSONNEL ISSUES

The issue of whether the United States should continue the all-volunteer force or reinstitute the draft raises difficult technical, military, social, and political questions. It is one of the most important issues, though by no means the only issue, affecting the numbers, nature, and training of personnel for the military services.

To rephrase the question: Can the all-volunteer force be expected to provide enough personnel of high enough quality to meet the military requirements outlined in the previous chapters? To answer this question it is first necessary to determine a baseline of force structure and personnel levels (active and reserves) required to meet the military capabilities outlined earlier. The numbers and nature of personnel required also depend on the scenarios assumed for potential conflict, even for a given force structure. The following discussion of manpower requirements and personnel policies is based on a force structure in 1982 of sixteen active Army divisions; three active Marine dvisions; twenty-four tactical fighter wings in the Air Force, along with the programmed strategic nuclear, airlift, and other support forces; twelve carrier battle groups; and a fleet in the neighborhood of 525 ships. The corresponding active-duty manpower requirements—which I consider appropriate—are about 190,000 in the Marines, 785,000 in the Army, 580,000 in the Air Force, and 555,000 in the Navy, for a total of about 2,110,000 active-duty personnel. Of these, about 500,000 are stationed overseas or at sea.

Reserve requirements for the wartime Army now include just over 700,000 in the Selected Reserve (organized and equipped Army National Guard and Reserve units that train as such); their expected end strength for fiscal 1982 (the numbers authorized at the end of the period) was 650,000. That planned for fiscal 1984 is 722,000, which would be the highest in peacetime history. The Individual Ready Reserve (individual replacements who have mobilization assignments and presumably are ready for them) number about 200,000, considerably further short of Army requirements than is the case for overall reserve requirements for the wartime Army. Reserve requirements for the Marines, Navy, and Air Force are not far from the present levels of reserve personnel in those organizations. Again, these requirements are appropriate for the force levels contemplated in 1982 for the mid-1980s.

The Military Services have often spoken of the need for increased force levels, and the Reagan administration has on occasion advanced figures of three additional army divisions, a 600-ship fleet, and five additional air wings. At the same time, the Reagan administration proposed to Congress as part of its fiscal 1983 compromise budget package some force reductions—the decommissioning of current active ships and the elimination of an active Army division—as one way of slowing down the expansion of defense expenditures. An increase in the force structure would require a corresponding increase in active-duty forces. The Reagan administration's five-year program for ship construction and overhaul proposed in the fiscal 1983 budget, for example, would require an increase of about 100,000 in naval personnel by the end of the 1980s, and many of the new personnel would have to be skilled petty officers who could handle the nuclear propulsion and flight operations on additional carriers. The estimated shortfall of technically skilled personnel was already 20,000 in 1982.

Numbers

In meeting the personnel requirements for both the active and the reserve forces, the task is to enlist and then to retain the needed people. The requirements, and the current and future nature of the problems, vary in the different Military Services, though all of them have some needs and problems in common. The Army has traditionally had, and will continue to have, the greatest problem in raising, training, and retaining adequate numbers. The Air Force and the Navy need more personnel with advanced technical skills than do the Army and the Marines. The last two must place particular emphasis on ground combat forces—infantry, armor, and artillery. Military actions involving a few divisions, a few air wings, and a few carrier battle groups would be met by active forces without reserves. Larger forces and more protracted wars would require the use of reserves.

How well has the all-volunteer force met these personnel needs? In the regular forces the performance varies. The Navy and the Air Force have been able throughout almost the entire period to recruit the necessary personnel, and the quality of their prior education has been reasonably good. The Marines and the Army had significant recruitment problems during much of the 1970s. The Marines were able to solve these in the late 1970s, but the Army was not able to recruit what it considered adequate numbers of high school graduates until a major pay increase was passed in 1980. The Navy and the Air Force experienced an increasing problem in retaining experienced personnel, especially those with technical skills, after the introduction of the all-volunteer force in 1973. That problem continued through 1979 and is cumulative; it takes years to cure. But it is not a simple function of conscription versus the all-volunteer force. Successive major pay increases in 1980 and 1981 and the recessions from 1980 through 1982 have eased both the recruitment and the retention problem markedly, but not fully or permanently.

The previous chapter discusses the need for the United States to rely heavily on advanced technology and equipment to balance some of the advantages of potential adversaries. As a corollary to this, U.S. military forces must include an unusually large component (as compared to the forces of other nations) of people with special skills and training, to operate and to maintain complex mechanical, aeronautical, and electronic equipment and weapons systems. To maintain the aerodynamic, hydraulic, engine, and electronic components of advanced jet aircraft requires ground crews with advanced training and considerable experience. This requirement will be reflected in the grade structure; more higher-ranking noncommissioned officers are needed in those services and units that demand technical skills. This situation holds for Army helicopters, Navy nuclear propulsion units, and the Marine Tactical Data System. The skills of officers serving as fighter pilots or operating submarine detection equipment and of noncommissioned officers handling the electronic counter-countermeasures equipment for antiaircraft acquisition radar are also central to combat capability. No less essential are the training and inherent skills that enable a combat platoon leader to show initiative, or a tank commander to react to an unexpected situation. Recruiting incentives, including educational ones, and retention benefits that attract and hold on to people with such skills might solve these problems for the regular forces. Six-month or one-year conscripts with subsequent reserve obligations might well help to solve the analogous problem for the reserve forces.

The all-volunteer force has performed quite poorly in achieving the desired level of reserve forces, although the situation has improved as a result of actions taken from 1979 to 1981 and as a result of the recession in the national economy from 1980 through at least 1982. The principal problem among the reserve forces is in the Army. The Army's Selected Reserve can be expected to meet anticipated strength goals over the next few years, mostly because of better pay and bonuses; but the Army's Individual Ready Reserve (IRR) must be expanded. Most of the easy gains in the Army's IRR have been made; but a series of steps, including filling the active Army Selected Reserve, reinstituting reenlistment bonuses for the IRR, increasing the length of the military service obligation from six to eight years, and using more retirees could add anywhere from 300,000 to 600,000 more reserves to the Army mobilization pool. In 1980 the Army mobilization requirement was about 1.75 million, with availability somewhat under 1.5 million. The projections for fiscal 1983 are almost 2 million required, with just over 1.7 million available.

Except in a major war between the United States and the Soviet Union, substantial political constraints will exist on calling up the reserves. The experience in the Berlin crisis of 1961 and in the Vietnam War suggests that planning for the use of reserves must take such constraints into account. If the United States is to be able to fight smaller conflicts against other adversaries, the active-duty forces will probably need to expand their support capabilities so that reserve units will not have to be called up to provide that support.

Overall, with the all-volunteer force, the United States in 1983 has about 2.1 million people in its active-duty armed forces. This level represents a drop of about 25 percent from the early 1960s, before the Vietnam War. Measured solely in numbers, this indicates some decrease in U.S. military capability. A judgment of the sufficiency of the present level involves the complicated matter of requirements. But unless the United States is prepared to make the additional outlays on expensive equipment for a higher number of personnel under arms, there is no great value in increasing the number of active-duty personnel.

Moreover, increasing the number of reserve combat units, and with that the number of reserve personnel, would not improve the U.S. ability to put larger combat forces into the field in overseas theaters in a short time, even if the United States were willing to make the required expenditures to provide them with equipment. That ability would be limited by U.S. airlift and sealift capabilities. Because the reserves for a protracted war could not be delivered overseas, in many cases, in less than six months, and because training could be accomplished within that time, the limiting factors are the availability of lift and of equipment, not the numbers of trained reserves. Thus there is no compelling need for trained reserves beyond those already required in the approved Army planning documents. In meeting these requirements there is, as indicated earlier, a modest deficiency.

Quality

Whether the all-volunteer force is producing the quality of personnel needed is at least as important as whether it is producing a sufficient number. The quality issue is made more difficult by the lack of an agreed definition of what constitutes quality. Bureaucratic pressures to lower the standards in order to meet recruitment goals will always exist. Senior political leaders will want both to avoid conscription and to keep the armed forces as open as possible as a safety valve in a low-employment economy. Recruiters will want to meet their accession goals.

How can and should quality be measured? What should be the standards? There continues to be legitimate concern whether enough people with technical aptitudes and a record of educational achievement are entering the military forces to run the modern, often complex equipment on which the military forces are dependent now and on which they will be still more dependent in the future. In this connection, the use of so-called intelligence tests has played a sometimes questionable role. Experience in the military suggests that the ability to do technical tasks falls off gradually with lower performance on such tests. The correlation is not precise, although those in the lowest test category (Cat IV) do seem to experience considerable difficulty. Such training takes longer for the lower categories and must be updated from time to time; as this retraining becomes excessive, senior noncommissioned officers and junior commissioned officers can become discouraged, and their retention suffers. In my view, much of the alarm about these test results is overstated. But it is highly desirable to attract into the military larger numbers of motivated young people of whatever economic background who can acquire technical skills, especially those who seek or have had some education beyond high school.

Suppose that the all-volunteer force provides enough genuinely qualified personnel to meet the present enlistment standards. Is that sufficient? It can legitimately be argued that all competitions, including military conflicts, are usually won by exertion and by doing more than meeting some minimum standards. The need to carry out in combat or under emergency conditions some tasks that are not included in the normal job description also makes an ability to function beyond minimum standards important. The question, then, is what change would result in the quality of the military forces if the United States were to reinstitute the draft to make up for the perceived deficiencies in numbers of high-quality recruits, either for active duty or for reserves.

One way to answer that question is to use as a criterion the attainment of a distribution of test results similar to or better than those of individuals in the same age cohort employed in the civilian economy. In my judgment, by that criterion the quality of personnel in the Armed Forces would not be significantly improved by conscription unless the draft were either to take between a quarter and a half of the age cohort at random or else preferentially select those with higher test scores. Thus getting 10 percent of the force from the draft, selected from the population at random, would not change the present test score distribution by much; neither would getting 25 percent if the conscription procedures tended to pass over the more highly educated, as has been the case in drafts in the United States since the end of World War II.

Women in the Armed Forces

What can the present or increased participation of women in the military do to help solve any deficiencies of numbers or of skills? The exact issue is, what kinds of military positions can women fill, considering physical and social factors, in combat, combat support, and noncombat roles? Because so many military positions now involve a higher degree of technical training and a lower degree of physical exertion or of direct exposure to combat, some of the distinctions among those three roles have eroded. Perhaps better distinctions would be based on the physical strength or endurance required and the degree of direct exposure to enemy fire. By both criteria, service in an infantry platoon or in a tank crew fall toward one end of the spectrum. Headquarters service in a materiel, administrative, or clerical capacity would fall toward the other. Service in an air defense battery, as an aircraft pilot, or on some naval vessels would fall in the middle. Even headquarters are sometimes attacked by enemy fire; with the increasing importance of command-and-control and communications facilities as targets, this will be even more true in the future. Women have served as military nurses at the front—and been wounded or killed. Women served as ferry pilots in World War II. Women as fighter pilots would be exposed to a greater risk of death or injury, but their ability to perform the task would depend on the physical condition and reflexes of the individual woman; after all, few men qualify to be outstanding fighter pilots either.

There is no doubt that women can perform a substantial number, perhaps a majority, of the tasks required in military functions, and that they can perform them as well as men. But there is also some evidence that combat involvement of women lowers the morale and performance of men. It is noteworthy that the Israeli Army dropped this practice after the 1948 conflict in which Israel was born and that the Soviet Union has dropped its World War II practice of using women in combat duty as well.

Women are a less flexible part of the force because their assignments in wartime would be limited for various reasons: lower physical strength, a concern that the fighting ability of men would be impaired when women are killed and wounded around them, and the incidence of pregnancy. This means that the percentage of the force that should be female must be limited. Whether that limit is 5 percent or 20 percent should be decided only after careful and repeated examinations of the mix of skills and abilities required, not as some preconceived percentage derived from an impression of the appropriate degree of female participation in the military. The limit will probably not be the same for each of the services.

To the extent that unfilled personnel requirements exist and women who can fill them are willing to volunteer, I would lean in the direction of accepting them. The disadvantages of some reduction in flexibility seem more than offset by the advantages of an additional pool of personnel thus made available in peace and in war. The key to determining a proper role for women in the armed forces is to move gradually toward expansion of the number of functions available to women, on a voluntary basis, and to insist that women accepted for such positions meet the same standards as the men who serve in them.

Improving the Forces: Pay and Benefits

What actions could be taken to make the present all-volunteer force function better? Pay increases are clearly one possible tool. But what should be the criteria for military pay? Three alternatives present themselves. One is that pay should be comparable to that in civilian jobs requiring similar training and skills, so that military personnel will not be worse off than their civilian counterparts. An alternative view is that some differential is acceptable, that pay should be slightly lower than for comparable civilian jobs in light of the extra support that is given by the military community to its members, including special privileges and retirement options and the sense of belonging. There is a third view: that military pay should be *higher* than in comparable civilian jobs to compensate for the special hardships and dangers of military service.

The distinctions among these views are somewhat blurred by the difficulty in practice of determining comparability to civilian jobs. This is done formally by comparing federal civilian jobs with those in the private sector and by using a roughly equivalent rank structure to compare the civil service and the military. In the case of the all-volunteer force a substitute measurement exists, namely, the market test. Federal civilian agencies are deluged with qualified job applicants except at the top executive levels, but the military still has difficulty meeting its requirements with recruits of the quality it seeks. It is thus clear that the military is relatively underpaid at the margin, in comparison with the civil service, in purely monetary terms and for the present force size. The larger the force, the higher the pay required at the margin to fill the force. But it is also appropriate to note that in the military, more than in most civilian professions (teaching and the ministry may be exceptions), the nonmonetary rewards—the attraction of the profession and the way of life, the associations and the community spirit, and the stability in a particular career and organization—provide a substantial portion of the incentive for joining and remaining, at any reasonable level of pay.

It is difficult to disentangle the effects of the reduction in relative compensation for the military from the simultaneous effects of erosion of the nonmonetary attractions of the military that came about in a period during which the general public held the military profession and those in it in low esteem. In any event, from 1973 to 1979 military pay, which had been set in 1973 at a level judged comparable to that paid for civilian jobs competing for the same personnel, failed to keep pace with pay increases in the private sector. Relative compensation fell to 25 percent below that available outside during a period of sharply higher inflation rates. Moreover, living conditions worsened as compared to those on the outside: Military housing fell below civilian standards, and family separations increased, especially in the Navy. Public atttudes toward the military went through a negative period that began to change only after about 1976. And civilian competition increased greatly for personnel with the technical training possessed by those with engineering ratings and nuclear reactor training in the Navy, by pilots and aircraft maintenance people in the Air Force and the Navy, and by electronic technicians in all services.

Given these factors, it should be no surprise that retention fell sharply in the late 1970s. It has recently been restored to the levels prevailing in the early 1970s, though the loss of people with six or twelve years' experience cannot be made up in a year or two. Military pay increases and the poor performance of the outside economy have reduced the competition for recruitment as well as for retention and thus have contributed to the increase in the level of educational qualifications of those who entered the military service in 1980 and 1981. The numbers of recruits had never fallen far below what was required to fill the force. By the test of the marketplace, military pay and benefits are not now so badly out of line. They should not again be allowed to become so.

My own judgment is that the military in an all-volunteer force should be compensated with sufficient pay and benefits so that they will not be substantially worse off than people doing civilian jobs that are in some sense comparable. Such a policy, together with the naturally strong pulls of the patriotism, the service ethic, and the esprit that draw some people to military service should serve to attract and retain roughly the numbers that are needed. Special cases, especially highly skilled and trained technicians, will warrant and require bonuses, as should special hazard and hardship. If the United States were to move to a mixed force, with a substantial portion of the lower ranks filled by conscripts, the pay of that group could appropriately be lower, especially if they remained in service for a relatively brief time, for example, no more than a year. But some difficulties could be expected if different people doing identical tasks were paid at substantially different rates.

A second approach to improving the effectiveness of the all-volunteer force is educational benefits. The best way to improve the quality of the active-duty armed forces is to attract larger numbers of upwardly mobile recruits of all economic classes, and educational benefits would be an extremely valuable tool. It is probably worth trying a program that ties all individual federal educational benefits to the performance of some term of national service at low pay. Some have suggested either civilian or military service. Making eligibility depend on six months of military service would allow enough training for subsequent inclusion in the reserves. Because military and civilian service are not equivalent, the requirement for alternative civilian service should perhaps be set at a year. It is far from clear that civilian service of various kinds could be adequately organized, but existing volunteer agencies should be asked to try. Such a program would also serve the purpose, claimed by many who advocate universal service, of providing a degree of discipline and orientation toward achievement for young people. I have some doubts about such a purpose; people who have not attained such discipline and goal orientation by age eighteen are not easily brought to it later on. Nevertheless, it is a worthy subsidiary aim.

There are likely to be many difficulties in working out the details of such a program. Alternative civilian service would be difficult to define and even more difficult to administer. Requirements for women or the physically handicapped would pose problems. In the end, it might be simpler and sufficiently equitable to devise a scheme according to which physically qualified young males could, through a year's voluntary military service and an extended reserve commitment, gain educational benefits at a level much higher than shrinking federal funds make available to other segments of the college-age population.

CONSCRIPTION VERSUS THE ALL-VOLUNTEER FORCE: THE LARGER ISSUES

Even if the technical military requirements for personnel can be met by an all-volunteer force, there remain broader questions of military and social policy arising from the absence of conscription in the United States. In political and military terms there are implications for the image of the United States as a superpower. Not only the Soviets but all the continental European powers in NATO employ conscription, even if in some cases for relatively short terms of service. The presence or absence of a draft in the United States could have a significant effect in retaining the support of U.S. allies for such politically unpopular actions in their own countries as higher defense expenditures, deployment of modernized intermediate-range nuclear forces, or restrictions on economic relations with the Soviet Union. Some allies ask whether the United States can be considered serious about its commitments when it does not practice conscription and whether the people of the United States are prepared to sacrifice in order to defend their own and allied interests. The presence of a draft could also convey the seriousness of U.S. intentions to the Soviets. These questions are separate from the issue of how well the United States can perform its military missions with the mix of people currently drawn into the all-volunteer force.

In the area of social policy, the draft has long been thought of as an instrument of socialization, bringing about a desirable mixing of races and classes and instilling a degree of discipline. It has also been thought to provide a route for education, training, and upward mobility. The question has often been raised whether the United States can expect to defend itself as a nation and as a society when only a small portion of its population is prepared to engage in combat in its defense. It has also been suggested that the all-volunteer force separates the professional officer corps from most of the rest of society. But as long as a large fraction of that corps continues to be recruited through Officer Training Schools and Reserve Officers Training Corps (ROTC), the somewhat unrepresentative nature of enlisted personnel in the all-volunteer forces is unlikely to have a major effect of that kind.

There is also concern about the racial composition of the Army, particularly of its combat forces. It is a negative comment on U.S. society, rather than on the Army, when the proportion of minority group members among enlisted personnel in those forces approaches 50 percent. This is a troubling trend, even though the educational qualifications of black soldiers are, on the average, as good as or better than those of white soldiers. To the extent that an Army drawn significantly from conscription would reflect more closely the racial composition of society, that could ease the serious consequences, both for the cohesion of U.S. society and for the conduct of particular conflicts, if (as would be likely today) the first Army casualties and the first reinforcements would be heavily black.

These questions, the answers to which offer an implicit argument in favor of conscription, have some validity. But it is hard to know how much weight to give them. Often the contrast between the Army of the late 1950s and early 1960s and that of the late 1970s and 1980s is ascribed to the difference between conscription and the all-volunteer force. But the attitudes, habits, and composition of the entire cohort of American youth reaching age eighteen in 1982 differ enormously from those of its counterpart in 1957. That difference is primarily attributable not to the presence or absence of a draft but to changes in society during the intervening quarter century. And, unless the draft took a large percentage of the eligible males, it is not likely to answer these concerns about the quality or the composition of the present all-volunteer force.

Thus one must balance potential gains from the reinstitution of conscription against its problems. Given the probable attitudes of young people during the 1980s, not only in the United States but in all of the industrialized democracies, such a system would work only if a substantial fraction, perhaps most, of those eligible do in fact perform such obligatory service. In this regard, the demographic trends are helpful: The number of youths reaching eighteen will decrease each year during the late 1980s, so a given number will constitute a higher percentage.

Can the United States devise an equitable draft system to meet the military personnel deficiencies that may arise? Unless it does— and the test of equitability would have to be that those who are drafted regard it as so—the social divisiveness engendered by the reinstitution of conscription could well outweigh the force improvements that resulted. It is not clear that conscription would lead to significant financial savings. The age at which service would be required, the treatment of conscientious objectors, and the treatment of women—all would present problems. These could probably all be solved, but it would not be easy. Without fully convincing evidence that conscription would improve the general manageability of military personnel issues or the overall quality of forces, the burden of proof—which must lie with the advocates of conscription—has not been met.

CONCLUSIONS AND RECOMMENDATIONS

Discussions of military personnel needs have inevitably tended to focus on one of the proposed solutions—the reinstitution of conscription. But it is probably a mistake to begin with a solution. The various participants in the debate undoubtedly have criteria—often worthy ones—that go beyond the needs of the military forces. They would like to have those criteria met through the functioning of the Armed Forces and their means of enlistment and retention. But it is necessary to separate the various criteria and deal with them individually. And the primary criterion must remain what meets the personnel needs, in numbers and skills, of the U.S. military. The number of active-duty forces now meets those needs. But the skills and educational levels of recruits and the rate of retention of experienced noncommissioned officers leave considerable doubt about their current adequacy.

Many of these deficiencies can be treated to some extent by the specific measures outlined above. Retention could be improved in large part through adequate pay for officers and noncommissioned officers now faced with recurring remote tours and family separations; by an increase in the pool of those eligible for such tours, so that such hardship situations represent a smaller part of a military career; and by bonuses. Skills currently in short supply could be attracted by financial and perhaps educational incentives. The number of upwardly mobile recruits who score high on qualification tests could be increased by expanding educational benefits. Reserve force deficiencies could be met by a variety of incentives. The United States may thus be able to staff its armed forces satisfactorily with volunteers at least until the mid-1980s.

But, given the demographic trends, the United States may well not be able to do so after that. At that point, a dual system of reasonably well-paid volunteers who enlist for terms of three years or more and a larger number of conscripts serving obligatory tours of six months or a year may be necessary, with service in the latter category constituting the beginning of a reserve obligation and involving up to half of those eligible. The issue of young women would have to be handled separately. But if conscription of men proves necessary, it should not be prevented by disputes about the obligations of women.

Universal service of this kind seems to be theoretically possible, but it will surely founder on the details without procedures and even concepts yet to be developed and set forth. Conscription for nonmilitary service, moreover, poses problems of constitutionality. I would have greater confidence in the workability of such a program if it were accompanied by some imposition of sacrifice on the rest of society. An example would be some sort of defense tax or combination of taxes—whether a windfall profits or wellhead tax on deregulated natural gas, a surtax on present income taxes, or a consumption tax. That sort of corresponding demand on the material well-being of older people (who pay most of the taxes) is likely to help justify to young people the service required of them.

It is important to begin working now on plans for possible substitutes for the all-volunteer forces, especially those that would involve obligatory service, to ensure that they meet concerns about equity, universality, constitutionality, and need. This will enable us to avoid unfairness and mass divisiveness should such a program prove necessary.

Until such a system has been devised, and until the suggested improvements in the present system have been tried, my own judgment is that the reinstitution of the draft would do more to create or exacerbate divisions in the body politic than it would do to solve military personnel problems. But the United States may need such a system some time in the second half of the 1980s, so the design and public examination of various alternative obligatory service arrangements should be discussed now. The reinstitution of registration is a salutary first step in this direction. If Congress can summon up the requisite political courage, the registration requirement should be extended to women, on the grounds that if men are to be drafted for military service, at some later time women might be drafted for nonmilitary service or noncombat military service. A program to tie some federal educational aid to a period of voluntary service should be seriously considered as a further intermediate step.

16

A Program for the Future: Making It into the Twenty-First Century

In the coming decades, the United States, no longer enjoying military or economic supremacy, will find it more difficult to formulate and implement a national security policy than in the past. The Soviet Union, now in a process of political succession, will be militarily strong but economically and ideologically weak both internally and in its Eastern European empire. Western Europe remains politically fragmented, and it will experience economic stagnation, with political and social effects in general more severe than in the United States. Japan will continue to be economically successful but will remain highly vulnerable because of its enormous dependence on outside markets and raw materials. It will probably continue to rely on the United States for military protection and to lack a visible foreign policy aside from the promotion of a large positive foreign trade balance. The People's Republic of China will seek an independent but not isolated international role and probably a more pragmatic domestic path that encourages economic expansion by avoiding further disruptions of the kind that repeatedly prevented such growth in the 1950s, 1960s, and 1970s. The other East Asian nations in aggregate will become a major economic force and a significant political force. Southwest Asia, a region of critical importance to the industrialized democracies, will remain politically unstable; its proximity to the Soviet Union will increase the threat of Soviet military intimidation

or manipulation of internal factions. Other parts of the Third World
will experience some leveling off of the population explosion, but
they will continue to face massive economic, political, and racial
problems, with poor prospects for the future.

DOMESTIC GOALS, RESOURCES, AND PROBLEMS

In these challenging circumstances, a U.S. national security policy
for the 1980s and 1990s, and the very security of the United States,
must be derived from the fundamental principles, values, and aspirations of the nation. Security must depend on the nation's internal
political and economic strength; the will of the people and their
ability to persevere in a given course; the quality of U.S. education
and technology; the state of national leadership; and the degree of
confidence the public has in that leadership.

Future U.S. national security policy thus requires an economic
program successful enough to provide resources both for domestic
programs and for a fully adequate defense establishment. Without a
strong economy, the United States will not be able to achieve a
consensus in favor of the military expenditures that are required to
support a global foreign policy, nor will it be able to conclude the
agreements necessary for a stable international economic order. In
particular, the United States must become much more nearly self-
sufficient in energy. Beyond that, it would be advantageous if the
United States were able to provide from its own resources a major
percentage of allied energy needs.

The U.S. Government cannot be passive domestically while attempting to play a major role internationally. The strong domestic
political leadership prerequisite to an effective foreign and military
policy depends on economic and political success at home. Internal
cohesion is needed to build both a strong national security program
and an effective economic program. That cohesion in turn demands
a recognition that a consensus on social welfare programs and on
economic equity is not only compatible with but necessary to national
security and continued economic growth. U.S. international policies
must take advantage of particular U.S. strengths—economic weight,
technology, agriculture, political freedom—and publicize the achievements of the industrialized democracies, the well-being of their people,
and the advantages of voluntary alignments and coalitions over
compulsion and domination.

Along with the other industrialized democracies, the United States
will confront major domestic economic and political problems in the
1980s and the 1990s. Most of these have been widely recognized

and discussed over the past decade: the very governability of a democracy in the face of single-issue constituencies and "hypercommunications"; the decrease in the work ethic; the existence of structural unemployment; the lack of resilience and flexibility, leading to stagnation in the industrialized economies after more than twenty-five years of steady and substantial economic growth; the prospect that the same international economic interdependence that has brought unparalleled economic growth will now cause disruption because it is accompanied by political disunity and because protectionism is now growing; vulnerability to such outside shocks as the massive increases in energy prices; the collapse of public education; and the decay of social stability that results from the decline of public confidence in political, religious, and economic institutions.

Unfortunately, the United States cannot base its future national security policies on assumptions of future improvements in economic performance at the rates experienced in the 1950s and 1960s. For the economies of the United States and Western Europe, the 1980s are likely to see a continuation of the 1970s' pattern of slow growth, continued high unemployment, and high inflation (though well below the levels of 1979 to 1981). Japan will probably do better, but not nearly so well as it did in the 1970s. Thus, severe competition for resources will continue among social programs, consumer demands, investment in civilian plant and public infrastructure (transportation and utilities, for example), and military expenditures. Political leaders of the democratic countries will be severely tested in their ability to manage their domestic situations and to strike a balance between domestic and foreign policies that can gain the support of their electorates.

The United States will also face some particular problems of its own. One is the search for economic fairness (which is not the same as equality of income) in a society that has wider income and wealth variations than those in most other industrialized democracies. In the past, this difficulty has been mitigated substantially by higher average incomes than elsewhere, twenty-five years of economic growth, the relative lack of class distinctions, and generally higher social and economic mobility. During the 1960s many black Americans, previously excluded, achieved this condition of mobility. But the subsequent economic slowdown has threatened to reinforce the special U.S. problems of racial and ethnic division (especially among blacks and Hispanics) and of structural unemployment, which has created a permanent underclass spanning generations. Unless the United States can solve these problems, it may no longer be able to gain domestic support for military or foreign aid programs or for other political or economic policies toward the developing countries of Africa, Latin America, and Asia.

Despite these difficulties, the United States and the other industrialized democracies will continue to outperform economically both the Soviet bloc and the Third World (especially its socialist regimes) and to offer the advantage of political freedom. Soviet assistance continues to be welcomed on occasion by aspirants to internal power in the Third World as a faster and more certain road than the electoral and political processes, and as a road to more absolute power; but attraction to the Soviet ideology in other parts of the world has faded almost completely over the last several decades. Still, the democratic economic and political system, whether capitalist or as democratic socialist, have also failed to capture the ideological imagination of either the poor or the politically active in the contested regions, because of the democratic systems' materialism, their inability to promise quick solutions, and the lack of the necessary economic, political, or cultural underpinnings in those regions. The United States must make more of the advantages of its political and economic system without denying its own faults and excesses—even as it attempts to correct them.

BALANCING THE ELEMENTS AND MEASURING THE BALANCE

A workable national security policy requires a combination of political, economic, and military elements. The military and political elements are the most immediate and visible in establishing both the national security policy and the national security of the United States. Obviously they are the most essential in countering the effects of the Soviet military buildup over the past two decades and the expansionism that characterizes Soviet policies. They are also essential to maintaining access to such natural resources as must be sought outside U.S. borders, to ensuring our alliance relationships, and to preserving the existence and physical integrity of the United States. Military power has its limitations, and U.S. security policy will often confront problems in some particular geographical or functional area larger than not having enough military strength. In cases in which the ability of the United States to bring military power to bear is insufficient, however, that lack will often become the dominant problem. It is extraordinarily difficult to compensate for clearly inadequate military strength through some combination of political and economic policies.

The military balance is important for two main reasons. First, the United States must deter a wide variety of potential military conflicts and be prepared to defend U.S. interests through the use of military force. The likelihood of conventional conflicts in various parts of the world is high. A conventional conflict between the United States and the Soviet Union remains a possibility, and a dangerous one. A nuclear exchange between the superpowers is highly unlikely, but it is conceivable, so preventing it must be the central purpose of U.S. strategic nuclear policy and force structure.

Second, the military balance can affect the peacetime political situation. A military balance viewed by the U.S. Government and public or by U.S. allies and friends as unsatisfactory—or even as becoming less favorable—raises the possibility of explicit or implicit Soviet political intimidation. This could influence morale, attitudes, and actions on all sides. Perceptions of the military balance—regional, strategic, or overall—cast long political shadows before them. The decline of Western European confidence in the reliability of the U.S. commitment to their security during the 1970s had many causes, but surely the perception of a relative increase in Soviet strategic nuclear forces played a part. The Persian Gulf nations' assessments of the comparative capabilities of the United States and the Soviet Union have affected their willingness to build closer political ties with the industrialized democracies. The lukewarm support for U.S. nuclear force modernization in Western Europe and the Saudis' reluctance to accept a visible U.S. military presence are in substantial measure results of the Soviet increases in their nuclear arsenal and conventional force projection capability, respectively, combined with perceptions of American will. Nevertheless, the United States must guard against attempts to justify, on the basis of perceptions of the military balance, the acquisition of military capabilities that have only a tenuous justification in military need and usability.

Military balances are hard to define. There is not one measure but many, and military requirements depend heavily on the choice of scenario and region. Determining the adequacy of a balance is also difficult because judgments must be made not only on military comparisons but on their political implications in the particular context. It is probably easier to determine when a balance is inadequate. The military balance in a geographic region could be said to be inadequate when it would cause U.S. policy to fail no matter what the political, economic, and ideological factors. An adequate balance is one in which the United States and its allies have enough military forces in areas vital to their interests to prevent a military victory by the adversaries or (preferably) to deter military action by denying them confidence of victory, or the possibility of a quick victory.

In strategic forces, the United States is still within the range that constitutes parity. It leads by some measures but is behind by others. The trend has been adverse. If the United States is to maintain strategic parity and improve stability in the strategic balance, it must make improvements in several areas—command-and-control and communications, ability of land-based ICBMs to survive an attack, capabilities for penetrating Soviet air defenses—or Soviet forces must be decreased by arms reduction agreements.

In Europe, the Warsaw Pact ground forces are clearly superior to those of NATO, both on the central front and on the flanks. Air forces are more evenly balanced. Whether the Warsaw Pact's conventional superiority would be enough to assure it a quick victory would depend both on NATO's political will and logistical capability to provide rapid reinforcements as well as on the reliability of the non-Soviet Warsaw Pact troops.

In East Asia, Soviet land forces again dominate, but the resolve of the People's Republic of China and the size of its forces must give the Soviets pause. Japan and South Korea are vulnerable to conventional attack, but the presence of U.S. air and sea power would again erode Soviet or North Korean confidence of a quick victory.

In Southwest Asia, the relative proximity of Soviet forces combines with the probable Soviet perception of a lesser likelihood of nuclear escalation to make the balance more precarious in purely military terms. But as elsewhere, the determination and skill of the indigenous forces will be the deciding factor both in deterrence and in the outcome of a conventional conflict.

In a naval conflict on the high seas, or in a conflict on land south of the Tropic of Cancer, U.S. seapower and long-range transport capability generally retain an edge. But the outcome of any conflict on land will again be influenced critically by the political allegiance, military capabilities, and determination of the inhabitants.

The major problem for the United States in the overall military balance is that it cannot bring its sea and air power, or its central reserve of land forces, to bear in all regions at once and would thus have to set priorities in a multifront conflict.

Perceptions of the military balance are derived primarily from the statements of public officials. Those who assert U.S. inferiority or understate U.S. military capabilities—whether through hope of political gain, through misjudgment, or in an attempt to rally support for needed funding increases—damage U.S. interests. At the same time, the overestimation of the relative capabilities of the United States by its political leaders would be dangerous. The proper situation is for U.S. officials to see and describe the balance accurately, but to point out and seek correction of adverse trends. If adversaries take a more cautious view and are thus further deterred, so much the better.

How much real growth (after accounting for inflation) is required in U.S. defense budgets to ensure the needed capabilities as well as perceptions of an adequate military balance? The answer will depend on the actual characteristics and capabilities of the U.S. force structure and weapons programs, the extent of Soviet capabilities and those of U.S. allies, and assumptions as to the "acceptable" degree of risk. My personal judgment is that a real growth in U.S. defense programs (that is, in Department of Defense appropriations) of 5 percent to 7 percent a year from fiscal 1982 through fiscal 1987 would produce an adequate balance (though far from overall military superiority) and would serve as an example for allied efforts. This would bring U.S. outlays on defense at the end of that period to 6.5 percent to 7 percent of the GNP.

For the longer term, the U.S. military budget cannot grow substantially faster than the overall GNP. But the military budget fell as a percentage of GNP from 10 percent in the early 1960s to just over 5 percent in the late 1970s. The United States should find it possible over time to maintain a level of 6.5 percent to 7 percent of GNP.

The goal of 5 percent to 7 percent annual real growth in the military budget will inevitably be hostage to economic conditions in the United States. The Reagan administration originally programmed a somewhat higher rate, but it may now be hard pressed to achieve even the middle of this range. Still, in the absence of radical U.S. and Soviet nuclear and conventional arms reductions, the United States should firmly set at least a 3 percent to 5 percent real annual increase, corresponding to the plans of the last two years of the Carter administration, as a floor, even under poor economic conditions. The United States will need to make correct choices of equipment, strategy, tactics, and training and to operate its military establishment efficiently, even with increased military budgets. But it would be a serious mistake to believe that U.S. security commitments abroad at or near present levels can be sustained, without significant military budget increases, by efficiency and improved choices alone.

THE UNITED STATES AND THE SOVIET UNION

A national security policy for the United States in the 1980s and 1990s must include a policy toward the Soviet Union that is founded upon a picture of the goals and behavior of Soviet leaders, the internal political, economic, and military situation in the Soviet Union, and the likelihood of that situation's evolving in various directions. It would be foolish, however, for the United States to have confidence that it can have any important effect on Soviet policies, given the limits of U.S. knowledge about the details of internal Soviet politics. Instead, the United States should try to avoid actions that could encourage dangerous miscalculations on the part of the Soviet leaders.

U.S. policy toward the Soviet Union must be founded on a strong military posture essentially equivalent in capability to that of the Soviets. It must also define a political attitude toward Eastern Europe and Soviet policies in various other parts of the world. Existing Soviet hegemony over states contiguous to the Soviet Union is not reversible by U.S. pressure even if the United States were willing to accept great risks. Any changes in the relationship of those states to the Soviet Union will have to come from within, as happened in the People's Republic of China during the 1970s. Where Soviet military power is dominant, as in Eastern Europe, such a major change is not likely—at least not for a long time. Distant Soviet successes are reversible by a combination of internal developments and U.S. encouragement, principally with nonmilitary tools. This happened in Egypt. It could happen even in Vietnam or Cuba. Soviet actions, direct or through surrogates, in Angola and Ethiopia do not directly endanger U.S. security—unless they portend similar Soviet behavior in Southwest Asia, which is vital to U.S. and allied security. The United States must be able to protect its vital interests, but it should not be distracted by every temporary growth amid the fluctuations in Soviet influence.

U.S. policy toward the Soviet Union must include a position on economic relations. Actions on trade, technology, and credit can appropriately be used as incentives or reprisals for Soviet policies and actions, at least at the margin. But their effectiveness, especially when used as sanctions, will be limited in time and will depend greatly on the cooperation of U.S. allies and friends, who have substantial freedom and can to a considerable extent replace the United States as suppliers of credit, agricultural products, and industrial goods.

U.S. policy toward the Soviet Union must recognize that U.S.-Soviet relations are adversarial by virtue of the respective political systems and historical conditions and that they are almost certain to remain so, at least for the rest of this century. The major U.S. goal should be to resist Soviet physical and political expansion in collaboration with those who are threatened. At the same time, the United States should cooperate with the Soviets to minimize the risk of nuclear or conventional war, negotiating both to achieve arms control and to reduce tensions in the Third World. U.S. policy should encourage any tendencies that may exist among Soviet leaders to adopt less expansionist foreign policies as a way of helping to solve their internal problems. Firmness in regions of vital U.S. interest, a policy of linking economic cooperation to Soviet political behavior, and U.S. steadiness of policy would be the best way to maximize the chances of what is at best a hope for such an evolution in Soviet policy.

ALLIES

U.S. policies towards its allies must be based on the recognition that their interests are sometimes—and their perspectives are usually—different from those of the United States. Most U.S. allies in Europe and East Asia consider Soviet intentions toward them less threatening than the United States does. Somewhat paradoxically, Europeans and East Asians probably overstate Soviet military capabilities. Most disturbing, Europeans have a sense of having little influence on their own fate. The fear of being incinerated in a nuclear war initiated by the superpowers cuts across a wide political, national, and generational spectrum. Europeans also feel (and correctly so) far less economically secure than Americans. At the same time, the largely competitive economic relations among the United States, Western Europe, and Japan have grown from a irritant to a serious political problem among allies. Western Europe's economy has grown to exceed that of the United States, and Japan has become more economically effective and self-confident.

The United States has lost its clear military and economic dominance of the world. Western Europe and Japan feel much less secure than they did in earlier decades, when the United States was able to decide, and *did* decide (with some consultation), what the alliance military, political, and economic policies would be. The Western Europeans and the Japanese are also concerned with the decay in effectiveness of the U.S. political process, which they may now judge to be enduring its sixth consecutive incomplete or failed presidency.

Isolationism in the United States, never very far beneath the surface, is stimulated by these increased difficulties in alliance relationships. It expresses itself in the call for the withdrawal of U.S. troops from Europe and for the development of a so-called offshore strategy. According to the offshore strategy, instead of relying on overseas alliances and stationing of forces there, the United States should be prepared for unilateral military intervention around the world, rely on control of the seas, and if necessary withdraw into the Western Hemisphere. Such an approach is certainly not preferable and may not be feasible. But the United States cannot—and should not—try to keep military forces in place as guarantors of Western Europe and East Asia if U.S. allies show either by their explicit statements or policies or by their behavior, that such deployments are not in accord with their wishes.

To protect its own interests as well as those of its allies in Western Europe and Japan, the United States must station some forces in, or rotate them through, Southwest Asia and the Indian Ocean. Furthermore, the United States must now plan for the rapid deployment of military forces worldwide. Future increases in U.S. reinforcement capabilities for the defense of Western Europe and East Asia will thus be less than what had previously been planned. The Western Europeans, Japanese, and South Koreans will accordingly have to augment their own reserve and reinforcement capabilities. The Europeans should be expected to increase their real defense spending by at least 3 percent a year and, in addition, to supplement the goals in the NATO Long-term Defense Program to achieve that augmentation of capabilities. An analogous situation holds for Japan. It should be expected to undertake most of the burden of defending its own territory against conventional attack (as Western Europe now does) and of air defense and antisubmarine defense in the air and waters above and around Japan, as well as of the first 1,000 miles of its sea lines of communication. The United States will find it difficult to maintain its commitments and deployments in defense of allies who reduce their own defense efforts while the United States is increasing its own. The United States should not, and cannot over the long run, be more dedicated to another nation's military security than that nation is itself.

THE THIRD WORLD

U.S. policies toward the Third World must be tailored to complex internal political situations, and they must appreciate that the U.S. ability to influence events is often quite small. The People's Republic of China (PRC) is a major factor in the world balance of power, both because of its sheer size and because of its geographical position bordering the Soviet Union. The United States should maintain increasingly cooperative political relations and expand its economic ties with the PRC, but military relations with the PRC should be kept at a modest level, recognizing that the two countries are not allies, but that they have no reason to become adversaries again during this century. U.S. military relations with the PRC should include the transfer of dual-use technology and selected nonweapons military equipment. As time goes by, this might be extended cautiously on a case-by-case basis to the transfer of manufacturing capability for such defensive weapons as antitank and antiaircraft missiles. The United States should participate in discussions and exchange expert visits that cover military organization, logistics, education, and tactics. U.S. policy should emphasize parallel or even cooperative geostrategic and diplomatic actions with the PRC in support of similar political aims, where such aims exist. But major sales of weapons—let alone joint military planning—should not be pursued, barring a crisis in U.S.-Soviet relations that goes well beyond the strains and actions that have so far characterized them in the 1980s.

In the near term, Southwest Asia is an even more important factor than the PRC in the security of the industrialized democracies. The United States should give priority to an energy program to ease U.S. dependence on the resources of the Persian Gulf region. The U.S. military presence in the region should be expanded through the prepositioning of equipment and the rotation of units in exercises, insofar as that can be done without severely damaging the political situation. Finally, the United States needs to strengthen political stability in the region through economic development assistance in the poorer countries, through an active U.S. role in pressing for a settlement of the Arab-Israeli disputes, including the question of Palestinian autonomy, and through an attempt to reduce Soviet influence in the radical states.

HUMAN RIGHTS

U.S. human rights policy should be based on the ideals that are fundamental to democratic principles and institutions. Yet it cannot require of others a perfection that the United States itself lacks. Moreover, international relations must give primacy to whether a government mistreats its neighbors rather than to how it treats its citizens. Nevertheless, while recognizing the differences between friends and adversaries, the United States should exert pressures on *both* to conform to standards of personal and political rights, making it clear that their denial of human rights is a political liability as well as a moral failing.

U.S. MILITARY FORCE POSTURE

The U.S. military force posture should be derived from these foreign and military policies. But military force postures at any given time will rest in large part on past policies, so changes can be made only gradually. Military forces (especially such capital-intensive ones as ships) also have long lead times and long lifetimes. They must therefore be planned, designed, and assembled with enough flexibility to accommodate possible future changes and the dangerous contingencies that could generate or accompany such changes. Among present concerns about U.S. military force posture, five issues now require particular attention.

The Alliances

The most critical issue is the extent to which the United States should continue to plan for the protection of its interests through alliances, as opposed to concentrating on control of the seas and defense of the Western Hemisphere. The answer will play a major role in determining the future sizes and characteristics of the four military services; the balance between land and short-range air forces, and naval and long-range air forces; and the requirements for airlift, sealift, and prepositioned equipment. If the United States were to follow a unilateral course but continue to have major outside interests, it would have to expand greatly its military forces beyond those required for an alliance strategy. But with no allies and no substantial interests outside North America, the requirements for U.S. forces would shrink, at least in the short run.

The clear U.S. preference should be for the continuation of an alliance strategy, in which the United States and its allies are jointly responsible for the defense of common interests. The "offshore strategy" may promise lower defense costs and fewer problems in dealing with other governments, at least in the short run. In the long run, however, it is much more likely to confront the United States with either chaos outside its borders or a world unified against it by a hostile totalitarian state. Only if the alliance strategy were to fail, because of the military insufficiency or political disintegration of the various alliances, would the offshore strategy become an appropriate fallback. But to the extent that U.S. strategy, force structure, and procurement were concentrated on such an approach, the chance of its becoming a self-fulfilling prophecy would increase; confidence in U.S. alliances would erode, and adversaries would be emboldened to take actions to destroy or fragment the alliances.

Basing

A second, related issue is where to base U.S. forces: either overseas to defend U.S. interests or in the United States with the capability to move them and their equipment rapidly over great distances by airlift and sealift. Forces overseas cost no more to operate, though they adversely affect the U.S. balance of payments. Refurbishing bases in the United States to accommodate those now overseas would be expensive. Stationing forces in the United States would require an increase in airlift capability for their initial movement overseas in crisis or war, and an increase in sealift capability for subsequent resupply. The effectiveness of such an approach would depend on U.S. ability to maintain access to bases en route. An intermediate approach would be to preposition equipment and supplies close to potential scenes of conflict in order to reduce airlift and sealift requirements in an emergency.

Prepositioning five or six division sets of equipment in Europe makes sense if the Western Europeans are prepared to provide storage sites and other host nation support. The political situation for prepositioning remains favorable in Europe, and the likely combat zones are predictable. But beyond those five or six division sets, strengthening U.S. capabilities for Southwest Asia should have higher priority. Because the locations of potential conflict in Southwest Asia are both less predictable and more politically sensitive, the United States should plan over time to position a total of two or even three division sets in rear locations in Egypt, Oman, and on shipboard at Diego Garcia in the Indian Ocean. In the Far East, U.S. forces will play a lesser role. The appropriate approach there is to provide some war reserves and consumable stocks for U.S. allies. Most reinforcement supplies in both the Far East and Southwest Asia should be delivered by airlift in the first few weeks and by sealift thereafter. Present airlift capabilities should be doubled. Enough fast sealift capacity should be procured to move an armored division from the United States to the Middle East in two weeks, to be followed with another two weeks later.

Sustained Combat Capability

A third issue is what balance should be struck, given limited resources, between military capability for an initial defense and that to sustain a war for a lengthy period. The answer will depend on judgments about such factors as the probability of a long war between the United States and the Soviet Union or its surrogates; the likelihood of U.S. allies' being willing or able to join in fighting conventional wars of various lengths; and the estimates of how long a direct U.S.-Soviet conventional conflict would last before one side or the other resorted to nuclear weapons. But two other judgments may be more important. One is how far the Soviet Union would be deterred from undertaking a major direct attack by doubts about its ability to win a decisive conventional victory within a few weeks. That ability will depend on the initial military capability the United States and its allies can bring to bear. The other judgment is whether the Soviet Union would be encouraged to undertake a conventional attack by the belief that after some substantially longer time—say a few months—the allies would run out of materiel, ammunition, and combat personnel while the Soviets would not. In making these judgments, force planners will have to consider what the political forces of disruption might be on both the Soviet side and the allied side after several weeks or even months of indecisive combat. My own view is that it is much more important to show Soviet planners that they cannot count on overrunning Western Europe within a month in a conventional attack than to show them that they cannot count on exhausting allied personnel and materiel after six months or a year.

Theater Nuclear Forces

A fourth issue is what number and kinds of U.S. nuclear forces will be required in the various potential combat theaters. They are obviously necessary to deter Soviet use of their own nuclear weapons or intimidation through the threat of such use. For more than twenty-five years, the United States and its allies have also sought to solve the problem of unsatisfactory conventional force balances by posing the threat to use nuclear forces in combat outside the United States. These nuclear forces in turn often served as an excuse for not building up conventional forces. By now it is reasonably clear that they are at best a limited substitute for conventional forces. But in the absence of adequate conventional forces, the United States must provide for the possibility of first use of nuclear weapons. While the first use of nuclear weapons, even short-range tactical ones, would entail a high risk of escalation to mutual destruction, a no-first-use doctrine could encourage Soviet military intimidation or even attack. (The hope that such a doctrine would not be believed by the Soviets but would be by the Western Europeans, whose political support would thus be sought, is a remarkable combination of cynicism and naiveté.) If the U.S. and Western European publics are willing to make the sacrifices to achieve a fully convincing conventional defensive posture—currently highly unlikely, but conceivable in the future—there would be political advantage and moral satisfaction in adopting a no-first-use doctrine. But even then it would probably be unwise to relieve Soviet anxieties that a conventional invasion would involve a significant risk of escalation to a nuclear war.

Strategic Nuclear Forces

The final issue is how much is enough for U.S. strategic nuclear forces. Central to deterring a strategic nuclear war—which is by far the principal purpose of U.S. strategic forces—will be maintaining a diversified force posture. The United States needs enough strategic forces that would surely survive any Soviet preemptive attack to assure retaliation against a wide variety of both urban industrial and military targets. Moreover, U.S. strategic forces must be diverse enough to prevent the Soviets from concentrating their development and deployment efforts along only a few lines in any attempt to gain a preemptive capability. To my mind, this is a strong argument for a U.S. land-based ICBM force that could not be overwhelmed except by an attack so large as to divert a major fraction of Soviet resources from potential attacks on other U.S. strategic forces. This is a matter of prudence rather than fundamental principle.

U.S. nuclear strategy, and its strategic forces and command-and-control and communication systems, should be designed to deter Soviet aggression by demonstrating that the Soviets could not at any level of nuclear attack expect to gain a military advantage that would be useful in political terms. Thus, even though any strategic war is likely to end in a massive exchange, the United States must be able to retaliate selectively against various categories of targets in order to hold at risk whatever the Soviet leadership prizes.

Unless it is grossly unequal, the strategic balance can no longer be used by either side as a substitute for conventional military forces in a regional or a global conflict. Perceptions of an imbalance do nevertheless have a political effect. The United States need not match Soviet strategic forces in each category, but it must show an overall balance by being ahead in some categories if it is behind in others. Success in these endeavors will continue the paradox of the nuclear age: a need for massive expenditures to ensure that the resulting forces are unusable by either side as instruments of policy.

During the 1950s, the United States concentrated excessively on strategic capabilities. At that time it was possible for the United States to have a clear strategic superiority over the Soviet Union. But such a concentration starved conventional forces at the margin and served as an excuse (for the United States as well as for its allies) not to have sufficient conventional capability. The United States should be careful not to repeat that mistake, especially because it will not be able to reacquire strategic and tactical nuclear superiority over the Soviet Union. Moreover, though strategic forces are allocated only about one-fifth the resources given the conventional forces, the availability of additional funds at the margin for conventional capabilities can have a disproportionate effect on the magnitude of those conventional capabilities.

ARMS CONTROL

Arms control negotiations and agreements, covering both nuclear and conventional forces, must continue to be major elements of U.S. national security policy. Arms control agreements are the best way to limit the nonproductive and dangerous competition in strategic nuclear forces. Agreements on controls, limitations, and reductions in this area also have a unique objective: avoidance of mutual annihilation, which is equally in the interest of both superpowers. Few other disarmament measures or attempts at political cooperation will appear so valuable to both sides. A different approach would be for one or the other superpower to say, "We have enough strategic nuclear forces; the other side can go ahead and waste its resources on more strategic forces if it wishes." This would be militarily risky. The ability of its strategic nuclear forces to survive an attack, and the capability of the residual forces to retaliate after an attack, could be threatened by the other side's continuing buildup. That would erode deterrence. In my judgment it is also politically impossible for either side to abandon the competition unilaterally.

In many cases arms control negotiations will become instruments of political competition, with each side attempting to make political gains among domestic or neutral publics, or the population of contested areas (Western Europe, for example). But agreements can serve a useful, if limited, military purpose. They can inhibit areas of competition that may serve neither side but that would be likely to be pursued in the absence of agreement. They may be able to improve stability, reduce the possibility of surprise attacks, or alter the balance to the disadvantage of an attacker.

Arms control agreements cannot, however, substitute for the political resolution of conflicts. Nor will they make political competition, the main source of such conflicts, go away. But they can reduce the extent to which weapons developments and competition aggravate the inherent political conflicts. National security decision makers have few enough instruments to that end; they cannot afford to discard this one.

DOMESTIC ISSUES

The United States will face some difficult domestic issues that affect national security during the next few years.

The U.S. national economy has been badly disrupted over the past decade. The causes are many: stagnant productivity, low capital investment, high inflation, and large budget deficits (with even larger ones projected) that combine with low savings rates and a low rate of money growth to produce high interest rates. Budget deficits flow principally from rising costs of social programs, massive cuts in personal taxes, some unproductive subsidies and corporate tax loopholes, and an economy in deep recession, but increased defense expenditures also contribute. To reduce projected deficits while ensuring an adequate defense posture will almost certainly require higher taxes than those established by the tax legislation of 1981 and 1982, even if the growth of entitlement programs is cut back, as it must be. Responsible options include a wellhead or windfall profit tax on a deregulated natural gas industry, a tax on imported oil, postponement of the income tax reductions scheduled for July 1, 1983, and an abandonment of the indexation of income tax brackets to inflation. Encouragement of savings by moving the tax structure toward consumption taxes rather than income taxes could be a useful long-term approach.

U.S. military personnel requirements are expanding while the size of the population reaching service age is shrinking the recruiting pool for the all-volunteer force. As a result, the United States may soon have to face the question of whether to reinstitute the draft. Any future draft must guarantee that a substantial percentage of those eligible to serve do serve, that exemptions are rare, and that postservice reserve obligations are used to solve the problem of reserve forces. A program to tie federal education aid to a period of voluntary service should be seriously considered as an intermediate step.

The future organization of the Department of Defense is a critical factor both in managing defense resources and in planning military strategy and operations. The role of the Service Chiefs should be separated from the planning and operations responsibilities of the Chairman of the Joint Chiefs of Staff and the Joint Staff. Service staffs and the Office of the Secretary of Defense should be streamlined. Weapons development and procurement can be made more efficient and responsive to user needs by clear statements of requirements that are not to be changed lightly; by an insistence on correct cost estimates; by stable development and production schedules; by clear lines of authority and management accountability; and by program offices staffed with teams with operational and management experience, whose members are assigned to the job for at least five or six years. Development and procurement competitions should be decided more on past performance and less on brochures and promises—technical or financial. The lead enjoyed by U.S. technology must be used to provide superior weapons performance without stretching for the last 5 percent or 10 percent of performance at the cost of reliability, maintainability, and affordability.

All of these changes face major political obstacles. Without leadership from the President and the Secretary of Defense, supported by Congressional trust in both the executive branch and its own knowledgeable and responsible leaders (a trust not seen for nearly twenty years), they will not be possible. Existing local, industrial, and service parochialism will otherwise combine with honest differences of opinion to prevent improvement.

PROSPECTS FOR THE FUTURE

The United States should be able to find the internal resources to cope with an increasingly difficult international scene, despite continuing political instabilities and the prospect of economic stagflation and social unrest. The United States has major problems of governability, but it also has the natural resources, the people and the technical skills, surviving elements of the work ethic, the institutions of self-government to correct adverse political and economic trends— all the necessary elements to provide the potential for continued world leadership.

National security and the national welfare are inseparable. The United States exists amid the dangers of a world of nuclear arms, of rapid movement of people and almost instantaneous transmission of ideas, and of economic interdependence and economic competition. Without a strong military capability and an effective foreign policy, even perfect domestic equity and cohesion will not preserve the economic well-being, safety, or peace of the United States. Without a sense that U.S. society is both cohesive and fair, and that the economic situation of its citizens will at least gradually improve, the political attitudes and military capabilities needed for national security will be difficult or impossible to sustain. Unless the economy enjoys the needed features of capital formation, advanced technology, and labor and management skills and practices, it will not generate the resources to sustain the necessary policies and programs for either social welfare or defense.

At the margin, resource trade-offs among social needs, security requirements, and future economic health will always have to be made, often on political grounds as much as on policy or program criteria. But the goals are mutually supportive, not antithetical. If the decision makers and the public recognize that all three goals are both necessary and interrelated, the decisions are likely to be more rational, less politicaly divisive, and more clearly correct—though still difficult, and their results far from perfect. To choose either guns or butter in peacetime is a mistake. The more fundamental mistake is to insist on one or the other without examining what kind of guns, what kind of butter, the requirements for each, and how these all fit into a program to increase the human and material capabilities on which both national security and domestic well-being depend.

Each of the industrialized democracies has its own peculiar domestic problems, its own international relationships, and its own internal style of political leadership. The differences between the industrialized democracies and the developing countries are even greater. But all of these nations need leaders who will have the courage to take steps that produce long-term advantages at a cost of short-term sacrifice and who also display an ability to convince their populations to support such policies.

Correspondingly, leadership must be exercised on the international scene, not solely but especially by the United States. It remains by far the strongest of the industrialized democracies, economically and militarily. Japan may run more efficiently, but it is enormously more vulnerable to external influences on its economy. The proper combination of persuasion, incentive, example, and arm-twisting will not be easy to find in each case, but only the United States can exert it on the international scene.

The United States and the other industrialized democracies—even Japan—have seen too little such leadership and too little public willingness to postpone gratification even minimally. As a result, the trends have been adverse or at best mixed for more than a decade in relations among the industrialized democracies, in their international security, in their economic growth, and in their internal social and political situations. Competent and effective political leadership, with a popular commitment to long-term consistency of policies, can bring underlying elements of strength to bear to reverse these trends. Otherwise there is likely to be a considerable further decline—in international security, in internal social harmony, in productivity, and in living standards. Such a decline could come from anarchy in the Third World, from a breakdown in international trade and finance, from a fragmentation of industrialized Europe and Asia leading to Soviet domination of major portions of it, from internal malfunction, or even from a catastrophic nuclear war—or from some combination of these factors. Whatever course the decline might follow, it would not be the first time that nations and civilizations, having chosen personal ease and private gain over difficult tasks and sacrifices for the benefit of others, found that in rejecting the latter they had made it impossible to retain the former. My own view is that the leadership and commitment to avoid such a decline can be found.

Democratic leaders need good judgment, credibility, and in the not-too-long run, some examples of success. In the 1980s and the 1990s, that is also likely to require a certain amount of luck. The approaches described here may not work, but they are our best chance of surmounting, or at least outlasting, the problems of the rest of this century, and they are the only course consistent with democratic government.

Index